"Haff" Breed

Leon K Reval

Fulton Books
Meadville, PA

Published by Fulton Books 2022

ISBN 979-8-88505-833-9 (paperback)
ISBN 979-8-88505-834-6 (digital)

Printed in the United States of America

I don't think I ever planned on sitting in a cubicle, in a building that I helped plan and strategize both funding and empowerment of designing and constructing, in my early fifties, making $11 an hour, wondering if I have become to jaded, cynical, or just a killjoy. I reflect daily now on my life and question if I had done enough, could have done something different, or even maybe I was deserving of phase 2 of my life, now unemployed, single, raising three children, and now that my middle son turned eighteen, fully responsible now that I had filed and received full guardianship of him.

I accepted a very kind invitation to help a department that is and has changed the dynamics of the do-over for adults who had not finished high school, as well as also taking a more proactive approach of reaching younger students to begin to learn and apply the skills needed to finish school but also be prepared to secure employment or even attend higher education when they graduate. However, the more I sit idle in my cubicle, the self-reflection tends to grow deeper. I have thoughts that keep me wondering if I am giving myself permission to hoard and retain so much internal anger and negative thoughts, emotions as to try and find that internal inspiration, again, by demanding answers as to how I got here today! I had always felt confident that I could balance life's twists and turns, like leaving my state of New Mexico to go to a technical school in Florida, graduate, and then move back to the Southwest landing in El Paso, Texas, discovering that my academic career path would hit roadblocks, to working as a doorman/bouncer in a gentlemen's club, which admittedly was very cool for about a month, then became the DJ, or more like a carnival barker, slinging drinks, reminding male patrons to tip and playing music for the dancers. I think that's where I began to learn to watch how group dynamics applied in any setting. I would observe how girls hustled or just wanted to party; how customers would hand fists full of cash in the hopes of getting more than just a dance—that never happened, by the way; and how my presence, voice, and demeanor would help balance and in turn make money for the dancers and the club and for me, as I relied on tips every night. I lasted about a year and a half before I started feeling stale. I kept asking myself if the nightly partying and few dollars, sometimes handed to me from shoes, or from a dancer's underpants, the places people keep their money, and it just felt it was time to do something different.

After being unemployed for a month, I found myself at the local college's radio station. I can't recall how I even was allowed to be on campus as I was not a student, but as nervous as I was, I had a show playing jazz music. It was pretty cool, and the stations programing director, a young kid, asked if I wanted to do a show, and so I created and hosted a Friday night show called "The Rock and Roll Friday Night Metal Show"—not the best title but I was able to play the music I love and built up a small following. I did the show for three months and loved being able to talk and connect through the airwaves. I had a connection and then secured my first paying job as a radio jock at a Top 40s radio station. From there, I took another job at another local station and went from doing the afternoon show to hosting a morning show. I found my niche, and I was good, but as I look back at the end of my radio career, I was being demoted. My ego says it was because I didn't pander to the stations manager. Maybe I should have, but there was no mutual respect. I later heard that manager embezzled and did jail time. I have to admit I smiled, but I try to keep my karma pure. During the radio days, I became a father and then had to make sure I could support all duties as a father and provider, both financially and emotionally, and yet what would that be? Do I take on any job, or do I find something that would be my white whale that would boost my personal life and career? I made a decision that would take me away from my new family but also would become my new muse and love, but I really think we need to revisit my youth so that you might see how that white whale could destroy one's world.

I was raised to be made from stone, yet I began to see some contradictions in that parental life lesson. At the same time, their teachable lessons were not verbal; they were based more through acts, and that is where I began to see the illogicalities of what I was supposed to be as a pawn piece of the family cohesiveness structure. Turns out, as much as my parents acted like they were made from stone themselves, their lack of understanding how to deal with their own issues became my childhood syllabus that would now mold me into a fearful, inconsistent emo, as the kids say.

Growing up, my parents would fight, argue, and usually because they were mad at each other, either because my father wanted to drink and my mother, I'm not sure if she hated that my father wanted to go, but maybe it was the constant cheating, which I absolutely understand could be a huge issue, although for me, I knew how bad it made my mother feel, which is why I never cheated in my relationship. But anyway, when my parents fought, they would find the common denominator—me —and I became the golden child while they were mad at each other. I can't remember exactly what age I was when I began to notice that I was a pawn in their game during their issues, but what I did know was when they fought, I would get what I wanted, and I was going to reap rewards, and boy did I feel like a spoiled prince. In fact, I became Pavlovian when I noticed my father getting antsy and needed a drink. That meant he would be leaving the house soon, and if I asked, I had a fifty-fifty chance that I would get to tag along. I say fifty-fifty because I needed to wait to see what kind of argument might ensue, and that could range from a yelling match to a go ahead and take him because it was a quick errand that needed to be done, like take the trash to the local dump. But I also knew it could end up with a full-fledged hangout party, and I wanted to be there. After all, I got to hang out with some older kids, and we played, ran around willy-nilly. There were times I got to sit on my dad's lap and got to steer and feel like I was driving and, best yet, got snacks whenever a beer run needed to be done. I think I became addicted to junk food during that time as I could really put away the sodas and chips, but it was fun in my mind, and I was feeling somewhat like the center of attention. By the time we got home, it was late, and as I began to wake up and make the walk from the truck to the front door, I might then have to be alert as to how I might have to intervene if there was a fight. If my mother was up, she would give that ninety-yard stare, and my dad would smirk, and he might try and give a snuggle, and she might say no, get away, or she might smile, embrace him, and I felt I could relax for the night. If on occasion my dad came home, and usually if I did not accompany him, then I knew things might get loud, even physical, and I would stew and began to loathe them both but at the same time also stand guard in the event I might have to be the peacemaker. I felt my father would never hit me if I got in between him and my mother when he would get aggressive, so I was fairly confident that in being the protector of my mother, I was safe if and when I heard what may be winches and/or punches and then needed to rush down the hallway, push the bedroom door open, rush in, and now be the referee. I found myself cringing if I saw my parents' bedroom door closed. Didn't matter if it was day or night, fighting or not because of my father's haste to want a guys' night out or not; if the door was closed, I would find myself sneaking up to it, leaning in close, all without giving away that I was just outside the door as to try and hear what may be going on. It was during one day that I had come in from outside, looked around for my parents, and noticed no one was around, but what I did notice was that their bedroom door was closed. I tiptoed down the hall and pressed my ear as gently as I could to the door and heard what I know now—was my youngest brother being conceived. I didn't know too much about those pleasurable bedroom noises, if my mother winced or cried out. It was because my father was hitting her, so these noises were a bit different, and I remember being mad. In fact, I gave the silent treatment to my parents later that day.

The old silent treatment, an emotional tool I would master in life and still use today. I look back and wonder how I used that to cope with whatever, but I surmise it began with my parents as I began to notice that my rewards of being the golden child were now becoming excuses to allow behaviors to surface. My dad would say he wanted to go hang out with us, and he'd declare a fishing trip to which was his chance to drink the day away. My mother seemed to allow or ignore this pattern as she let us go but then would give comments or grill us as to my father's actions. It was daunting being the reporter. I didn't want to tell as it was fun hanging out with my father even though he would get drunk, and at the same time, telling my mother how great it was would make her seemingly feel like we were siding with my father and ignoring her, but it also seems at some point they would reconcile, and then I would be the guy pushed to the wayside. And as much as I wanted to state how crappy that made me feel, I kept my emotions and comments to myself and felt that was the proper thing to do. On the plus side, I always had good intuition. I may have not known exactly what I was seeing or hearing, but I knew if it was bordering on the positive or negative. By that I mean, if I was being told something like the rules, then I saw those who were telling me of the rules bend or to break the rules, I would think, how, why, and if I did question, I was told because! *Because* began to be the go-to word that would have a very detrimental effect on me in a way that would begin to feed my silent treatment defense mechanism. I would think, *Why does my dad have to drink beer, if he had a six-pack?* I would try and dispose of two beers, thinking that if he had two less beers, he would call it a day and would not be too buzzed when we got home, and things would be cool. That never worked; there was always a beer run, and there were always treats for my brother and I. As far as my mother, she would hold me, and together we would sit on the couch, seemingly waiting for my father to come home. And when he did, I would be discarded, or it began to feel like that after a while, I was noticing that I was being used, and when I wasn't needed, I was left alone. Yet I remained on guard, waiting to save my mother from the abuse my dad would inflict on her. I didn't know it at that time, but I was developing very crappy coping mechanisms. I would eat my emotions and again practice the silent treatment. I started feeling that if I questioned the statement of "because," I would be scolded, and rather than be offered an open, honest opinion, I was met with, "Because I said." I then knew it was time to shut down and pout. I say pout as that would seem to keep my anger from surfacing. I had a lot of anger and defiance but never was overly violent, maybe just enough to cause pain but not damage. I started becoming sarcastic, used humor as a way to feel like I could communicate my angst, stay witty, and be able to bend but not break. After all, if I did crack, I would not be able to be the kid who could save the day by waiting outside that bedroom door. In becoming the comic and eating my feelings, I would be the target of nicknames from my father. He would call me Fats, Rollie-Pollie, and yet still feed me snacks from the many beer runs we went on. The names didn't really bother me all that much. I mean, he would laugh, I would laugh, and my mom would say "stop" in a joking way, and that would make me feel good, which in turn made me feel like these names were acceptable. I started encountering personality shifts. I tried to lock up and hide my happy-go-lucky persona, maybe in an attempt to assimilate to the family dynamics, maybe for the purposes of trying to promote and accept harmony. I see now that what I was doing was trying to form myself into plaster casings that I knew I didn't fit and, in doing so, squeezing to fit, would create cracks and chips that I think may have been my innocence. I don't know if I felt guilty at that time, but I think I did ignore the fact that I was crumbling, and because I couldn't conform fast enough, I would soon be plagued with the burden of craving acceptance and wanting others to like me, embrace me, just as I had felt I was doing with them. But at the same time, it began to feel one-sided, and I would soon feel lost and confused at the confusion of others not doing what they said they would do or are supposed to do what they are expecting from me and/or telling me what to do that, to this day, this one-sided feeling continually generates harsh criticisms of my inner child's character and, in turn, continues to feed my silent treatment protocols.

I had no intention of wanting to write or share my life experiences, but the surprising part to this personal project was how my trials and tribulations of my life and maybe my own need of emotional and mental self-survival have now flung open the many closed doors of my mind. And now I find myself reflecting way back, trying to weed through my new current events, of no career, relationship, and how I will provide for my children. Sure things are different, life has been good, and I also have a different perspective as a fifty-two-year-old man, but yet I am still feeling like I am continually overcritiquing myself way too much and by now should be more in control of my thoughts, feelings, and emotions. I thought I always felt I had a strong magnetic persona, had the ability to be able to adapt and not necessarily conform just because but to keep my standards high, ask questions as to make sure I and others were on the same page in order to establish a mutual understanding and outcome and that I didn't have to fear confrontation or feel like I had to sit with my ear to the door as a child in an attempt to be the savior. I could just be me, that ride-or-die person till the end. But as I reminisce, I realize that many times I questioned my convictions because I felt that if I did not conform—case in point, the radio station manager I should have kissed more behind—I was not the savior to myself. Did I let my ego get the best of me? Did that set a new outlook in motion that would have me contributing to chaos rather than standing up against chaos, like I felt I needed to do with my parents'? When I felt alone, I guess could see how I would now begin to lock up my inner child, protecting him from being hurt, ignored, or used. I was learning to hide my true persona and in turn replace it with what I may have thought was a safer and more passive Leon. After all, if I fought or lashed out, I might have hurt those I valued, and that began making me feel like taking flight was the better solution to fighting, even something as simple but important as allowing myself to express my feelings. So I wonder if I should have never taken the high road in life and just fought to stand my ground rather than sequester my thoughts and concerns and allowing assumption to be my new gauge. What has become the finished product of this new creation, well, I rarely share anything personal and will shut down emotionally, even if I knew and felt that what was right was right and wrong was wrong. But the good news is, I always stand by convictions as a decision maker, board member, or political figurehead, and that is the one constant that has made me a vocal endorser of the rules and staunch advocate of policy and standards, and that would prepare me for a career where if I had a million dollars, I would have bet that I would have never moved back to the town that I left behind but would come back too and find myself in that position. Again, if I had another million dollars, I would have said I would never do, but I would discover that both of these two new changes in my life were why I was meant to be but at the same time would also feel like my defeat.

I think it is important to look back a little bit more and share a common mutuality both my parents and their families share. They both grew up in and graduated from high school while living in the township of Dulce, New Mexico, a very small cattle town that grew into what is now the reservation of the Jicarilla Apache tribe, established in 1887. There is a backstory of how the tribe, now calling itself a Nation, which we can talk about that later, grew and became the origin of the now considered homeland of the Jicarilla Apache Nation in Dulce, and depending on who tells the story, there are a couple of different versions and heroes, but for now, let's just talk about me.

Growing up on the reservation, there were very fond memories, an enlightening experience that began when two high school sweethearts took a ride, and nine months later, I was screaming somewhere and for many reasons, but I think it was because I just wanted all the attention. I can remember some things more vividly than others but as far as the home front, in retrospect, was a very great way to develop some roots that would be of service to my growth in the future. It seemed that my parents were the popular kids in school, and that made me automatically popular with extended family and their friends in the community, and I would get a huge smile on my face when I would hear my name being called at the local community center or when I was asked how my dad is and how my mom is. It felt really great to have some recognition, and I never thought that feeling would go away.

I can recall normalcies in my childhood, playing with the dog, running in the hills that peppered the area behind our home, and watching what I thought was a normal family dynamic. I attended the local head start, had friends, was shy, and had a lot of love that was comforting and warm. For whatever reasons, my parents enrolled me in the local Catholic school some five miles out of town, and again, things seemed normal, outside of having to attend church services and pray, which, when you break it down, at least in my opinion, was a way to respect life, even though life was represented in persons associated in the Bible. I even was an altar boy. I was in charge of setting up the candles, buffing, and preparing the chalices to shine as they held wine before it was turned to blood. It's a Catholic thing. I even began teaching others on how to properly set it up, and to be honest, I can't remember how I was chosen to do that as I always tried to never volunteer, but I did what I was supposed to do and usually always did so as good as I could do.

Time rolled on as it does, and I can remember that my father, who was very well respected and a giant of a man in my eyes, would do his best to provide a sound, safe home but unfortunately hid his vice of alcohol. My mother was a strong, hardheaded woman and shared a ton of love and understanding, but in her, what I know now of, codependency, I felt regressed and found other outlets to release her angst. Being the oldest, well, there were times I felt I was the whipping post but looked past that and tried to respect the strong core values both parents had in order to cope and not question their actions. After all, in that time of the '70s and '80s, love and pain seemed to go hand in hand, and if you didn't dust yourself off, you were considered weak, a lesson that stuck with me but in ways that confused me as I had no real concept of properly coping at that young age.

I loved growing up on the reservation back then. It was filled with fun, family, and a way of life that was laid-back and fairly simple. In retrospect, I had no clue that this was a facade and that there were larger issues below the surface. I say that because I was able to see things and always wonder, I'd think to myself, why is that being said that way and why if I am being told to do something, others who are telling me are not following suit? I had no idea that I stumbled onto what I think now are called convictions. I still was programmed to be what my parents wanted me to be, and as I explored these actions later in life, I realized they were somewhat living vicariously through me. My mother was the dominant force, and my father followed her lead. We may never agree on that, but that is from perspective. Now that I've said that, I always was inquisitive about things and not really knowing why or how, just kind of thinking, *Okay, I guess*, especially since I am being told and in that being raised. A few memories remain that I feel had molded me into a passive-aggressive person, and maybe it was learned behavior, but I definitely perfected it. I remember being at family gatherings and my parents laughing and being jovial. They were always great hosts, and my great uncle, from my mom's side of the family, cigar in tow dangling out of the side of his mouth, asking my mother in a joking way, in his Oklahoma accent, "You still whim-whamming these kids?" And a great big smile came across her face, and she'd answer, "I sure am!" I would look at all the dynamics of things like this and then question the reasoning of these hows and whys. I don't remember ever being sad or disappointed, just wondered. I had so many questions but always did what I needed to do and in that maybe felt that my questions didn't need viable answers since I felt the adults around me knew best, and that's how things were supposed to work, you know, be seen but rarely heard.

As the years went by, again I don't recall life being bad. I mean, I'm sure there were far worse issues happening in homes on the reservation, but I was legitimately happy. My parents seemed at in those moments between my father's drinking and my mother's attempt to cope, which is now called being a codependent, which makes me one, I think? I do recall some outbursts where my father would try and manhandle my mother in an attempt to, I guess, force her to forgive him for his running off and binging, even in his infidelity, to which I didn't know what it was, but I did sense it at that young age when I was the excuse to go somewhere and he would run off. I vaguely remember if I ever looked my father in the eye, but I do remember looking at him and desperately wanting to ask him why he was doing these things, but I don't remember if I was asking because I was concerned or I was mimicking my mother's coping mechanism as to the why. I do remember the time I may have begun to hone my passive-aggressive coping mechanism. When you're young and you are feeling a rush or power in getting anything you ask for when I was with my father, I often wondered when we might go "hang out" again, so I would ask things like, "Dad, can we go here or there?"

and then getting mad if he said no. Now that I think about it, did I force my own personal agenda on my father so that I could get what I wanted even if that meant he would be able to quench his thirst of alcohol, or were my younger brother and I my father's scapegoats because, after all, a good father wants to take his sons out and about to show them how to do things boys should later know when they are men? Hmmm? Interesting concept. Nonetheless, I felt I was living the good life. I often found myself one of the guys, hanging out with my father and uncle or some friend he said he'd give a ride to when we would stop at the bar for beer and, here's what I thought was the greatest thing ever, chips, soda, and candy. In fact, the tagline, dare I say slogan, of father-son hang time, "You want pop and chips?" became my addiction to the best time ever! I was being bought, but who cared, I was ecstatic with my reward of being able to hang out with my dad because he was so cool and generous, and in reality, he was in his own right. As the day's light turned dark and evening set in, I would still be hanging out with my father or at times hanging out with his buddies as they all reminisced of boarding school and then high school days. I would sit and listen, maybe even be the source of some stupid joke my dad would proudly ask me to do, and I would oblige. I mean, after all, I am hanging out here, and it's awesome! Soon it was time to head home, and it's always very late. My mother would be waiting, questions at the ready of, "Where were you?" You know, I cannot recall any other questions, and I do not recall her pressing in any aggressive manner, but there would be the rush to the bedroom, door close, then be pushed open and closed again and loud muffled speech and, sometimes, a tussled sound of not screams but saddening moans of oohs and awes. To this day, that sound haunts me, but I would learn that this act was my cue to sneak up to the door and listen, ready to rush in and save my mother from some violence. It would be years later that I questioned my mother when we had a conversation about our lives, and she mentioned that she felt that she was not abused or ever hit by my father, words that cut deep inside my core, to that little kid who sat patiently just behind the bedroom door, listening, at the ready to rush in and get between them. You know, I never ever felt that my father would hurt me, which is why I thought that me rushing in would create a safe place for both my parents. I don't know, but those fun days of hanging with my dad became fewer and fewer, and after a while, each sibling would find themselves replacing me in those dad hangout times.

I remember my mother saying to me, threatening or like an ultimatum because before I started second-guessing my desire to hang with my father. All I wanted to do was go with him when it was his time to run off, and I would cry, scream because my mother would tell me I could not go, and that made me mad! I lashed out and to the point of severe tantrum. After all, I was missing out on pop and chips and being able to run around and do whatever I wanted with the other kids who were all waiting for the dads at these group beer chats. But my mother said to me, "Maybe I should go out and do whatever. Maybe you want that, instead of me being here at home!" That comment stuck with me, and I questioned it in my mind because it made some sense, even though I thought, *Well, Mom, you can't because you're Mom*. It was strange, but I felt that if I had said anything or didn't comply, then I would be adding more issues, so I didn't say a word and went off to my room still mad at not being allowed to go with my father.

Those comments still stay with me, and I think that is when my passive-aggressive coping skills began. To be fair, I am not blaming my mother or my father. I, in fact, did so for far too many years, and it only drove wedge in our relationship, but again, we didn't know how to communicate and then forgive in a way that was uplifting. I think we said the words, but the act of doing so fell short and usually just to appease our feelings and demands. I think that could be defined as ego?

My mother did have wonderful survival instincts, and she once mentioned to me that she learned those survival skills when her father was killed in a car accident when she was very young, mostly because she felt she didn't fit in with the maternal side of her mother, my grandmother, and related much more to the paternal side of her father. Again, I discovered that tidbit later in life in one of our conversations. My mother and I had a volatile relationship. I really had such a great respect for her, and yes, she was the enforcer, and it was usually at the hand of some corporal "whim wham" and usually with whatever was in arm's reach, but she was also loving, and as I think about it, at a distance but not miles away, metaphorically speaking but inches, enough for me to recall hugs but maybe on her own terms, I don't know. Example, my dad was an avid hunter, but this particular time, he was employed as a game and fish officer, and one night, he came back with a fawn, baby deer, he found wandering alone, so he brought it back to town but stopped by the house to show us. My mother was in the kitchen, and my father pulled his work truck to the back next to the back-side screen door. The lower part of the screen was ripped, and our dog, Princess, would stick her head through the rip in an attempt to feel like she was in on the action of the house. My father called my mother's name, and of course, as kids, our hearing was spectacular—selective but spectacular—and my brother and I ran to the door, and my mother followed. My father showed us the baby deer, and in an instant, my wonder turned into a hmmm moment. My mother, in trying to vie for my father's attention, because when things were good, I say "normal," then they were once again high school sweethearts and the only two in the world. As I leaned over the truck bed, my mother said, "Watch it" and, in what I thought was an attempted shoulder bump, simulated a push-away. I scooted over, but it made me wonder how I was actually in her way, when there was a whole lot of room and an entire truck bed, but I think it was because I was closer in proximity to my father. I mean, that was my thought and what I think now. As I look back, another lesson in becoming passive aggressive, and I was gearing up to use this practice more and more.

Back to mother's survival skill. My mother decided to go to college and, although I don't think she wanted to, had some great people around her who inspired her to do so. My mother had been working for the local school district as a secretary and, in that environment, had a blossoming attitude of value and professionalism. She made the decision to move, and I am not sure if her decision was derived out of survival or a need to grow. After all, there were some very scary moments where my father had threated her life and even held my brother and I hostage. I don't think we were in harm's way,

13

but there was a rifle, and I do remember a peace officer on a megaphone or maybe shouting to try and talk some sense into my father. I can't remember too much more, but I'm here, so it ended peacefully. Then there was the time my father had went off drinking and came home and, in an attempt to get back in my mother's good graces, began working on making a concrete patio area in front of the house. My mother pulled up in the driveway. I remember looking up and smiling as, one, my father was home, and two, I liked being a part of the surprise. I can't remember the fight or what was said, but I do vividly remember my father cussing at my mom, and as my mother was leaving, my father threw his concrete trowel at my mom, and it missed her and hit the wooden post that held the gate and stuck like an arrow hitting its target. Did I mention there was the time my father shot himself in the stomach in an attempt to have my mother take him back and forgive all his transgressions? I didn't see the actual shot, but I do remember the neighbors carrying my brother and I to their home across the street. Yeah, my mother's feeling like it was time to leave probably came at a good time.

In 1979, my mother, my younger brother, and the bundle of joy that all of sudden was here, by the way, remember when I mentioned that my new practice after my father would come home, I would try and sneak up to the bedroom door and listen just in case I needed to rush in. Well, this time I did exactly that, and well, these particular ohs and awes were out of passion, and baby made five. So off we go, on an adventure to someplace totally new for all of us, the baby, the furniture, our memories, clothes all loaded and packed up into a horse trailer headed some 200 miles south, to Las Cruces, New Mexico, and the home of the New Mexico State University.

I mentioned that my mother was not only tough but also resilient and a real problem solver. It took her a while to get clear because there were more reactions than strategy, and being the firstborn, I had what felt to be an open season pass to be the whipping boy. I don't say that to be mean, maybe a little facetious, but don't well play the victim sometimes? Growing up in Las Cruces was really cool. My mother was a great student and very committed to her studies. I always felt she thrived not out of need but desire. Again, having to traverse through emotions that she could not shed. Oh, I forgot to mention, my father enrolled as well, so yes, once again, we were a complete family living in student family housing that was made entirely out of block.

Looking back, if you widen the optics of what we are and who we have become as adults, then metaphorically speaking, we were all in prison, and this time, the warden was not my mother but my father. Engulfed in studies, my mother must have handed over the job of homemaker to my father, and he actually was very good at it. I remember he would sew, cook, clean, and help us with our studies. He would yell and shout and bang the table if we weren't quick to give the right answers, but helping is helping. My father really blossomed while we lived in Las Cruces, and everything seemed to click as far as being a family dynamic, then coincidental or not, he would either get phone calls, or family, on his side, would visit, and he would succumb to his weakness. I don't know what made him feel so vulnerable around his siblings. I mean, I don't think anyone forced him, maybe coerced in terms of "egging" him on, but I never saw anyone holding my father down and pouring beer down his throat. My father's family meant everything to me. My father had three sisters and one brother, and I had great memories of my grandfather, whom I still can see him in me especially when I smile and laugh. I held my aunts and uncle on a pedestal and loved every one of my cousins, and they loved us all. My mother was even highly regarded, and my aunts and uncle really looked out for us, and it was both safe and fun.

When they would visit us in Las Cruces, my parents would be so welcoming, and what little we had we made the most of, and it all worked harmoniously. I don't ever recall being upset that part of the fun came with alcohol. It seemed part of the course when the family got together, but that feeling of harmony would soon change. Laughs and jokes would turn on a dime to arguments and fists. I remember one time having a sleepover at one of my cousin's house. We were all congregated in a bedroom, sleeping bags and blankets covering six kids who had a long day of play and, all of a sudden, a shake and push as the bedroom window flew open, and shouts of get up and get out filled the peaceful slumber. There was a fight, and all I remember hearing was, "He has a gun!" There was no shot, and as we lay in a nearby ditch, waiting for the all clear, I remember thinking, *How the heck am I in a ditch in the middle of the night, and why was I not allowed to put on my shoes?* I think that night, I began part 2 of my new journey to accompany my passive aggressiveness; say hello to cynicism. When the family got together, it was not if but when would there be an issue. I didn't know at the time or even what to call it, but I always got a sense that my mother was resistant but accommodating to the family visits, and I'm sure at the bequest of my father, it didn't leave much room for negotiation. In picking up on this sense of doubt my mother would give off, I think it was because of that uncertainty of not if but when something would happen, and that usually started when my father would say, "I'll be right back," which usually meant he would come home drunk. My mother had a pretty good poker face, but her will to contain any sense of relief and/or trust was broken, and there would be many times when she would use her passive aggressiveness to help what I felt was give her some comfort in being able to release her angst. That's usually when I would be the whipping boy, and she had a stare that was piecing to the soul coupled with the threats and then "whim wham" for not listening. Well, my approach to coping was getting stronger and stronger, although I still has no idea what I was learning and eventually mastering. Again, that was also my cue to be on guard, stand by as to make sure I could intervene when that bedroom door shut. Right about this time, I would now have thoughts of anger, real deep hatred at how my father could do what he did and then come home and completely disrupt what seemed to be some serenity. We really didn't communicate openly. Our dialogue consisted of humor and usually at the expense of someone. My mother never really shared her emotion and maybe rightly so. Again, this decade was still in the hierarchy of child to parent and listen and don't speak until spoken to, to be fair in various degrees, but the substance of this philosophy was relevant. I don't remember asking why my mother felt it would be a good idea for me, and I think I was the only one who was mandated to attend an hour or so of counseling, but I remember having

16

to go to a building, and in this room were toys and other stuffed animals, and I was able to play and, I guess, talk. I honestly do not know why my mother felt the need for me to see this person and in retrospect thought it was something she was learning in school, and if she saw some light, then why should others and I volunteer without volunteering? I don't remember the conversation, but I do remember these foam bats that we used to hit for a feeling or word, and I just complied, again questioning as to why and how this would help, especially when I knew there were others who needed to hit something with a foam bat more than I did! I don't recall these sessions helping and, other than a handful of times, became a blur, but a piece of that stuck and grew my cynicism and enter a new feeling called hypocrisy. The biggest memory that stands out from those sessions were that, for some reason, I would be dropped off, and it was just me and this person, counselor, after work hours, alone in this office in a huge building, and I guess it could have been worse. In being dropped off, the counselor would walk me out, and I would wait in front alone. This is where and when I discovered the Reval curse of time, a curse that meant we were either late going or, in the case of my parents, coming to pick us up. The day would soon be dusk, and in the fall, the days grew shorter, and I would be sitting, and then as the shadows disappeared, I would stand against the building feeling that I was covered and created a feeling of security. I would look down the street for headlights, and when I did see a car pull into this large lot, I would get excited, but then the lights would stop, and people would exit their vehicle to enter into a Pizza Hut that was in proximity of the office building, and again I would lean back onto the facade of the building. I did think that if I did go to the Pizza Hut, I would at least be inside and could have sat on a bench, but I never did move. I don't remember why, but it may have been because I was afraid I would get in trouble and stayed up against the wall. Soon what seemed to be hours, headlights would appear, and it was my mother. I don't ever remember any dialogue of why she was late or even an apology, but I do remember my anger and what I wanted to say, especially after being in a session of counseling where I was supposed to release and not bottle up my emotions, but I would regress, and in that, my passive-aggressive friend would allow me to be quiet and when asked questions would give one-word answers, and that was it. Being passive aggressive became my cape. I got to put it on, and it made me feel safe. I could be opinionated but then laugh as to try and sequester an act of defiance as to not get into trouble. It worked. I mean, after all, when my parents were in their own emotional tirade, my dad would reward us, and it became a warped system of who was the better parent. For a while, my dad always won that contest.

My mother was not weak; at least I never saw her as weak. And I have a ton of respect for her. Whatever her reasons were, she kept us safe, fed, happy, and was our greatest cheerleader when it came to sports. My brother and I excelled in sports, and soon we would be finding ourselves competing in baseball or soccer games and doing very well and holding our own. We always had a knack for being able to learn quickly and in some regard not master but do more than enough and then be able to want to do something else, maybe out of boredom. That statement can be very dangerous, not for a lack of doing but for a lack of allowing the mind to say, "Yeah, you're good, and you should be getting more attention!" My ego was forming, and there is time now, later in life, that I wish I had been cognizant of ego and how I could have managed it better, but ego did serve its purpose on occasion. The thing about ego is that it is more of a coward than we realize. It festers and wants to explode, and when it does, after the release, it leaves you hanging and in a place to which you find your-self on two paths—fight or flight!

The one thing I discovered while growing up in Las Cruces was my sense of power. I am a big guy, and I can't ever remember using my size to overpower, but I did have a brief moment of what it meant to be a bully. My mother enrolled us in the local Catholic school, and our daily routine consisted of getting up early to take the ten-minute drive to be dropped off and then picked up, much later than most students, again the Reval curse. I never minded going to Catholic school. After all, I had my earlier years while living in Dulce, and it seemed normal even now. I did all the same old routines while in school: served as an altar boy and set up for regular church services, funerals, and other special days where the church was involved. To be honest, I do not ever recall volunteering. The only thing I can surmise, which I discovered later and it became a real pet peeve, was that my mother volunteered me to all sorts of things, but I complied and later in life complied with disdain. I enjoyed my late elementary years at Immaculate Heart of Mary school. I was somewhat popular. I was a decent student, had good friends, and learned two new things that would change my life. The first was heavy metal! The school had a custodian, young dude, but as I could recall maybe just out of high school and was working and keeping the classrooms clean. We would see him doing his job and, while doing so, would play on his boom box cassette player, with the volume just loud enough to hear but go unnoticed, Black Sabbath's album *Paranoid*! My brother and I were instantly hooked. We would go to whichever classroom he was in, and he actually was really cool and considerate in letting my brother and I just hang out and listen to the music. After all, this turned out to be one of those times when it was great to not have my parents be on time to pick us up after school.

The other learned lesson was the irony, although I had no idea what irony was at the time, but the irony of being taught kindness, treating others with respect and regard and that God was always watching us, so always be on your best behavior. Not bad values to share and teach, but the irony I found was that the teachers, usually nuns, rarely if ever practiced what they preached. I must have repressed my memories of going to Catholic school in Lumberton, just outside of Dulce, because it was the same mixed signals as it was there in Las Cruces. I always questioned and never saw any answers. I've always had great intangible luck, that sixth sense if you will, that guides you with an inside voice as to stay safe or sound, and it was that luck that I was always called upon to either help or do. In this case, the school had an old movie projector, and the old projector had a tension spring that was stretched out and worn out and kept sliding off the tracks that basically tuned the film stock projecting the movie. So somehow, I found myself being the projectionist for the school principal. I won't say her name, but she was Sister Blah Blah Blah, and she pulled me out of the class and assigned me the job of setting up, showing the movie, and putting the projector away, and I always did my job and did it well. However, I could never count on old equipment and in that compassion from someone who supposedly took a vow to follow the golden rule they were teaching and molding into young minds. There were a few occasions when the projector's tension spring, again wobbly and trying to hold on as tight as it could, would slip and eventually falling off. It would stop the film, and if I was not Johnny on the spot, it would backlash the reel. If you do not know what backlashing is, it's when the spool basically unravels, dumping its contents. In this case, the film stock or, worse, if the projector was not turned off quickly, the lamp would burn the film stock because the light was so bright and hot. Well, I discovered this problem firsthand, and when this wonderful event occurred during film day, Sister Blah Blah Blah would come up to me, smack me in the head, and blame me for not paying attention and doing my job of being the projectionist I never volunteered for. I would take the smack and don't recall getting mad or defensive but really just stopping like a deer in headlights and wondering how I did just get hit and why this was acceptable. My new hate and I know *hate* is a strong word, but at that young age where there was nowhere to turn or no one to talk to, my darkness for nuns grew, and to this day, whenever I happen to see a nun, especially if they are smiling, a thought of wanting to confront comes over me, much milder now, but maybe writing about it will allow me to fully release this repressed anger.

Overall, life in Las Cruces, in our comfy prison-walled home, was very pleasant. My brother and I would find ourselves always doing something. We would be gone from the house for hours, and there was no worry or concern. My parents were busy, and we cut our teeth, as explorers, thriving in the dessert and looking out for each other. We would often find ourselves comingling with the college kids who were doing all kinds of things, and we really never were pests, but it was cool to be able to hang even from the fringe. We always had luck with fitting in or adapting to group dynamics, and that is one value I am happy to have received from my parents and a skill that I added to my mental toolbox, which would also serve a purpose later in life.

It was 1984-ish when my parents had one of their domestic agreements. Again my father was not doing what he had always promised he would do, and as a result of choosing the bottle, he would have to face the music. The tune, at least from my perception, was getting pretty old. I would always wonder why it was acceptable for my mother to keep forgiving him and taking him back. It was conflicting because as kids, we were told to listen and be responsible, accountable, although a term I didn't know too much about then, but I thought I complied to the rules. So to allow my father who was the adult and had to be more responsible, it was confusing, and in and around that time, my passive-aggressive friend became stronger and grew with me. My father must have been kicked out of the home. I can't remember exactly why we moved back to northern New Mexico, but in his absence, he took a job with an oil and gas company, and I thought maybe my mother settled for economic safety versus being able to prolong a career to make ends meet. After all, she had three kids to support. My mother being resilient also had a very strong quality of not settling in, and that demanded the best, poshest amenities. I not talking designer clothes or even living beyond her means, but for example, she would make sure our living conditions were good. She wouldn't settle even if it meant a few dollars more to provide a clean, well-maintained safe haven. Again, we never lived rough. We had clothes that were new, and sure, we were unable to get name brand, and after all, the one benefit of going to Catholic school was having to wear a school uniform. But man, how cool was it when my brother and I were able to get a fresh pair of Chuck Taylors. Come to think of it, we were pretty spoiled. I did try to scream and yell to get toys from Sears, to no avail, but we always had new bicycles and nice cars and very nice homes. I spoke briefly about being a bully living in Las Cruces, well, talk about karma, when we moved to Bloomfield, I somehow lost my toughness or perceived toughness. It was like a light bulb that just dimmed and then stopped lighting up. I never got into any real altercations, but if push came to shove, I would ball up on the inside, and blood would rush throughout my body, creating a flood of emotion, not to attack but to wonder why I was being accosted. It was very strange, and I still feel that sensation today. I often thought about it, and I think it became a way to cope, suppressing many things as to not upset the herd, and then at the same time, I think it was divine intervention as I never wanted to hurt anyone. I tried, but either my punches or hits, whenever those occurred, were held back.

I began middle school in public school, and the first day of school was intimidating. I am a big guy, but in my mind, I make myself small, maybe to fit in or maybe to hide, I don't know. It was during this time that I think I leaned more on my passive aggressiveness to help me adapt in this sea of new people. After all, in my younger life, I was in small spaces with small crowds at Catholic school, but now, there are tons of people. I also think this is around the time I began to also hone my anger stronger toward my father as we once again were a family unit, and we were supposed to mimic what I called the Cleavers, you know, from the show *Leave It to Beaver*. My father would work and provide, but the interesting thing in his returning home was he would cater to my mother, and in that, my mother, maybe feeling secure in this rejuvenated love, would embrace every bit of it, and I often felt that I was pushed aside. I mean, when my parents fought, I was the go-to guy, not man of the house, but I felt I was able to help my mother and in some small regard was even asked of my opinion, and we gelled trying to create some harmony within the home. It was when my father would return that my mother would then absorb all the attention, and since we never talked about our feelings, I regressed and began my journey of teen angst. My mother and I became adversaries, and we would argue, and I would lash out, and she would threaten, and the more my father was around, the more it made me angry. I kept wondering how one moment we were close and the next moment we clashed because she would endorse my father's rule since he was back home and now parenting. I always took umbrage with his allowability, but he was the man of the house, so I tried to ignore. It was a volatile time for me, new emotions, and I felt I could never really be open about my new thoughts of being a teenager and talking of knowing about sex and other general things about mind and body with my parents, so I repressed yet again. This was when I developed my insecurity that plagues me today. I was shamed of my body and the image of ever wanting to be naked in front of people outside the home. We were active, but I also liked to eat, and we ate large meals and sweets, and it was comforting and safe to be able to eat and laugh. I don't know if this next move to go see a counselor was for me or my mother, maybe both. I mean, after all, I'm sure my mother wanted to help, and maybe I complained, or maybe she could sense my shame, but she took me to a guy who did hypnosis, and I remember thinking, *This is crazy*. But I went, and he attempted to put me under as they say, and I remember closing my eyes, trying to breathe, and go to a place in my mind to which he was directing me, and I remember feeling that I had to act like I was in the labyrinth of my mind and we were going to find the root cause of why I liked to eat so much. Funny as I think about that time, but since I had very little positive coping skills, I let my mind take over, and that was in hindsight a mistake. The mind is so powerful but quite the instigator and trickster. This is the time I learned how to project, allowing the mind to devise an alternate reality or truth as a mean for survival, survival of getting out of a problem, but that usually meant starting the bus and driving over someone. So while I sat, eyes closed, using a monotone voice to answer, the only thing I could think of was sharing a memory where my mother had hired a babysitter, while we lived in Dulce and she worked, and the lady was nice enough, and I never felt unsafe, that I could recall. But I threw the babysitter under the bus and said it was because she made us eat everything, and if we didn't, we should get in trouble. I thought that was a nice enough pearl of life to share to try and expedite this session. So I said what I said to the hypnotist. My mother was also in the room, and I remember I had a subtle hint of guilt, but again, the mind is quite the smooth talker, and so I went on with my fib. We wrapped up the session, and that was probably the first time my mother and I really talked about my feelings grow-ing up, and it felt really good, so I had to continue with my ruse from this newfound discovery of repressed emotion, and my mother stated, she felt there was an issue but never questioned her feeling with our babysitter. I seemed to feel better and had less guilt as I then thought, well, maybe something did happen, and it must have made some sort of impact on me. I mean, I retained that memory, but then again, I could remember many things and was the record keeper of events and proud to be when my parents would tell a story at family gatherings and then say, "Well, Leon remembers." I remember feeling important, even for a minute, during this older group discussion. I don't ever recall being too shy. I do recall not wanting to participate in group activities outside of family events, and maybe I was hiding my insecurity of being a big kid. I don't know, but the confidence I created in my head in Las Cruces somehow left me when we moved to Bloomfield. I remember not wanting to go to a new school, but my mother was pretty tough when it came to honoring commitments. Those things you have to do and say you will do and need to get done. So we walked up from our new house about a quarter mile to the main road where the bus picked us up, and off to school we went. I remember after school getting on the wrong bus and being the last kid sitting there on the seat as all the other kids got off and went home. I don't know why all of a sudden I froze. I mean, asking a simple question might have directed me to the right bus in the first place, and second, asking the bus driver the same question about the bus number and route would have both got me home quicker and developed my confidence to be able to adapt to even someone giving a half-assed answer, but I remained quiet and reserved, and that seemed like the safest plan at least in my head. So we pass the bus stop, and I remember thinking that's my stop, and the bus passed. I still sat quiet, and I was the last student to be dropped off about four miles away from bus stop when the driver finally asked me where I lived. I told her we passed it, and she said I was on the wrong bus, and I thought, *Yes, I know*, but that was the last time I ever missed my bus stop.

High school was okay. It helped me develop better than junior high, and the only thing I really remember is again as a freshman, still being or feeling like the fat kid! I had friends, great friends, and we were tight as a unit and still are today as best we can be, but it was freshman year. I really was pushed to my innermost insecurity of being chubby. Back then, there was this allowable ritual now called hazing these days, but back in 1984, the seniors and other upper classes got hold and conduct a freshman "slave sale!" This was where seniors would "pick," more like coerce, freshman students to partake in a sale to which we would have to go onstage at the school's auditorium and spin in a circle in an attempt to garner the most money, to which came from bidding upperclassmen/women. Two things further fueled my insecurity and fear, the first, not being popular. There was a hope, I remember, that maybe I will get very high bids. A mere fantasy of reality to help me not die from embarrassment. To no avail. In fact, I was then put with a group, which happened to be my friends, and I have to think that made more sense as to be protected in numbers versus being alone. I can't exactly remember what we "sold" for, but we were now at the beck and call of our owners, and we had to do whatever they said! Now mind you, my bully days were not only short-lived, but karma felt it best to teach me a life lesson and leave me exposed without and layers to be or act tough. I just went along and felt that accommodating would be the safer, bet but I also felt not only like a puppet, but I kept wondering how this practice of holding a "slave sale" on school grounds was allowable and acceptable.

We did various tasks—carry books, open doors, and the one thing I had to do and not directed by my owner but by some senior who came up to my owner and said, "Tell that guy," pointing to me, "to go up to that teacher." We were all in the cafeteria having lunch and to go up to that teacher sitting at a foldout bench table, and tell that teacher, who was heavyset, "Those who indulge, bulge!" I sat and looked at the guy giving me my new order, and it felt like twenty minutes went by before I got up from the table me and my friends were sitting at and began the slow walk toward the teacher. I got to the table and begrudgingly belted out the words I was told to say. I said in a calm but shaky voice, "Those who indulge, bulge," and I looked back as to deflect the statement I just repeated in an attempt to show where it really came from as the senior laughed, and the teacher gave a chagrin smile, and I walked back to the table, not proud but perplexed as to what I thought the teacher wanted to do because way deep down inside myself, I wanted to punch this dude. But that feeling subsided very quickly, and I never gave it another thought, and that feeling remained buried. Again, family members got a different version of me, but to everyone else, I never bowed up! In that lack of being able to express myself properly, I buried a lot of emotion and hide from others except from my family. I would now freely lash out and find myself being much tougher and more disrespectful in my demands for respect, and that became a habit that I have found to be very unfair!

I still wonder how that moment affected me and why I froze. In fact, writing this right now, I stall to make a call to ask about something important, but my mind is saying no, as I could be upsetting the flow of things. I don't know if I built a wall of protection from wanting to or needing to hear bad things. Out of sight doesn't mean out of mind, for a second maybe, but the only thing that happens is in procrastinating, I still end up still hearing something I didn't want to hear in the first place because how can I control things that are out of my hands? It is a really strange phobia to have. At the same time, I mentioned I have wonderful intangible luck. Those series of events that happen to be good, I may not have necessarily asked for something specific, but I've either been rewarded or kept safe. However, in not being more open and direct, again a classic symptom of passive aggression, I feel like that insecure junior high student even today if I have to call and inquire about something, especially if it is personal in nature. The question that arises is, if I call to complain, have I changed the course of things, you know, upset the yin and yang of life, and therefore my intangible luck will go away. After all, out of sight out of mind has been pretty fruitful and benevolent to date. Why should I care if someone gets upset because I asked a question, why do I cower, and why am I afraid? It's been an issue, and even when I want to so desperately say that it has not because it has served a purpose, well, it sounds crazy, but yet I still balk at having to ask simple questions especially when it comes to personal business things. This style of coping would continue to stick to me like it was welded into my psyche and coupled with now seeing that I developed the need to please everyone around me, who was not family. After all, it's family. Their feelings don't matter because that's what families do; they just do. Well, that was wrong on many levels, but again, it was how we dealt with feelings, emotions, and situations in our circle. However, when it came to others, we were the Cleavers! We or, at least I felt, my parents put up a facade, and this facade was to show how wonderful we were as a family unit. I'm not faulting my parents in anything I have said. Whatever skills they developed, they used those to survive and in that cope with the trials and tribulations of life. I, even at a young age, had questions, and these feelings are now issues of what I felt at the time, and today and now as I look back, now having some real-life experience and wherewithal with lingo describing the mind, I can maybe understand or even be able to accept what is and those things that could never be. I still think, *Okay, what if you were the Cleavers? Now what?* I can't answer that. I am at this point of my life, just trying to understand what it means to be in a safe, happy, genuine mentality and in that maybe make the cycle of dysfunction cope healthier especially so that my children may be able to cope and much sooner than I have or doing today.

After I graduated high school, I got a job at an oil and gas refinery with a subcontracting company hired to construct new fuel pods and other devices used to turn oil into fuel. I don't know how it worked. I just know I was working, and it was pretty cool as I got to work with a dear friend, and it was a lively environment, and I actually learned things that I would apply throughout my life. I had no clue then, but learning something you never thought you would ever do or ever thought you would be doing is still a wonderful platform to help be an ever-learning person and, in that, a real professional. I lasted a year as a go-for of "gopher," which was someone who hustled to get things done when asked, and I excelled and was quite proud of seeing something I worked on, being used to complete the maze of pipe the refiner used to make gasoline. It was a few months into the job. I allowed a door in my mind to open and released my newest trait that also fueled my passive aggressiveness—ego. The independent contractor I worked for at the refiner was just that—independent —and had their own rules and policies to which employees had to follow. And on the opposite side, my friends worked directly for the refinery, where they followed a completely different set of rules, but because in my eyes, I was a hard worker and a great friend, my ego told me I could do whatever I wanted without question. Needless to say, I was terminated, and I remember why and actually in my mind knew that this termination was valid. I played the victim, stormed off, and blamed the site supervisor to which I carried that grudge for many years and never addressed it, just carried the weight, the unnecessary weight of my own demise in not following policy.

There is an adage, "Everything happens for a reason," and in that, I was so lost in my mind because now I had no job, was not working with my friends, and lived off my grandmother, who fed and catered to my needs, and I justified this reason by saying I was helping my grandmother and I was great. As I write this, it is embarrassing, and I have some desire to wish for a moment to apologize, but maybe the battle of the mind is to find balance, and when you tender too far to one side, refocus, remember to love yourself, and respect yourself to do better, that lesson would have been really good to have back then. Maybe I would have had a understanding of keeping my passive aggressiveness in check.

I found myself lost as far as what life is and had in store for me. I recently had a very profound phone conversation with a dear friend, whom I met in college, and he mentioned that he was not in agreement with someone who says, "Find your own destiny." I am inclined to agree. I think the only time your destiny is a factor in defining who you are as a person is during a eulogy. Destiny is to me the final curtain, that paragraph to which is read that gives a biography of one's life. Is death the person's destiny? Then how can destiny occur when you haven't even lived it? Wouldn't that then just be plans or planning? Well. what he also mentioned was adage of, "If you don't like it, rewrite it," or something to that affect. Again, how can you rewrite something that already occurred? Sure, you can learn from something and even choose not to do the same thing twice, but his last comment, it was what really landed and retained in my mind—don't rewrite something; change the plot of your story! That was a very powerful statement to me, and what I shared so far in my memoir is not to change things, more to understand, embrace as to realize that these facets and variables that happened also made me who I am today. It is not that I could ever share my memories or felt like I couldn't; it was that in my passive aggressiveness, I became content and lazy and felt that all things had to come to me, and if things or people did not, well, it was their loss. I learned how to ignore and not face the trials and tribulations of life, and I thought it was a skill. Well, it most certainly was a self-induced curse, and I am now choosing to change my plot, and I also choose to no longer be a prisoner to my ego and insecurities derived from being a passive-aggressive person. In my phone conversation to my friend, I mentioned that when I was young, I had older friends and cousins touch me. It's a very tough word for me to say, *molestation*. I've even asked myself if I thought I was molested, what if I didn't see it as being a bad thing or feel like I was meant to feel bad? Then again, what if I suppressed all emotion and thought and somehow now in the latter part of my life, it is a big issue? Sexual abuse is defined as abusive sexual behavior in which an older adult or adolescent uses a child for sexual stimulation. So as I explore this deeper, absolutely no pun intended, see, right there I tried to diffuse and deflect the act with humor as to try and deter the reader away from my situation. I honestly do not think I was forced. Do I recall it being wrong? Maybe. Did I fight? I don't think so. Did I ever tell anyone? No. Am I really a victim and somehow convinced myself that this act was innocuous and just something kids did to experiment. Now that I think about it, maybe a viable argument if the kids are the same age, but the act from someone older to someone younger, then I do fit the definition of a victim.

It was during junior high school that I felt lost as far as accepting my indemnity. My father was enrolled as a member of the Jicarilla Apache Nation, and although my mother's family were lifelong residents of the Dulce area, well, before the establishment of the reservation for Jicarilla, they were not eligible and deemed outsiders, to which I later found to be very ironic, but I will get back to that later. I really felt both my parents had wonderful insight and, although they may have had emotional needs that were absent, were very proud and loving of their lineage and background. It was around my junior

29

high years that I felt that I had my indemnity crisis. Bloomfield was a very nice town, but it also had its share of racism. I never really remember being the target of direct racism. There was some good old-fashioned ribbing, but I felt that my large stature coupled with being Native American was going to create jokes at my expense and, in retrospect, yet another unfortunate way to cope and hide within myself, so I claimed only my Spanish heritage. It was also around that time that my parents became hotter and colder in their relationship. In fact, it had to be one of their discussions where they agreed to but their very first home, as we had always been renters, and we all of a sudden were living in a newly developed suburb. It was nice, and although we had some nice memories, I would bear witness to an ebb and flow of communication, love, and ridicule and also find myself caught in the middle of this tryst. When my father would want to be naughty, as I called it, my mother would once again turn to me to help, vent, and continue to create the facade of happiness. This feeling became comforting, and I tried to comply, but unfortunately, my father would eventually come home, and then they became the happy couple, and I was pushed aside and then started reacting and becoming more and more volatile with my coping. I never crossed any lines of bad behavior, but I did push the envelope and am glad I never broke through. But again, I had great friends, and we were pretty tame when it came to the sun setting. As I lashed out more and more, I developed a real hatred of my father, and when I started finding out he was coming back to Dulce to "tom cat" as I heard it described a few times, I wanted to understand and ask my mother why she allowed his actions to be exonerated when he came home. It always bugged me that my mother would yo-yo in her relationship with my father, but I also understand how uncertainty can lead to fear and fuel that little voice of reasoning, and I don't fault her, especially experiencing life and knowing and facing my own little voice. So I built a wall around my emotions and began hating my father and then Dulce as that seemed to be the base to which all issues began. I continued to hate Dulce and began to distance myself further and further away, even in visiting family. I wanted no part, and if I did, I did so with resistance and a chip on my shoulder. I began feeling more distant from my father as well and in that began to project my fears and doubt upon him as an excuse to say, "Because of you, I am not more successful," or "Because of you, my life is tough." That mentality overthrew the wonderful core values I did inherit from my father, but at the time, I ignored and developed a habit that if I blamed, I did not have to be accountable to myself, an unfair trait that I am trying to reverse this day.

Never say never! A lesson I not only learned but a lesson that also gave me a new life. I always thought I was tough, mostly surface, but down deep, I tried to avoid issues and flew under the radar or trouble and maybe life. I had the decision to move away from the state of New Mexico and didn't know where yet but felt I just needed to go as far away as possible because I also knew that if I was close to home, I would use that as an excuse if and when times were difficult when leaving the nest. I saw an advertisement for music recording, and I always had a love of music, and even though I was a virtuoso air drummer, I never learned how to play a real instrument. I always had the knack to be able to adapt to anything I put my mind to, just was lazy and complacent, especially if I was bored or if the desire or fantasy felt too long to live up to. So I had many opportunities to learn how to play guitar, just never disciplined myself to do so. This mentality suited me at times, but it would also limit me, and since I never volunteered but was chosen because others saw my value when I did not, I was also able to achieve all tasks assigned and do it with professionalism, a wonderful trait I did inherit from my parents, who were very professional in career duties. I was adamant that I was leaving New Mexico, so I applied for a scholarship the Jicarilla Apache Nation had for aspiring students of some higher education and with the help of my mother completed the application to the scholarship office and was approved to attend the Art Institute of Fort Lauderdale. I had attended class at the local community college in town, but I never felt inspired, but I also had some dreams, which I refer to as fantasies again because if I didn't obtain or that particular fantasy I created changed, well, I would quit and complain and then become complacent in life. I think, and this is an assumption, but maybe I have ADD. I should research the symptoms, but then again,

31

I may wait. I messed around my hometown for a bit, and it was in December of 1989 where I boarded a flight, my first airplane ride anywhere, but this one was bound for Fort Lauderdale, Florida.

I always thought I was tough and strong-willed, that nobody can tell me what to do. Then I got on the flight six hours—well, three hours with a layover in Dallas, Texas, which in and of itself is also a journey to get from one gate to the other. You never know how tough you need to be until your feast for survival, and then your instincts kick in, and then you realize what a wonderful instinct you have, another positive trait that you inherited from your parents. I landed at the Fort Lauderdale-Hollywood International airport in the evening. In hand, I had three pieces of luggage that carried clothes and no memoires but enough items to get my student career started. My mother always surprised us kids with gifts, not extravagant gifts, but in her frugalness was able to spot a bargain, and it was hit or miss, but the thought was always there. I don't know where my mother purchased my three-piece luggage set, but she had bought me very nice going-away gift, a matching set of plastic faux wicker, leather print gray suitcases to help carry my small possessions. I actually still have the middle-sized one holding some stuff from my Florida days.

I was actually quite proud of myself for actually committing to such a long trip so far away; however, you soon find out that you're not as tough as you thought you were. I have landed suitcases in hand in a strange place, having to catch my first taxi, wondering how much the fare was going to be to get to my room, to which I would now have to live and also in the back of my mind have to live with somebody; a roommate was it to be. I kept imagining somebody who was not very clean. After all, three boys growing up at my mother's house, well, us boys were the ones who were taught how to clean and clean good at a very young age. I also imagined somebody whose personality would clash with mine, but then thinking and accepting that any choices in that moment would be limited coupled with limited resources, my options were pretty few and far between. Being so far away, I had really come to terms with all those things I had wished for. I wished I wasn't here in Bloomfield. I wished I was living on my own. I wished no one would tell me what to do. If I was alone, life would be fun, and I could do whatever I wanted. Reality can be a wake-up call, a slap to the face. I remember it was the second day after I woke up from my long flight. I found a payphone, made a collect call to my mother, and I said, "I can't do this. I want to come home." I'll never forget the words mother said. This actually was a turning point in my life. It taught me about commitment; it taught me about being a person of my word, and although not knowing at that time, it taught me about accountability. If I had quit, the large ripple effect that would have created would have been embarrassing and a waste of time, the time and effort of others had done to get me accepted to school, to get me the funding needed for school, to give me the plane ticket to fly to Florida as well as all the support that came with a decision that I had made. Her words were like a much-needed gut punch. She said, "You made a commitment. You can do anything you set your mind to because you are strong, and I have NO money to pay for any plane ticket back, so do what you need to do and do it right!" I remember feeling sad because I wanted her to see me in that moment, and she had actually done with her words, which I will never forget.

I absolutely fell in love with my classes. I was learning a new trade, the trade of rock and roll. I had so many opportunities, met so many new people, and forged some great long-standing relationships with friends I still value today. I was thriving in my new environment. This is actually where I started learning a new life lesson, the value of listening to people, learning from people, and taking a little part of that person and then applying it to yourself for a greater good. The ability to do that doesn't mean you're trying to act like somebody; to me, it meant seeing something I thought was valuable and then trying to find the best fit this person was doing and then applying that trait so that I could start utilizing this new tactic or positive piece of energy, which I call it today, in a way that was now going to help do better in whatever I was doing professionally!

Professionally, I seemed to excel. Again never volunteering, I had been chosen for class projects, some administrative duties, which were all new to me, in fact, a funny story. I was asked to participate with school faculty members, teachers, department heads, and administrators, to which I tried to gracefully decline, but there I was, the student representative sitting in discussions that talked about curriculums, dual credit planning, and strategies and other topics that committees discuss to provide solutions. I remember my first meeting showing up, large conference table chairs filled with adults, and I walk in, and the room looks at me in their silence. Okay, in my mind, there was silence and judgment and other scary scenarios I built up in my head, but I sat down, and this was my first time ever hearing, forget knowing but proper protocols of committee responsibilities, you know, chairpersons, secretaries, treasurers, and other related officer roles. As the duties were delegated, I looked around the table try not to stare. *What the hell am I doing here?* So the duties were delegated, and I was chosen to take meeting minutes. I remember thinking to myself, *What are meeting minutes, and how am I supposed to help this committee when I know absolutely nothing about anything?* The first meeting presides, everybody shared their comments, and another meeting was scheduled. I left the meeting feeling uncertain how was I going to help win. I only knew a little bit about even being a student, but the good news is, those on staff saw something inside me that I could not see, and they made sure that I was going to step outside my comfort zone. So lo and behold, I show up to the next scheduled committee meeting. This time, I'm feeling a little bit more confident, that is, until the chairman of the committee looks at me and asks, "Can we get a copy of the meeting minutes." I looked at him and said, "What?" He said, "The meeting minutes, the notes you took from the last meeting, do you have a copy available for us to see and approve?" I remember feeling stunned, tunnel vision. I couldn't breathe. I felt the gamut of things, one from ignorance, stupidity, to embarrassment, but I've always had this wonderful guardian angel, and now they tell you about it. I hope you forget about it because I've also believed that if in talk about something or boasting, that I now have jinxed things. It is a strange habit, but it's served me. In that moment of being asked about my responsibility, the mood shifted. All of a sudden, somebody made a comment, and the discussion turned from me being asked about meeting minutes to an issue that needed to be addressed right at that moment. I felt I still was sucked into the back of my chair and waited for those words to call the meeting adjourned, a new word that I found comfort in. I can't remember the exact reason, but we have about two more meetings, and with sheer luck or a complete disappointment, I was never questioned about meeting minutes again. I still look back at that moment, that moment of uncertainty, that moment of fear that as a little boy, they keep telling me I didn't belong, and there are still days, but I feel like I'm sitting at the table, but it was such a great practice for other things to come, discovering the ability to function and find my place at every executive table from that moment on. I can't believe how fast the school went. I found myself wanting to do more but also missing family. I had completed the associates program the Art Institute had, including a bachelor's program, to which I received a marketing degree, and I also paused for a moment thinking about the possibility of attending Florida Atlantic University, where I could have tried to get a master's degree in business, but for whatever reason, that little voice in my head convinced me that we had other plans.

It was in 1993 that I packed up my little two-door Honda Civic and headed West to El Paso, Texas, where my mother was now residing. In a spontaneous adventure, I hit the road late afternoon and ended up missing Interstate 10 and ended up in Atlanta, Georgia. Not planning accordingly, it was in my head that I drew a map to drive through New Orleans, Louisiana, Houston, then up to El Paso. Well, that plan flew out the window when I stopped for gas and asked if I was on the right road and clearly not. With the right questions, I received answers that was the opposite of where I was going. I got back in the car thinking I should've asked, but again, that little voice in my head said, "No, you'll be fine. Besides, you don't want to be a bother." Those words of "being a bother" still continue to hurt me to this day and one of the reasons that I rarely ask questions and rarely do follow-ups in my personal life. Mind you, in my professional life, I cover all bases, again going back to that whole meeting minutes debacle as a student representative, but in my personal life, I'm both complacent and fearful of making sure I understand or that I am heard clearly. On that particular day, I find myself a few hundred miles off coarse but nonetheless made it safe and sound to El

Paso, Texas. My plan was to hang out for a while. After all, I deserve a reward for my hard work in obtaining my degrees. Complacency can get ahold on you pretty quick and keep you tied down, and it wasn't before long I started getting on my mother's nerves, which, I mean, sure, but she had to know that I was cooking and cleaning and was helping pay back for my room and board. It was around the time that I received another wake-up call, another life lesson that was called assumption. It's true, assuming only provides further issues. I had assumed that since I was now a recent graduate that finding a job and any job of my choice was going to be a piece of cake and that once I walked into any office, I was going to be the guy they were looking for who was going to be a benefit and fix all problems. Don't laugh. This attitude is still rampant with all early twenty-year-olds, but unless you're a Kennedy or a Rockefeller, this fantasy will surely burst. I looked at a few places for a job that would be in the background of either audio recording and/or in marketing. I found not one job opening, not one opportunity to even start from the bottom and work my way up. It was a real blow to my ego and a real wake-up call to reality. However, life has a way of being a gut puncher to benevolent opportunities one is provided.

During this time, it was uncertain as to where I was going or what I was going to do to survive both financially and as an adult. I soon would come face-to-face with realizing that I had to do what I have to do especially since what I wanted to do was not happening, that being able to work in an environment to which I went to school for. I don't call it being pressured. Call it tough love, especially knowing that now in retrospect. My mother was really pushing me to find work because she knew I had something inside me that once I got started, I was unstoppable, and although I didn't understand that at the time and I had some displaced feelings about her motives, but I absolutely am grateful she provided that tough love. I ended up going to a gentleman's club. I walked in and looked around in this dark room that was dimly lit with flashing lights and music playing. I had been to this type of club before but never as a possible employee. I asked for an application. I talked to a manager, filled out the application, and walked out the door. No less than a few days later, I got the call telling me to show up back up to the club I initially went to for an audition. I remember thinking to myself about auditioning to one of these clubs, what that was about. So in an attempt to go there, never mind, I remember that phone call back to my mother where she told me that once I made a commitment, I should see it through, so I paused, did what I had to do, show to the club, went behind the bar to a little DJ booth—basically a 5 foot × 5 foot space with two CD players and a microphone—and was told to say, "Introducing Mercedes to the main stage. Don't forget, beer is still on special, so get them while they're cold." I remember saying the words but not meaning them, not being able to sell those words, not being able to enunciate in a way that basically marketing had taught me to do in order to sell a product. I had customers. I had some of the ladies come up to the little booth and say, "Who is this guy?" I look back at that moment and remember how much I wanted to flee. Everything I knew about myself, or convinced myself who I was, turned out to be a fallacy, but they hired me on the spot, not as an emcee but as a doorman/bouncer/bodyguard for both the club and i's dancing ladies—oh, and at a sister club located a few miles from the Fort Bliss Army base. I think that was when I learned that not everything seems to be what it is, meaning just because I was in this specific club that was pretty high end with a nice respectable clientele, at least based upon their suits and ties they wore. I was finding myself in that club, that no less than forty-eight hours before I applied, I had to throw an irate customer out, and that person came back and shot at the front door that opened to the inside of the club. I remember driving up to this round building to which I met the manager outside who was smoking a cigarette, a giant of a man, tall as wide as a Volkswagen bus, and as he said in a questionable hoarse tone, "Leon?" I said yes. He said, "Follow me." As we walked to the front entrance, that was where he had pointed out the three bullet holes that had just punctured the door. I thought, *What in the world am I doing here, and what if I have to throw someone out of the club?* That moment was actually another life lesson because in my attempt to not ask questions, and only assume, I had created quite the scenario in my head that was just going to be bad. However, I would be truly mistaken and also realized in hindsight that anytime a door opens, shot up or not, it's an opportunity to learn and practice doing your best because of the commitment made. I really enjoyed working in the gentleman's club, and soon my doorman/bouncer/bodyguard days would soon come to a close because of one opportunity that arose to which I found myself being directed by the manager to do a job because, after all, my job was to also perform duties assigned, and because the regular emcee had not shown up, it was now my responsibility to introduce dancers to their posts or stage. There was a center stage and a side stage. I had talk up drink promotions, count customers, and then also watch the door. Little did I know then that I would have found my true passion, talking into a microphone. I excelled at my job. I could director the ladies like a traffic cop, I could sell drinks, and I can do so with a drink in my hand. I even got pretty popular with the regular customers who were coming up shaking my hand and buying me drinks. The ladies were even tipping me well because I made them look good dancing songs that made them move provocatively. I even found myself being requested to work at the original club I applied and did so happily. I lasted just under two years in that environment. It was one day where I was just waking up in the late afternoon and just realized suddenly and asked myself the question, *Is this my life?* In that moment, I had a flash of the future, of me being burned out showing up to this club day after day, playing music, living off tips, drinking mixed drinks, smoking a pack of cigarettes a day, having bags under my eyes, and never being able to excel within this company. I don't know what it is, but I've always had this ability to learn quickly not to be the best but to be able to be good enough to excel, but in that, I also have this little voice that made me feel that in my conquest, this challenge was no longer challenging. And so I became bored and even though in my mind, before I started anything, I was trying to convince myself that I couldn't do something or that this task would be the hardest thing I would ever do, so why try? I still was able to complete any assignment and do so with extreme professionalism. I am not sure if that is irony, but it sounds crazy when I say it now.

So with that, I had resigned my position with the organization that hired me to be a doorman, bouncer, and bodyguard for dancers and then taught me how to use my voice for promotion, selling, and in return making a pretty decent living during that time, while learning my new trade. I can't fault that time. It was a blast, and who knows, maybe I would have become a manager, but I just had a feeling, one I could not explain, that made me feel it was time to move on. I can't say anything bad about that time. It opened a whole new world for me. Oh, yeah, that was also the time I met my then girlfriend, who would also become my partner for the next eighteen years.

It took me a while to get another job, and fooling around was maybe necessary or part of my curse, meaning that even in my downtimes, I've been really blessed to be lucky. It took a while, but a cousin of mine was working at a local pizza shop, and I don't know how he found out, but the local university, the New Mexico State University, had a radio station KRUX. Somewhere somehow, my name was dropped, and I reluctantly made a call to the station, and it was during the summer, so there was not a whole lot of students on campus, but they still need to keep operations running at the station, and there were drives or times that needed to be filled. I showed up and met the student program manager, nice kid, and he asked me if I had any experience. I said no, but I did work at a club where I had to talk on a microphone. Again, through sheer luck, he asked me if I was free and if I could start that minute. I balked and said yeah. The student program manager walked me to the booth. I was basically in the room where the CD player them either far, and he showed me around and showed me all these lists I had to fill out. I had a log of what songs I played at what time. I had to take readings from meters that gauged how the equipment was operating per FCC laws, and I could talk, but I had to watch my topic of conversation and my language. I felt like a stranger in a strange land, but boy, I quickly found my niche.

I had always been inquisitive even at a young age and also had a hundred questions lined up at the ready. Sometimes I asked all those questions; sometimes I didn't. However, in this circumstance,

my first interview, my natural curiosity, which I know call my ignorance power, was getting ready to serve me well. I was told I would
be receiving a call from a gentleman who was rolling cross-country. I
can't remember his direct cause, but he was a paraplegic, and he had
this sports-style tricked-out wheelchair, which he was rolling through
all major cities, and just so happened that on the day I started at
the college radio station, he was going to be traveling on Interstate
10 through Las Cruces. I had no idea what I was in store for as this
assignment literally just appeared. Actually another life lesson, when
stuff happens, be prepared to do your best try and figure it out and
make people go wow. The station phone rang. I put his call online,
which meant people could hear the interview over the air, and I proceeded on asking questions, and it was a natural flow. I remember
being curious, and in this heartfelt curiosity, that came out during
our conversation over the air. The student program manager came
in and said, "Wow, that was a great interview." I looked at him with
a not surprised look but a "hey, you're here in front of me" look and
said, "Oh, well, thank you." And I was a little stunned because I
thought, *Wow I was just talking, just having a general conversation, and
I was actually curious about this person and his life*. I have been blessed
with an ability to actually be able to just listen and, in any conversation, be able to make the conversation be about an individual, which
I felt would make them feel like they were 100 percent the topic of
our conversation, which transpired in my interview. In that moment,
it was just him and me. The gentlemen rolling cross-country just
wanted to share, and I was there to listen, and our dialogue exchange
came out naturally, and it did not matter if two people or a thousand
people were listening. People, including the student general manager,
felt the sincerity, and I was hooked from there on.

That particular time helped me hone a new set of skills, which
carried me into the next phase of my career, broadcasting. Turns out
that one of the faculty members who hired to help run the college
radio station at the university also was working as a reporter for a
couple of radio stations in Las Cruces. I remember him coming up
to me and saying, "You know, Leon, you should think about trying
out and applying for this open position at one of the radio stations I

work out." I remember looking at him with a blank stare but smiling as to seem like I was listening intently. I thought, *Yeah, sure, why not?* and went down to the radio station, met with the program manager who was this former beauty pageant contestant, and whether I agreed with her skill of broadcasting at that time or not, she still held title over me, and I was merely the guy coming off the street lower than pond scum and had to get on her radar.

Very interesting when you think about things, when you reflect back on life or back on how you handled the day's events. I have always been spontaneous, but that came with the cost of overthinking and then hindsight, a by-product of overthinking, so I always would question myself or my actions even if those actions had not occurred and was basically all a prediction of what may have come. That little voice in the back of my mind would raise up, and questions would form, like, *Why did I do that? That's not going to fare well, and I'm wasting my time because I can't do this, and if I don't do anything at all, nothing bad is going to happen.* The good thing about having guardian angels is they are always looking out for me, and they know which doors need to burst open and which doors I need to be pushed through because my value is not only luck, but I know deep down that I am skillful enough to do any job, complete any task, and create positive outcomes.

I was offered the job of nighttime air talent at KMVR, which was a top 40 radio station. My new shift consisted from six to midnight. Despite my difference in musical taste, I actually enjoyed learning how to find my fit with the small radio market. I pretty much did what I had to do, which was play music, talk up a product using a liner, tell the time and the temperature every half hour, and introduce the artist and the artist's song I was playing or going to play in the next few minutes, creating a cliffhanger of sorts trying to make sure the listener stuck around long enough to hear their favorite song through the commercials. I mean, after all, listeners were there to listen to music, but the money was on advertising, and to try and not make one more than the other, that was a real art. And at the same time, if you were good, your ego is the next thing that will try to surface. And radio jocks are a fickle bunch. There are all experts who look down on newbies. I remember my ego surfacing every once in a while especially when I started gaining a little bit of listenership. I was still honing my voice, not to be a puker, a colloquialism that described how some jocks sounded, like a bad game show host. I really was trying to be a natural, and since I had learned how to be more baritone from my gentleman emcee clubs days, that was my style. I would do these funny bits and share these funny stories in between breaks. I would pull from news feeds funny stories from around the world about people doing crazy things and edit them to cut down on time, again all pre-internet as far as ability to see videos, so I had to make sure I could also help the listener visualize, or else I was just reading and likely losing the listeners' interest. I would actually get people calling in saying they enjoyed hearing these stories, who did not enjoy hearing my anecdotal news articles, where the program manager and program director felt that I was distracting from the music and cutting into the customer base or advertisers because people listened to the radio to hear their favorite song, not hear me, which I always disagreed with that logic. To me, it wasn't complete if you did not have somebody. I was capable of tying the two wins together, and to me, that was somebody who had a personality, had a good voice, and could keep the listener hooked, but what did I know? I was the new guy. Besides, I thought, this was six to midnight, and I was only doing these stories after nine o'clock, so all younger listeners we're all getting ready to go to bed, but I complied with the "experts" and followed the rules and then discovered a little trick called voice tracking. Voice tracking is the ability to record your voice, add it to a certain time frame of an hour, and your voice would then be triggered to come on seconds before a song or commercial break, all without having to be sitting in front of microphone because everything was prerecorded. Since I was limited to doing what I could do, this particular allowability served its purpose at this particular station. However, I soon fell in love with the ability to be able to go live, talk into a microphone, and share with the listener every part of my persona through my voice.

I don't ever remember wanting to learn the actual business side of radio, but I do remember retaining enough knowledge to do my job and be able to be able to regurgitate the lingo when need be. What I was really in love with was the ability to connect to somebody listening to my voice in their car, from a device in their bedroom in their home, and I was helping them get through the day; that was a really powerful feeling.

I can't remember how long it lasted at the top 40 radio station, maybe a year or maybe a year and a half, but that was around the time that I found out I was going to be a dad. My then girlfriend and I found out that she was pregnant, and I remember the world stopping when I heard that news. I remember feeling that at thirty years old, I was not ready to be a dad and unfortunately held on to that thought for a very long time, which also saddens me when I think back, considering I raised a very nice respectable young man.

I knew it was time to move on from the top 40 radio station, and even though it helped me add to my jock repertoire and I was learning things, I wasn't happy in the environment. As I mentioned, ego between jocks ran rampant, so I was really never allowed to blossom or develop any new skills like voicing and editing commercials. It was because of being able to voice track that I had a lot of time to learn how to teach myself how to create commercials utilizing the latest software and through a lot of trial and error became pretty good. And even though I was getting a lot of work voicing commercials, I was coming into my own despite some criticism from my jock colleagues.

It just so happened there was another opening on an oldies station, KVLC, and I went to this station, met the general manager, armed with some experience and background, which landed me the afternoon drive time spot, which was from 2:00 to 6:00 p.m. This is where I learned so much more, had the ability to do much more, and where I really think I came into my own with my newfound passion and newfound career. I started creating more commercials, voicing more commercials. I started doing more live remotes, which are basically on-site broadcasts, and I made a lot of customers happy because we were bringing business to their establishments, and by that time, Nicolas, my new son, was born and doing very well. My mother also remarried and seemed happy, so yeah, life was pretty good. I really enjoyed being a dad, and I thought I did pretty good. My schedule was flexible, and it allowed both parents to be able to function as one. While my girlfriend, Nicolas's mom, slept, I would be up with him, and I get pretty good at changing diapers too, and while I slept, Nicolas's mom took care of him. The schedule worked out very well. As new parents, we actually did really well, and as a couple, Nicholas's mom and I had an upside down, but for the most part, I think we both understood that we know what we needed to do, why we needed to do it, and felt safe in the company of each other doing what needed to be done—a real family. However, my vices, my passive aggressiveness, my cynicism, and my sarcasm would begin to grow stronger and stronger in my relationship. I was never abusive, but I sure was vocal, and without finger-pointing, what triggered my outbursts was the lack of affection from my partner. It really bothered me to not be able to touch and hold my partner. I mean, we had a baby, so we did things, but we never had any real intimate moments, more acts. I grew up in a very touchy, saying I love you, going up and giving hugs environment, and now I had fallen in love with someone who was the opposite. I know that took a toll, but I repressed those feelings and would only bring them up to try and make a hurtful point in our arguments. But I also think I was too afraid to leave the relationship for the greater good. I mean, I had a baby. I had to do my part. I had to provide. That was the manly thing to do. But I could never really articulate a decent conversation and understand that my opinion may have mattered to me but not necessarily matter to somebody else even if they were somebody I said I love you to. That was a very interesting lesson that took me a long time to learn.

One thing I learned during the radio years was how to really become comfortable with my interview skills. To me, there was an irony being in the field of radio broadcasting as a talent. You are told to talk less, to not say anything more than you have to, again the whole time and temperature thing, but I never really felt that made me more relatable to the audience, therefore connecting on a human level. I complied and did my job, but I also found ways to be able to stretch out a conversation over the air to try and really connect with people and make them feel like they were in a conversation with me, and it was a pretty powerful and wonderful feeling to be able to get a phone call from different listeners and hear that you made their day. I really felt that I was an asset to the radio station, and maybe I was. I don't know. I just did my job, and I learned from some really good people, but things change, and this maybe was about the time that I started learning about office politics. Even though I really didn't know what it was, it was there, and I was a part of it. My leaving the radio station was at the time a gut punch—a sucker punch is a matter of fact. The general manager of the station for some reason felt it in the best interest of the station to demote me from the morning show, which was an ideal spot for on-air talent because you had your biggest listing base being so early in the morning. But the GM wanted to replace me with a dynamic duo, and I felt completely slighted. This is where my ego came into play because again I was building an audience. I had listeners. I was being requested to do a lot of the voiceover commercials, and yet I never felt the need to kiss anyone's behind, and maybe that was part of my demise. But I still don't want to do that today. I just want to do a job, and I want to do it well, and I want to be rewarded for doing so. We had a meeting in the morning. The general manager, the program director, and myself sat in the booth where I was doing my show, and they made their decision. I said okay, and I walked out. I forgot I had some personal items, so I carried three big boxes of stuff, items I had put up in my little workspace, and each time I had to go back inside to get a box and carry out made that open wound sting much greater. To this day, my mantra has been, that if I can't carry everything from my office in both my hands, it's either staying or going in the trash, and ever since then, I've never decorated any office I sat in with any personal items. I separated my personal space from my workspace, and I think that has suited me well.

I had found myself unemployed with a newborn mouth to feed and a girlfriend who was a stay-at-home mom at that time. I didn't feel lost, but I do remember feeling mad. I had done a lot at the radio station and felt unappreciated, but I also may have let my ego, along with spite, talk me into proceeding on an issue that transpired when

I first started at this particular radio station. When I started my first day at the radio station, I was being introduced to the staff, and the general manager walked in at the time and did a hooting noise, a "woooo wooo wooo" chant, because one of the staff had mentioned I was Native American, and I remember laughing but also thinking, *Wow*. And rather than make any comment in that moment, maybe because I didn't want to rock the boat or maybe I was too concerned about hurting anyone's feelings, again bad coping ability, but because I didn't address this issue, it stuck with me for a very long time. And then to have a tumultuous relationship with the general manager, well, it seemed like a recipe for disaster. Anyway, after I quit, I filed an EEOC complaint, and it failed miserably. No staff member could recall the incident and rightly so, but I put them on the spot anyway. It was a lesson learned, and I felt strongly about this incident that I preceded to press the EEOC complaint. A meeting had been conducted with the mediator. I said my piece, the general manager said their piece, and so did the general manager. Long story short, my case was not strong enough to prove any point. Not to mention, I left and was not terminated. There was a lesson learned from that day on. I made it a point to document and preserve based on facts and wrote all narrations in a lengthy manner that would give more than enough backup if any issue were to arise, and let me tell you, there would be a lot of business issues that would arise.

I've always felt that fate has a plan in store for you. Now whether you agree or disagree is irrelevant because fate's plan is still your plan. My middle brother had decided to move back to Dulce and was working and doing really good. He bought himself a new pickup, had a new girlfriend, and he also knew that I was unemployed. So in one of our conversations over the phone one evening, he had asked me, "Why don't you move back to the Dulce?" I laughed and said, "Never!" What did I say about fate, lesson number 200 and something? Never say never!

I stayed out of work for a couple of months, and all of a sudden, call it soul searching, call it survival, call it doing what needs to be done as an adult and parent! I found myself applying for a job with the Jicarilla Apache Nation. There was a vacancy in the Nation's accounting department, and the Nation was looking to fill this vacant accountant position with someone who had some light accounting experience, for all the Nation's enterprises, which were basically the retail businesses that the Nation owned and operated. I received a call based upon the application I filled out and had an interview scheduled. I made the six-hour drive up from Las Cruces to Dulce, and I remember sitting in a hallway waiting to be called into the room where a screening committee sat, whose duty it was to ask questions, take notes based on the responses of each question, and then at the end, reach a decision as to who the best suitable candidate for the position would be. I kept thinking, *What am I doing here?* I really was in deep thought. I had no real experience in accounting, and all I could think about was the salary for this position. It was almost triple of what I was making in radio. So the door opened, my name was called, and I greeted the committee. Some knew of me from my parents, and some had no clue, and the questions began. Question number 1, "What's your background, and how will that relate to the accounting position you are applying for?" "Do you have any understanding of accounting and finance?" My answers were vague. All my answers were basically no, no, no, and no. One of the last questions was if I had any questions or comments. I said, "Well, I know there's no homes here, and I will not have any place to live, so if I don't get the job, that's okay because there is probably someone else who is more qualified than I am." I left the interview feeling confident that I flubbed the interview. After all, I didn't want to live in Dulce. I had vowed all those years ago that you couldn't pay me enough to live in Dulce, so by saying no to all the questions during this interview, I felt fine knowing that I did my part by showing up to the interview and therefore fulfilling my commitment, and now I could go back to Las Cruces and be with my family and hoped something in the form of a job would come up. That's the thing about having this fantasy of reality. You could blow things off and then wish for something, forgetting that everything in life takes hard work, dedication, and sacrifice, and in that if you had to start from the bottom, you started from the bottom but could then work your way up. I had felt at that time that radio was the only thing I could ever do. I was so in love with it. The job, the ability to connect to people, and the ability to use my voice to be a louder voice was addicting, and everything else in the world ceased to exist, a mindset I still have to this day.

I had thought that Dulce job was behind me. I mean, blowing the interview like I did, they'd be crazy to hire me, and I felt confident that I was to never hear of Dulce again. It was September of 2001, 9/11 had happened, and I remember feeling that this was unimaginable as I watched this unfold on television, being all those miles away from Ground Zero but feeling the impact, the fear, the uncertainty, and possibly call to war! I had thought, *Wow, now there's going to a draft, and I'm going to be recruited to fight.* I'm a pacifist. I think there are some out there who call it being a wuss, but that didn't bother me none. I can be a big wuss at times. About a week later, the phone rings. It was the Jicarilla Apache Nation human resource office telling me that I was selected for the position of principal accountant for enterprises or enterprise principle accountant. I can't remember the exact title of the position, but I do remember feeling like twenty minutes went by with nothing but silence as I'm cradling the phone to my ear and thinking, how the heck do I get out of this? How do I say NO? How do I say I don't want the job? But it was also at that moment a little voice said, *Remember, you made a commitment. You started the wheels turning in this chain reaction, and now you are selected, so you have to do what you need to do.* And so I said I accept and asked when I needed to show up for work.

I knew there would be some challenges when I moved to Dulce. One was a new job, two was leaving my family, and three was figuring out where I was going to live. I had mentioned to my father that I was moving back home, and he offered his home to me. He had just been married, and I wasn't sure how my presence would go over with the new wife, but I was grateful, and I knew that I would have to mind my p's and q's as the saying goes because after all, it was my father and his new bride's home, and regardless of my past issues, emotional angst, and inability to cope in a healthy manner, I had to abide by the rules. It was actually pretty interesting, and despite the lack of technological advancement, no internet, and no cable television, we actually grew pretty darn close, and having to sequester my angst especially since I let it fuel me for so long, I rediscovered how great of a guy my father really was despite his vice of alcohol. We actually went for drives, we went hunting, I would join him and his wife when they went to the casino, we cook and have meals at the table, and we talk about general topics. I'd visit him at work, and he would visit me at work. In retrospect, I wished I had more time with them. There's a little part of me that might have said things differently in our man-to-man conversation, especially beginning to realize that my thoughts and my misdirection of life, which I created in my mind about him, were really about me and my ignoring and repressing my inability to succeed in life.

One of the fondest memories I have was when my father surprised me by coming down to the office where I worked, my cubicle. I worked in the Nation's tribal administration building, and I had worked in an office space with all women, and I actually had some comments about working with all those ladies, but the reality was, those ladies were very smart and very talented, and I got along very well with all of them. It really was a very professionally experience and environment. Part of my job was data entry; in fact, a huge part of it was data entry. I thought to myself, *Why are they calling this an accountant position when really it's just entering data?* But again, the salary was pretty good. There were other duties like counting inventory at the four enterprises the Nation was operating in, but beyond that, it was really just data entry and pulling reports. When I first stepped foot into my new office space and was led to my new cubicle, I looked at a desk covered with stacked papers, all receipts that had not yet been inputted into the departments accounting software, where they could be filed and compiled into spreadsheets and other sources of data for momagers to use as information to gauge profit. I sat down in my chair and thought to myself, *What the heck am I doing here? I'll never be able to figure out this system. Look at all this work that was left for me. This really sucks!* When I looked up and I saw my dad standing in front of me, I wanted sympathy, that moment where you look at somebody and go, *Please feel sorry for me. Look at how tough my life is. You don't understand. Look at all this work I have to do.* In fact, I might have even stated that to him, but he looked at me, and he said, "Just do what you have to do. Just start with one piece of paper and then another and take your time doing it." My father's words stuck with me. I really wanted to say, "What the hell! Why aren't you trying to save me?" But in that moment, I didn't realize it, but he had saved me. The advice I had always been given about committing to something and doing it right was primarily from my mother, but to hear it from my father and already knowing that deep core value because I had planted it and followed that advice was powerful because my father's reinforcement of what I knew solidified that he was right, and the right thing to do was do my job, and so I picked up one piece of paper, hunted, and pecked the computer keyboard and coded everything that was left behind. I had learned the system and with the push of a button could recall any vendor the Nation bought products from, how many times, and at what cost, and I could now show the enterprise managers what was going on with their budgets.

I had been the enterprise accountant from October of 2001 all the way through September of 2002 and during that year had really grown close to my father. I did feel myself reverting back to that teen child when he would go off on a bender, and I regressed back to those emotion of disappoint and anger. It was one midmorning where I found myself sitting at the small table in the dining room of my father. I was waiting to go shopping with a cousin of mine, who was going to pick me up. And as I waited, my father approached me. I can't recall how the conversation started, but I know that he was hungover and had that grizzled voice and that hangover smell. It smells like apples that are overly ripened. At least to me, it did, but we sat there, and somehow I was able to confide in him. I had shared my emotions and my anger, my sadness, and my wonder of how he could succumb to this vice and choose alcohol over his family. I don't recall his exact words, but he shared just a very tiny sliver of his life, and other than mentioning that he felt he had done the best that he could, he did mention that he felt he could never rely on anybody and so in that feeling of abandonment had buried his emotions. And when he was under the influence, he felt courageous enough to share his true emotions, but he then said this. He said, "Whatever you feel about me, I am still your father. I am always proud of you, and I love you and your brothers very much. You can blame me for things, but you have every opportunity to be your own man." I remember a feeling of peace come over my body. I felt no need to debate or blame, and although my ego wanted to chime in, I kept it at bay and left our conversation on a positive note. Soon after, he said he was going to lay back down in bed, the horn beeped, and my ride showed up. We never talked about that moment again, and I think, at least for me, our time up to then was erased, and we had a do-over. My father was a very loving man. He was an affectionate man. He would give hugs and kisses. He was a jokester and had many friends. However, he had an opposite side. He could be very moody and mean. He would lash out and throw things in a rage. He was impatient and would scream and berate if we could not keep up with his pace, whether that was learning, as he was the tutor, or if we could not bring him fast enough something he asked for like a tool. My father had a lot of pride, and maybe he geared that pride toward my brothers and I because it made him feel vicariously like he was an athlete, especially because we excelled in sports. I know some of his colleagues from work had sons who were playing football and were doing pretty good. I tried out for football, but I just found out that it wasn't my favorite thing, especially since I was being yelled at by coaches whom I felt had very little experience themselves in real-life sports. After all, none that I recall were Hall of Famers, and so why are they yelling at me when I'm doing my job and tackling who I am supposed to? But my angst would still go back to being yelled at during my Catholic school days, and I didn't know it then, but so I lashed out, and I went the total opposite of what I was told to do, and I came to the conclusion in my mind that no one can tell me what to do, and so I didn't play. My father, who kept hearing all the wonderful Monday morning stories of the Friday night football games, would come home, and he'd be in a mood. There was one time where my brother and I were going to throw the football around in the front yard, and he looked at me with a look of disgust and said, "Why you holding that? Only men play football. You're not a man. You're a pussy. Put that ball away." I remember looking right at him and so wanting to throw that ball right at his head, but I turned away. He was a huge pain in my gut, and I said nothing, and I can't even remember if we played football or not, but I think we might have because I also did things in spite of, so I'm sure we did toss the football around, and I'm sure I made a lot of noises, and I sure I was doing some champion catches and some nice spiral throws just to press him. Unfortunately, I learned that trait and is still something I do even now to my own kids, but I am working at that.

During my time away working, I had visited my family, who were back in Las Cruces, adapting to Dad being away. The great thing was the kid's mom grew up in Las Cruces, so she had her mother and father to help in watching Nicolas as a baby while the misses worked. This dynamic worked out okay for the most part. We finally had surplus income with my new job and were able to splurge on things; it was a good time. It was the fall of 2001, and my family had come to visit me and stay during Thanksgiving with me and my father and his wife. I rented a car so that the trip north was both safe and reliable, and it was nice for Nicolas to visit his grandfather, and boy was my father pleased with his new grandpa duties. My father would take Nicolas with him on short drives, and my father would proudly sit Nic on his lap as Nic seemed to drive down the road. It was great, and I was happy that my father was able to experience being a grand-father for the first time. My father proudly declared that he was going to cook a grand feast for Thanksgiving, and we were all happy. My father was a very good cook, and his last job was cooking for students whose residence was a dormitory, who all raved when they ate. It was three days before Thanksgiving, and my father had even bought the turkey that was defrosting in his little pickup truck. It was cold enough outside to keep the cab chilled like a refrigerator, and then all of a sudden, he disappeared! He went off on a bender, and we had no sight of him or his Thanksgiving feast that he was going to prepare. I remember thinking, Wow, I thought we had an understanding, and I even went as far as to get really upset and think that I was lied to, but in reality, our talk at the table while I waited for my ride to pick me up was more about me and my releasing of pent-up emotion. I had created an expectation that because I spoke, he was to understand and comply with my feelings. That was yet another learned lesson, a fantasy I created to help me feel better about myself, and my father failed me, or so I believed at that moment. My little family and I had picked up my mother, who was visiting and staying with my brother, to go to town. Now the town from Dulce usually meant Farmington, which was ninety ought miles away, so it was a drive, but it was a Friday, and that meant sales and just to get out of the house. We were about fifteen miles out of Farmington, and I stopped for gas. While the pump fueled the vehicle, I remember complaining to my mother about my father abandoning us, and she nonchalantly said, "Well, no matter what he does or what he chooses, he will always be your father." I sat puzzled because usually our conversations were talking about others, and that pearl, although true, surprised me because that's exactly what my father stated to me! I found out some time after that my father paid my mother a visit, and they reminisced and, I believe, tried to find some closure, although I don't think that happened with my mother, but I felt it really did from my father. My mother's rang true, and for the trip to town landing at the mall, I was in good spirits. It was in the next hour that my girlfriend received a call from her mother, stating that her father just had a major heart attack and was in the emergency room in the local Las Cruces Hospital. The plan was to wake up early and drive down to our apartment in Las Cruces so that my girlfriend could be with her family, and I would watch Nicolas. The following morning, the alarm rang, and we got up and prepared for our long drive. My father had finally come home and was sleeping in his bed. I went to his room and told him what had happened and that we were leaving. I told him he didn't have to get up. He said he would cook breakfast, but we were in a hurry, and then his track record of cooking was a bit tarnished. Nicolas just so happened to come see what I was doing, and my father acknowledged Nic from his bed. I told Nic, "Say bye to Grandpa. Tell him you love him." Nic complied, and my father responded with his I love and bye sentiment, and I said, "See you later, Pops."

It was a cold November early morning. There was no snow, but the car's windows needed to be defrosted, and the cold air made for a serene and peaceful drive. I kept quiet and listened to music while my passengers slept. We would usually stop for breakfast, but because of the nature of this particular trip, we pushed through, only stopping once for gas. We made good time, and we got to our apartment just a little before noon. The plan was for my girlfriend to head straight to the hospital after Nicolas and I were dropped off, and I would cook and feed Nic and relax from the long trip. My girlfriend went to the bathroom, and I lay on the bed to hug Nicolas. That second, my cell phone rang. It was my mother. I can't remember if we made small talk, you know, how was the drive, you guys eat, that kind of stuff. I just heard her say, "Your dad is gone." My mother's voice crackled. I said, "What?" Thinking to myself in that moment, we just left him and he was in bed, where did he go? My mother went on to say my father had passed away. I broke down. I made a loud noise before I burst into tears, demanding an explanation. My mind went to a place that envisioned my father being in a car accident or worse, a hit and run. I don't know why I thought that, but those were my exact thoughts at that time. By then my girlfriend heard me and saw me sobbing, so I told her what happened. As she began to cry, just then, there was a knock on the door. It was my girlfriend's mother and brother. They stopped to pick up my girlfriend to take her to the hospital to see her father who was in the emergency room fighting for his life. Needless to say, it was a tough day, but I told my girlfriend to go see her father and be by his side. There was really nothing I could do, and I was not about to leave my girlfriend and Nicolas back, especially with everything that had occurred that morning. I do not remember anything else from that morning. I don't remember asking for details. I don't remember how Nic and I spent the morning, but later that day, my girlfriend's father recovered and was moved from the intensive care unit to a hospital room. That was good news. We waited until that late afternoon before we made the trip back north to Dulce. The drive was quick, again no stops, deep thoughts and music playing. We pulled up to the driveway, cars filling available spaces. It was family and friends. I saw my brothers standing outside as snow began to fall. The skies were clear all day, even on our drive, but then just released what seemed to be tears

54

from heaven. I opened the car door, exited, and fell into my middle brother's arms. I said, "That fucker!" My words were a collection of emotions all rolled up into a ball that I felt summarized who my father was—a kind, loving, humorous man, who could be a moody, mean, hateful person that succumbed to his addiction for alcohol. So using the words "that fucker" was my way of acknowledging our loss and also asking why. I composed myself and got the family inside. I remember feeling bothered by all the people sitting around, photos were being passed around, and spirits were trying to be good. I even quipped a few remarks that got the room laughing, and one picture came my way. It was a picture of my dad wearing a red New Mexico State University sweatshirt, a ball cap, and a huge smile. My father had a smile that I gratefully have inherited, and it was that picture that sent a flood of loving, positive memories back into my mind, like a door that had been unhinged and revealed a whole new room. I sobbed and remarked in a firm voice, "He was a damn good man!" Silence filled the room, and I went to the bedroom and sat on the bed. This long day was over.

The next couple of days, we were planning the funeral, getting things set to lay my father to rest. At the mortuary, I was asked if I wanted to view the body. My first response was to absolutely say no, but my brother said he wanted to, and I felt it was an older brother duty to stand by his side, so we proceeded to the back of the building where my father was laying up on a steel slab. I could see the Y incision, which is I guess where they open up the breastplate and remove the organs. I don't know. It just looks like a giant Y that was carved into the chest and then stitched together. I saw his shell of a body but didn't see any glow or spirit. I thought his image was going to haunt me before I saw him, but I think I was more scared of the horror I created in my mind. His body was transported to the local Catholic church where we had his service, as his wife had chosen the venue, which was fine with me. I mean, I wasn't holding any grudges against the building itself for my youthful Catholic church experiences, and I was only occupying the space of the building for a short time, so I think I was pretty cool with the decision.

Cool or not, I was chosen to give the eulogy, which was surprising because again I didn't volunteer to do it. I was recruited by somebody, might have been my mother, but maybe that's just my mind regressing back to a time that I spoke about prior. When I was called to do the eulogy, I really had no idea how to do a traditional eulogy. I went up to the podium, looked into the crowd, and there was a sea of people. The church was wall to wall with guests attending my father's funeral service. I was absolutely blown away. I knew he was a popular guy whether he was on the straight and narrow or when he was partying with whatever friends he made. Whatever that was, it made an impact on people, and people wanted to pay the respect. It was in that moment I changed my thought process of the eulogy, and I directed my comments more toward forgiveness, more toward compassion, more toward the ability to love somebody regardless of their choices or transgressions. I had briefly told the story of sitting at the table with my father and our conversation and in that moment being able to really kind of let loose the baggage I had carried around all those years. At the end of my speech, I had mentioned the cliché that life is short and that the only time we really say I love you to somebody is when we are gathered to say goodbye. I pointed to my father's coffin. I left the podium saying, "You have today. Go tell that person you have always said you cared about that you love them and give them a hug." The pallbearers took the body, loaded him into the back of my uncle's pickup truck, and they drove him out to his grave site. There were some final words from the priest. They put my father into the ground with all his possessions since that's what the culture denotes as respect when a loved one passes, that they are buried with every possession that they have. The backhoe started filling in the whole or the grave site. I said my goodbyes, and I never went back to see his grave site again. Not going back was not a sign of disrespect. I mean, I had made my peace with my father. I was at peace. He actually taught me his last life lessons, and those stuck with me, and I may not have been on the right path at that time, but the path was a lot clearer, and that was the path that I knew I needed to go down and do so knowing I made a commitment, so follow through with pride and respect.

Every once in a while, I look up at the sky, and when I see a hawk, I remember walking into a conversation between my father and his wife. They were joking, and my father had quipped that when he died, he was going to come back as a hawk, and of course, in the teasing, his wife said, "Yeah, right, maybe a buzzard but not a hawk." And they both laughed, and I laughed as I said, "Maybe a turkey." But every now and again, coincidental or not, when I need to feel at peace or I am driving to get to town and I see a hawk flying or sitting on a high-line wire, it just appears, and I know he's looking down on me and his family looking out for us.

The days passed, and within a year, my girlfriend and Nicolas were now living with me in my father's wife's home in Dulce. I was working, and we were doing pretty good. We made it through the holidays and had a bit of a falling out within the family, but that was usually par for the course. If someone didn't create an issue, then it really wasn't the holidays, but we managed to go through the motions. Sooner or later when you live in someone else's house, two things happen. One, you want your own space, and two, you feel like you're walking on eggshells because it's not your space. Don't get me wrong. I was absolutely grateful to have a home for me and my family again especially moving to a place that had no homes, no traditional way to even buy your home, much less rent because there was a mile-long waiting list to get a place to live for your family.

Maybe that was around the time I caught the bug for community activism or politics. I had developed a sense of wondering, asking questions to myself and in usual general chitchat at the dinner table, how was not providing homes to accommodate a populace acceptable?

I had really developed an niche with my accounting job and was flourishing, and I remember one time that there was a memo written from our department supervisor stating to the affect that there was an issue that the tribal council had heard about and that the council had demanded that all behaviors or comments directed at the government shall cease and desist, and I thought, *Wow, how is this allowable?* Because I had not heard of anything derogatory, nor had I seen anyone in my office challenge any actions. People would literally just shut down. They would stop everything because no specifics were provided or any due process of any sort as to inform by facts as to these accusations. I mean, people would complain but only in a very small circle and with the select view, but no one ever challenged or questioned as to why employees were being directed to do this or that or not do this or that; it was very strange to me. The only comment I ever received was, "The Council said…" and that never sat well with me, but I did my job and thought, *When in Rome…* After all, I was the outsider. Who am I to question authority?

It had to be the summer of 2002. I used to go to work very early, 7:00 a.m. I was the first one there, and I would make coffee so that when the ladies arrived to work, coffee was made. There was no place to buy pastries, so the night before, maybe I'd buy a small box of doughnuts to lay out just to show appreciation and try to make a positive work environment. It was one of those mornings that I had gone out into the main lobby of the administration building and saw a dear old friend, a longtime friend of the family, and we sat and visited for a while. She asked how things were going, and I said fine. She had made mention that this year was an election year, and it was coming up quick. I replied, "Yeah, I mean, I vote." I just really never know who to vote for because I really don't know the candidates or their platforms, but now that I'm here living in Dulce, I'm a little bit more informed. She then mentioned, "Why don't you run?" I looked at her with a shocked look on my face, thinking that this was the most ridiculous thing I've ever heard. I did not say that out loud, but I did laugh and say, "No one knows me here," and we left it at that. I went back to my cubicle, started doing my work, and kept thinking about her comments. Days went by, and I had mentioned it in passing to my girlfriend. We both were clueless as to what a council person actually did, but she was supportive, but I dismissed the thought but also kept it in the back of my mind. I kept on doing my job and doing it well, but the more I started seeing things whereas before you heard things I actually started creating more questions in my mind as to how certain actions and abilities were granted to a select few. Well, everybody else had to conform and adhere to every rule mandated by those select few, meaning government officials. I can't remember exactly when, but I may have thought more about the decision of actually entering into the race as a candidate for the upcoming 2002 election, which were taking place in June and July of that year. And I thought, *Well, at the very least, I can shake up the system.* And by shaking up the system, I could have a platform where I could ask questions, to satisfy my curiosity and at the same time provide some response to those other questions everybody else had when we would engage in conversation about politics and, in turn, those acts of government officials.

I had officially made my decision to run for office as a legislative council candidate for the Jicarilla Apache Nation council election. The term legislative council was changed from tribal council in an attempt to try and steer those officials into understanding what exactly the role and responsibility of being an elected council person was, which was stated in an ordinance, that council members were responsible for law creation, law preservation, law amendments, and economic development, nothing more. However, the term *legislative* turned out to be a suggestion even though it had been codified. The attempt was valid but turned out to be unreliable as the point was missed trying to get those individuals who were serving to stay in their own lane. Since I had officially made my decision to run for office, I had to pay a fee of $50 and then undergo a background check, a resident and age verification. All candidates had to reside within the boundaries of the reservation for six months or more and had to be over thirty years of age. I remember walking to the local election board office, which was the office that was responsible for making sure that all certifications were conducted and approved before any candidate could be placed on the ballot. I stared at four large poster boards that were titled with position numbers. The Nation has no districts, so council positions are titled by seat numbers, and since the elections of these positions are staggered, alternating elections will have seat 1 through 4 or 5 through 8. In my first election, the seats up for election were 1 through 4. I stared for what seemed to be an hour. I had no idea what I was doing, so all of a sudden, a number appeared in my head, and I said out loud that one as I pointed to position 4. There was one name above me that turned out to be the incumbent for that position and someone who had never lost their elections. I did not know that at the time but found out later when people, including family, came up and told me I should change my position because my new opponent had never lost and was certain to retain his seat. I would indulge the comments and say thank you, but I can't make any changes, and whatever happens, happens. In my ignorance, I never was one for bumper stickers and decals and political signs. I just felt that if I could talk to people, I could engage them in some dialogue that would be positive; that in itself is an interesting lesson learned. I did show up to one campaign rally. There were other candidates holding a rally in a local park. They invited me, and I went up there to the stage as I was called up, and I purposely took Nicholas, who at that time was maybe going on three years old, and I did so because I knew that with a child's short attention span, I could use him as an excuse to wrap up any speech, so that I'm not up there just gawking or rambling on. And sure enough, it worked. All I said is I'm running for office because I have a lot of questions, and my questions are concerning, and if I can shake up the system to allow people to feel that they should be engaging their government that I've already won, and I joked as I pointed to Nic and said, "I even brought my campaign manager up here with me just to make sure that I say the right thing." That got some laughs, and I wrapped up by encouraging everybody to vote, and I walked off the stage.

The weeks went by, and all of a sudden, it was June, which meant the primary elections had begun; it was election time. The Nation follows the standard elections that are done during federal, state, and county elections, meaning we have two elections—a primary election to get the top 2 candidates based from popular votes, where those top 2 will now go to head in the general election held in July, which will then be determined by popular vote. The winner, that person will then serve a four-year term. June came, and all of a sudden, I found myself as a top 2 contender for the possible seat as an opportunity to serve as a legislative council member for the nation, but then I also went back to those comments I was still being told, that my opponent never lost an election, and I should have changed seats while I could have. And all these emotions started to build up, assumptions and expectations started to flood my mind, and I began overthinking, trying to act like I was able to cope but not being able to do so in a healthy manner. So I repressed all those feelings and in that created a facade, which then began to be my response to people and myself, which was, "I don't care if I win or lose. I really don't care. I've gotten this far. I deserve a huge round of applause, and if I lose, well, it's nobody's fault because I really don't care. Besides, I don't know what the job is about anyway." Turned out, I really cared, and it was important. Those lessons both my parents instilled in me came rushing back. I made a commitment, and I needed to do what was right and do so in a professional manner. Habits are hard to break, and hearing those words in my mind and knowing what the right thing to do was, I kind of ignored it and just repressed those feelings because again I was too afraid to admit defeat or admit that I was scared. And so I had those excuses that it didn't matter at the ready, just in case I needed to help me feel better about something that I had no direct control over but would then have an emotional effect on me.

Fate, as I had mentioned before, is a wonderful thing. It's scary, and all I really asked of fate especially now learning lessons of opportunities, doors opening, or things that happen in your life was just to keep us safe—me and the family, just keep us safe. I'll do whatever you want me to do, fate, but just keep us safe. Well, it was election time, the big one, the general election to determine the four winners who are going to be elected officials for the next four years. It was also during and then you will celebration that happens here, and also he called the little Bieber celebration, which is basically a creation of activity that would happen sometimes in the '60s. I believe that was just an opportunity to get the town energized to come together to celebrate, so there was a large rodeo, there was a powwow, there was a carnival, other different events, a huge parade, and I debated about going to the parade, but I had some family members talked me into it, and I thought, "Well, okay, why not could hurt?" So they rallied and put together a nice little float. I went down through the parade, and I waved, and I smiled, and that was it. I don't remember being scared, but there was always that little boy's back out saying, "Don't do it. Something bad is going to happen." But I did it, went through the parade, had a good time, and I was glad I did it. The polls opened at seven and closed at seven, and I forgot to mention this, but while I was living with my father's wife, my girlfriend and Nicholas and I, it was getting pretty, I would say, tense. But again, because you don't have your own space, tense might be a good word, and I just needed a place to live. We needed to move out, and we just needed to start our life together on our own.

I don't recall exactly, but an aunt of mine had heard I was looking for a house. She had a mobile home that she was no longer living in because she was also, at this point, a caretaker for a great on two of mine, and so she offered her home to me and my family. I was grateful. I was beyond words, and so we moved in literally overnight, and that was our home for the next few years. So the night of July, the celebrations were going on, and the carnival lights were flashing. We could hear the drum music from the powwow. We had some family and friends over because they were visiting in, joining enjoying the festivities. I completely forgot about the election. I really did again based on what I was told. I was still the newbie in town. I was going to lose, but that was okay. I did my part all the way up to that point, had to be maybe around nine o'clock, maybe ten o'clock. It wasn't late, but it wasn't early. All of a sudden, I saw a car zooming down the road, and you kind of look at those cars and go, "What the heck is this driver doing? This guy's crazy. This is a residential area. I need to slow down." Car zooms in all the way from the road into the driveway, where we had her home, person gets out, and it was a coworker of mine who shared the cubicle space next to me. And she came up, and she said, "Leon, Leon." And I said, "Hey, what are you doing?" She had a smile. She said, "You won," and I remember looking at her like, "Oh, cool. What did I win?" In fact, that was what I said, "I won what?" She said, "You won the election. You beat him." And all of a sudden, I had tunnel vision, kind of like those scenes in the movie where you're standing there, you see the character, and the cameras are moving away, but they're kind of staying in the same spot, but everything around him is going farther back. It was a strange feeling. I had people congratulating me, hugging me, shaking my hand,

and I sat there with a confused look on my face, just blank stare, going, "Wow! what did I do? I just do what did. I just do." It was a strange feeling. It had not hit me until the next day. The next day, I had taken the family to the fairgrounds where all the events were taking place. It was the last day of the annual celebration. Sunday it would wrap up, and we wanted to go and get some so food and check out the vendors who were selling their wares, beaded key chains and leather goods, and things like that, native crafts. It was so interesting because just prior to that day, meaning Friday before the election, yet everybody is saying hello, acknowledging me, saying, "Good luck." I was walking around the fairgrounds. I was still myself going, "Hey, how are you? Hi, how you doing?" and it was like all of a sudden, a black cloud was over my head. I was labeled one of them. I am now bad. I am now a councilman, and now I'm going to be bad. I'm going to abuse my privilege. I'm going to abuse my authority. Now I didn't know that, then going through the years, I kind of put two and two together just based still on an assumption, but two and two together based on actions and responses of people. But it was such a huge, interesting practice of assumption from us all, and I'll never forget that day. All of a sudden, I felt alone.

The inauguration was held in September. I remember trying to figure out what clothes I was going to wear, so I donned some slacks, tucked in my shirt, and felt like a whale. I was really concerned about what I looked like and really wasn't focusing on the magnitude of that day. Through the pomp and circumstance, each elected official took the oath of office as a group and then preceded to have an impromptu speech about what they were going to do or what they thought the job was. When it was my turn to give a speech, I knew that I had very limited knowledge, so to spew anything that were big ticket items, such as money or policy, would have been a ruse, so I felt it important to be honest with myself and the system and only wanted to convey one major point. I simply said, "Please ask me questions so that together we could both find out what needed to be done and why as to also be able to share relevant information with others so we all know what the answer was as to

LEON K REVAL

also alleviate rumors." My comments seemed to land, and I received some applause and accolades from my new colleagues.

All inaugurations take place on Fridays, so after the installation, there was a communal luncheon and lots of eager handshakes and congratulations. That day at the luncheon, I received my first real dose of sage advice. A dear cousin told me to always be myself, realize my strength, and keep moving forward no matter what I encounter. He also added, "People will shake your hand today and tomorrow, turn their back on you, and that's okay. You are in a job that is supposed to help, and people will always feel their concerns matter most. Remember you represent all but also yourself." It was an advice that I soon would come face-to-face with many times over, and each time felt like a kick to the stomach. But I also knew I had limited authority and that I swore an oath to the laws, so even when I disagreed with said law, I still had to enforce and promote and in that had to learn if I wanted to propose amendments to the laws. Those amendments came much later. For now, I was still feeling like a stranger in a strange land.

It was Monday morning when I showed up to my new office. I was the first one in the building, and I walked into the hallowed halls of the council chambers for the first time ever. I even looked around because I couldn't find the light switches, so I sat in the dark for a little bit. I walked into that conference room, to the chambers where all meetings were conducted, and stood idle, thinking, *What did I get myself into? I have no idea what I'm supposed to do. I can't do this job!* I remember sitting in this dimly lit room, the morning sun illuminating some parts of the walls but not yet filling the room, and then all of a sudden, in almost a dramatic way, the lights came on, and people started walking into the chambers, sitting down at already assigned seats. Idle chitchat filled the room, and it was just another day in the hood as it were. At that time, the Nation's president was a lady, in fact the first lady ever elected by tribal membership. She came in and sat down and gave some opening remarks. We received an agenda packet, the first time I ever saw one, which was also the moment where I flipped through the pages and thought once again, *Wow, what did I get myself into?* I remember thinking there was a whole

64

weekend thinking, *Why did I not receive this agenda packet early so I could have at least gone through it?* But I kept quiet, again feeling like I was the new kid on the block, and who was I to ask questions, feeling like my wonderful coping mechanisms sheltered me from embarrassment. I just sat there and observed how things unfolded my first day. The meeting was called to order, roll call was taken, and a motion was made to approve the agenda. I had no clue what the process was, but we jumped right into the agenda, and off we went!

The items on the agenda ranged from department matters to some light business approvals, based on the Nation's constitution. Any and all approval has to be done by a majority vote of the legislative council, and I didn't know it then, but that meant anything and everything. I remember just going through the motions. My vote of yes seemed to fall in line with the majority of everybody, so I didn't feel like I was just following the crowd. I really felt like I was trying to absorb the details and make a conscious vote of yes or no, and I felt pretty good. I felt like I was keeping up. I felt like I was doing my part, and I felt like I was making a difference, still not really knowing what this job entailed.

It was around this time, my first week, where I met my mentor, my new colleague who had grown up with my parents, who, although slightly younger, still knew them and knew of them. My mentor was a rebel rouser back in the day, and although I really didn't know him, I soon found out he would be the anchor we needed to make sure the government stayed grounded. Based on his training and work ethic, which he had gained rising through the ranks to become an executive director within a key department of the Nation, that allowed him to articulate the understanding and need to promote better objectives, including inclusion of the group so that everyone of us elected officials understood the rules and the process of how things were to be done based on current laws and policies.

He was able to talk about the why, why the rules say what they say, and how the rules should help his department for the betterment and benefit of the people we represented, and I was all in from that moment on. These simple yet effective and powerful concepts seemed to be selective from those who were chosen, via an electoral

process, and at the same time, my curiosity was now becoming satisfied as to the questions I had early on working in the finance office,
which led to my attempt of even running for an elected position.
So now I had a basis and platform to use as my personal foundation
to implement these concepts to which made me fall in love with
something—politics—that I had no idea would have such an addic-
tive effect on me, especially during my first term, heck first year. I
still was grasping at the concept of both the wording and meanings
of the constitution and how ordinances would then highlight parts
designed to be more specific. It was a bit confusing, coupled with the
many other things the Council delves in. It can become too much,
and in that, a person can deviate and then assume as to just try and
act like one knows what they are doing. I had seen this from my
colleagues at the time but also from me, but I was like a sponge, and
having a mentor to help direct was not only comforting but also gratifying. I never felt like I was coerced in any of my decision-making or
comments. In fact, I soon would complement the need to promote
the why even when I felt like I was being disregarded in my debate,
but I was hooked. I was now becoming a master student and, still
not realizing my potential, kept close to the sidelines because again I
was fighting stereotypes of not only being the new kid, my age, but
also the half-breed kid, a label that I would be branded with, forever
creating a scar!

I caught on very quickly and found a love for the ability to
empower and create accountability and promote a team concept. I
did have some minor experience in group dynamics and was able to
vouch questions according to logic and protocol. Although I still sat
idle, mostly observing, I developed a wherewithal and understanding
of process procedure and other policy-related matters. It was a very
interesting job, and the day's itinerary ran the gamut between listening to people's concerns, developing new concepts to help create new
policy, sitting in meetings that basically updated the government on
what was going on, and from time to time, pitching meetings from
those who wanted to do business with the Nation. The magnitude
of what tribal government dealt with daily was pretty extensive. But
the reality of it, at least from my perspective of having been in and

around consistently as long as I have, this job never had to completely be hands-on. However, the interpretation from sitting groups, elected officials, to be hands-on and then to also dip said hands into everything spouting a philosophy that the people elected them so in essence if they do not form opinions about everything, they are not looking out for the people. This to me was a complete farce and ruse to basically challenge anything new. Don't get me wrong. At that time, I was still learning, but I had the knack to be able to articulate a dialogue that would promote my ignorance as to ask even mundane questions so that any personal agenda could be exposed if there was a motive. I would also come to find out that my debate tactic would make me also seem like I was being a bully. That was something I never understood. I made points, may had even had a tone, but all my arguments were based on history and current law, so I was puzzled as to the allegations of being a bully, especially since the job of an official is to expose the most amount of layers to expose the best part of the fruit, which in my mind meant that, using a boat analogy, it was my job to poke holes into this vessel, idea, pitch, or something that was being discussed. And if it withstood all questions, also creating a vetting process, and this boat still floated, then it may have been something positive. The Nation has a three government branches, legislative council branch, executive branch, and judicial branch, to which we all follow and swear an oath to the Nation's constitution, which was adopted in 1934, and then from that body of law, twenty five permanent laws or ordinances and God knows how many resolutions. In fact, my opinion about temporary law or resolutions are that these laws are often passed and used as memorandums, which then create a negative way of communicating to the constituency by forcing them rather than informing as to the why, not to mention the issues that then occur when these temporary laws have no sunset clause so people know how to and what to do as to properly adhere to this new law. But because there is no real record keeping and dissemination of information, people have no idea what is really going on and then become acceptable to bad behavior and then disengaged because their government has not properly shared this information or made the people feel like they were part of the process of decision-making. To me, the safest and best way to be a leader of and for the people was to inform and share why I made my decision and why I either voted for something or did not, but this was a concept that was and is still taboo. I never understood why.

Unfortunately, I also saw that there was also another type of ideology that basically meant that if the council was not in everyone's business, which really meant gross micromanagement of departments, it meant a misunderstanding of the separation of powers, and in my opinion, worse, it meant trying to be business developers with no concept of profit and loss. For me, these negative concepts would be the toughest pill to swallow, especially later in my career.

During the first two years of my new endeavor, as I had mentioned, I had developed a knack for understanding and promoting good governance. What is good government? Well, to me, it was empowering, holding accountability across the board, and having complete transparency. Now as I learned and began to forge these powerful concepts, it was still a tough sell especially when it was from some kid who was considered an outsider, but I was really grateful to have colleagues who understood these same concepts, who also promoted good governance, whom I was proud to call my mentor. Good governance concepts were something that council members struggled with. Now I am not being mean. I completely understand that if someone has created in their mind what they felt their truth was, then this mentality becomes a practice and, in turn, a unwritten rule based on repetitive behavior. It had actually worked in some regard, and the Nation had developed a great amount of wealth, but my points were always directed at both consistency and longevity. If a business venture had been developed and the council voted on this project, what were the details of the deal, a valid question, but the debate always became one-sided because if the practice had always been, "We have done things this way before and we never had a problem," and that was the only basis of the argument, well, that usually came with a large price tag that meant the Nation would only receive pennies on the dollar and at times may have lost hundreds of thousands of dollars. So for me, that was the part of the pill I just could not swallow. Presenting to the legislative council meant one of two things. You had a fifty-fifty chance to get a yes vote or a no vote, and the basis of that vote boiled down to two things. If a council member liked you, then your chances increased. If a council member heard things about you or your department or company, then your chances decreased significantly, and since there was no vetting process, this practice became the catalyst for almost all decision-making, again part of that giant pill I could not swallow.

However, when good governments were practiced and things began going right based on the concepts of transparency, empowerment, and accountability, we saw some great things happening, and I was and still am proud to have been a part of the many positive developments that had occurred in this community during my tenure in political office. There are a few dozen things that were done positively. One was simply enforcing the Nation's personnel manual, creating better ways to which the government would not be a first party anymore, meaning prematurely intervene in direct complaints that may have occurred internally within departments. In fact, there were even laws created specifically dealing with personnel matters, making sure both the employer and the employee had due process. Unfortunately, when this process was circumvented, all matters that were designed to ensure a fair process became tainted and then became hit or miss when it became a council matter. Again, this practice utilized the fifty-fifty approach. If you were liked, then you had a chance of keeping your job. If you were not liked, then you might have been now unemployed. I saw this practice during the time I first started but was fortunate to also work alongside great folks who understood the same need for good governance and saw the need to have a vision and embrace the mission of the current laws and concepts that were developed by simply following the rules. There were a lot of people who were upset because they felt that the council should be able to do whatever it needed to help the people, again a very one-sided argument that never allowed any due process be part of the debate. When you think about it, this is a very sad practice that pushes the barrier of breaching people's rights.

Not everything was dire, and in fact, when the majority of the council understood the concepts of good governance, we were able to do some really beneficial things for the community of Dulce. I had mentioned one about following a process for personal matters; the other dealt with economic development. There's a misunderstanding that I have seen from elected officials specifically council members who think now that they are elected and now have the authority to be a part of everything and nobody can question why. The Nation's constitution and ordinances are powerful, and when you read these laws, the letter and spirit of these laws become fairly simple, the laws spell out the roles and responsibilities of tribal members and in some regard nontribal members, but also the allowability of a council person and the law boils down to two things. Council members write law and promote economic development. That's it. Unfortunately it is a very foreign concept, but when it works, it works, and in one of these times, things worked when we had set a whole new precedence of how to preserve and promote the need to allow the Nation's finances to showcase just how strong protocols were, based on good lawmaking. And when people follow the rules, we had discovered that in the process of utilizing bond financing to help in a new business venture, the Nation had been given a credit rating that scored AAA. In laymen's terms, the Nation had a credit score that equaled the city of Los Angeles, California! The ability to use credit, in this case bonds, to finance the community and have the ability to come to the table with a viable option to then be able to diversify business was still a foreign concept and not only tough to sell but hard to understand for some voting members of the Council. And in order for any action to occur, it had to receive a majority vote of at least five votes of yes. I know the Nation benefited quite well from fossil fuel and those companies who had the capital to drill and explore for the precious resource of gas and oil, but what always perplexed me was that even though the Nation created a revenue stream, in taxes and lease options, it was leaving millions of dollars on the table for oil and gas companies to benefit. Maybe in the heyday, money was rolling in, and it wasn't something that anyone benefiting felt would go away. After all, the demand was there. People needed gas to keep warm and cook and oil to run pretty much anything with a combustible engine, so yeah, why diversify when things are working well?

That question would bother me well into my full career as a law-maker and provocateur of economic sustainability and development, so I still have not understood or accepted how remaining loyal to the status quo philosophy was going to secure finances and create nest eggs to accommodate for communal growth and those necessities' townships provide for its citizens.

Nonetheless, we made enough traction to get the votes to pro-ceed forward, despite opinions that were off record. We needed to find a way to not only create a strong business-minded group to help do the heavy lifting, especially dealing with numbers, that we had decided to ignite and let shine an already approved and created section 17 Nation corporation. Section 17 corporations were devel-oped from the Indian Reorganization Act of 1934 that established a way for tribes to develop federally chartered corporations, with approval of Congress, to allow the ability of a tribe to benefit as a for-profit business on their reservation, therefore creating a means to help finance tribal needs and shield the tribe from corporate legal matters in the event a corporation was unsuccessful. However, in my opinion, there were clauses in our charters that hobbled any real accountability of both a board of directors and employees of these section 17 corporations. I paraphrase the clause, but it stated that these corporations under the Nation were for the benefit of provid-ing employment of Nation members. A strong and political clause should have had the ability to really help encourage these section 17 employees to excel and climb the corporate ladder for the benefit of longevity and consistency; however, because this clause was political, it tied the arms and legs of these corporations to be able to reward strong employees and/or terminate those employees who were cre-ating more issues than progress, which should have included board members and general managers / chief executive officers. Because of this clause in all charters, employees would run to council members and complain, or boards would request financing from the Nation to keep afloat, so rather than have the true autonomy needed to function as a fully accredited for-profit corporation, it made these federally chartered businesses a pseudo tribal department, and bare minimum would now replace steady income stream dependent on the Nation for support.

Back to bond financing, we had created a strong group and, in a joint effort, made sure we had enough information to make a sound decision but to also try and create new philosophies that could really change how business and politics could mutually benefit if they sat way across the table from one another. With our new bond rating in hand, we went to Chicago to go to market to secure the financing needed to try and become partners in the first deal that would allow the Nation to be a true partner with an oil and gas company to now quadruple profit, no longer just getting lease payments and taxes that companies paid directly to the Nation for the privilege of drilling for oil and gas on the Jicarilla. We in this deal could now not only be at the table as to who to sell to but also create more worth to do other deals, therefore really becoming an energy tribe and no longer just a tax tribe.

In 2002, we went to market, agreed on a sale, and at 5 percent interest received a total of $150 million for the new partnership deal. There were even more benefits to being a majority partner. We could now save $15 million that the state would have received, which would have stayed in the accounts of the Nation's corporation, not to mention be able to sell any oil and/or gas at retail, therefore getting more money drilling, which at that time had a total of $160 million, again all money for the Nation, even before any gas or oil sales occurred. And since the Nation did not have to put up its own existing money, we had new bond financing. This new deal procured $40 million for the Nation, money in the bank. It really was a first-of-its-kind deal for an oil and gas tribe, and I was proud to be a part and learn from some really smart people.

With bond money in hand, we got the group and our utility section 17 corporation running with our new venture as oil and gas exploratory partners. It was just before this time that the Nation took over the water and wastewater treatment plants that were being run and managed by the Bureau of Indian Affairs. Not to bad-mouth the federal government, but in my mind, when I heard the term *trust responsibility*, it made me flinch. After all, the federal government had a bad track record of being properly responsible for looking after tribes, and even though I had no idea before I was elected, I always wondered how ironic the term was used by elected officials who used it as a means to debate and, in my opinion, pass the buck because, after all, if we as a tribe were sovereign, another term that I felt was misunderstood, then why would we as a tribe not want to create our own opportunities, both financially and then politically!

We now had to find a plan to properly maintain and hire staff to accommodate the current structure and for future growth, the water delivery and wastewater cleaning for the community. The current structures at that time were working, but the issue then became the transportation lines from the water treatment plant to the community. The water delivery pipes were outdated and arguably were also delivering carcinogens to local water taps. Using the bond financing, we created a phase plan that would plan for and pay for new water distribution lines throughout the community so that everyone would have pure clean water. We started phase 1, but unfortunately, the other phases never got their start. Using the bond financing, we also created and approved plans for new buildings. We designed big as to try and accommodate as much space for departments to be housed under one roof, so we started with a new tribal headquarters, new shopping center, and new housing development. We had even joint-ventured on a new hospital that used Indian Health Services money to build a large state-of-the-art facility that encompassed health, dental, optical, and behavioral health serves under one roof. The plan was to then create a charter, establish a board of directors, and then become one of the first billing facilities that would be open to insurance, Medicare/Medicaid, and accept patients who were non-native. To be fair, the venture started pre-2002, so I do credit my predecessors. We just picked up the ball and ran further down the field. We had a plan ready to go, we created a proper vetting strategy to hire an independent CEO as well as experienced board and actually hired a person who accepted the CEO position, and we were off and going and on the verge of having a way to generate funds, secure good doctors, and provide the highest quality of care for the members and now all patients. We even built a whole new neighborhood with the fanciest homes I had ever seen here for doctors as a recruiting tool. Things were really moving in a very proactive manner, and the move towards becoming a full-fledged hospital was moving swiftly.

It was also during my first two years of my first term in office that I had to cast my vote in the impeachment of the sitting president. The president was the first woman to be elected and unfortunately was the first female president to be removed from office. It was during this time my second son, Dominick, would be in the fight for his life in a neonatal Albuquerque hospital bed intubated. Dominick was a surprise. Well, all three were a surprise, but needless to say, we found out we were expecting our second child. And although fiscally more secure, we still were surprised and excited with this news. The biggest issue we had was that in my new position as a public servant, I traveled out of town quite a bit and sometimes out of state. I would often feel guilty for leaving but at the same time excited because I was able to travel abroad to places. I never imagined I would visit, but I don't think I ever expressed that to the kid's mom. I just did and relied on my still girlfriend to be the homemaker. One of my first business trips was to Las Vegas. I remember buying a brand-new luggage set and trying to justify the need for the pricier set. After all, I was a representative now and had to reflect that with some style. So I purchased a five-piece executive silver set of luggage for my trips. Rather than fly, my new colleague and mentor opted to drive. I had never been out west, so I was a bit hesitant, but he had traveled the road many times, so I knew we were good to go. I loaded the back of my work vehicle with all five new suitcases, and it looked like something out of a movie where the diva travels overnight and has an entourage of bags. I arrived at my passenger's driveway, gave a quick beep of the horn, and my colleague came out with one bag. And as he loaded his one bag in the back of the SUV, he laughed and said, "Damn, you are moving out of your house." I laughed, trying to save face, and said all the bags were for souvenirs. We arrived in Las Vegas at the Excalibur Hotel, and I learned some valuable lessons that trip especially going to Las Vegas—one, it's polite and customary to tip per bag, and two, the registration desks are what seem like miles away from valet when you're too cheap to tip more to have your bags brought up to your room.

The really cool thing about driving with a colleague was the length of time we got to talk shop, which helped a lot because not only were we sharing opinions, we were learning more and more about the intricacies of the job and the need to maintain balance of the system for the greater good of those we represented.

Since I was traveling, my girlfriend did what she needed to do, and I had always envied how strong she was, but it was on the third particular trip to the doctor's office for her checkup that we discovered the news of our growing child. During the ultrasound, the technician noted something that the ultrasound showed, the doctor was called in, and it was determined that the nuchal test, which measures nuchal fold thickness in the back of unborn baby's neck, was thicker than normal. After another scan, the results were clearer that our unborn child would be born with a disorder; the disorder most associated with nuchal thickening was Down syndrome. I had a series of meeting that whole day as we were in San Diego, California, and I received a call about 6:00 pm Pacific time. It was my girlfriend who was very distraught as I was unable to take her calls earlier that afternoon, and as I sat at the dinner table joking and laughing with other colleagues and business associates, my phone rang. I told the table it was home, and I needed to take the call, so I excused myself from the table and found a silent corner in the restaurant. I answered happily, and all I heard was that crackling of her voice, which made the little hairs on the back of my neck stand up. I asked what was wrong, and she told me of the test results. I went silent for what seemed to be a good half hour but also stumbled to find the words to promote care and kindness and compassion. It seemed very difficult at the moment especially in a public place, and since I had driven to the restaurant with a carload of passengers, I felt compelled to not leave to go back to the hotel to talk more openly in my room. I can't remember my words, and usually, most of our arguments were me becoming defensive and then lashing out rather than swallowing pride to just be an ear, so I may have held back since I was in a public setting and said I would call when I got back to my room. I returned to the table and tried to keep up my jovial mood, but my mind was racing, and my comments were choppy at best when asked a question or was being the butt of a joke. One person at the table asked me directly, if everything was okay. I smiled and said, "Oh, yeah," trying to play off my shock. I remember hearing more about the test and its findings and how unpredictable the birth could be. I even had thoughts of being embarrassed of having a child with some disorder and even thought I should make the comment of ending the pregnancy. Add the moment to the short list of life regrets, and I even still tear up when I think of how selfish my thoughts were at that time. Still unsure of the nuchal fold results, as even though it was determined, it could have been a false positive, there was one test that could be conclusive. They would take a very large needle and insert it into the stomach to draw some amnio fluid, but it had risks and, well, huge discomfort to any mom. We talked about it for a second because the test could also determine genetics of which parent was more likely to be the carrier of any disorder, and I know that would have created huge issues especially for me if it was determined that my girlfriend was a carrier. After all, my ego told me it could have never been me, but we declined the test and decided to let fate show us what our family would be blessed with. Six months later, Dominick was born, and we were the proud parents of a beautiful special boy who had trisomy 21 Down syndrome. He was so strong. He cried, so we knew he had a strong set of lungs. In fact, when my girlfriend's water sprung a leak, we got into the car and saw that we needed gas to make the eighty-five-mile trip west to the hospital that was properly equipped to handle such a delicate delivery. And so as I was pumping gas, a constituent came up to me, and we started talking and talking and talking. Well, after I stopped pumping fuel, I finally said, "I don't mean to be rude, but my wife is giving birth, and I have to go." I was excused with a congratulations. I never felt that it was acceptable to dismiss anyone who came up to me to talk. After all, it was my job to listen even if I was being blamed, which is why I felt compelled to listen even during this time of my girlfriend going into labor. We got down the road. My girlfriend would wince in pain, and I tried to speed but wanted to be cautious as well. It was about forty minutes into our trip that she screamed, "I'm not going to make it. The baby's coming!" I had a shocked look on my face and tried to be encourage her to breathe. We were supposed to take Lamaze classes that week but instead found ourselves already ahead of that curve. I kept encouraging her and saying we were almost there; we were not. She would cry out again and this time started pulling down her pants. My eyes bulged, and I said not on the leather seats. Yeah, I know, but I was in shock and out of range for cell service. All I could do is think, "Oh, man, I am going to have to deliver my son. I can't do that!" We crested a large ridgeline of hills, and I made the 911 call where an ambulance met us in from off a seven to eleven. I thought, *Great, now I have to name my child Seven or Eleven.* We made it to the hospital, and all I had to do was wipe a small spot of the passenger leather seat.

So as the case for impeachment began, it was a very contentious time. We had a split vote, and of course, the membership were also split, and I heard a tape where the president was trying to force the police department to arrest us. And when the police department declined, the game and fish conservation officers were told to follow suit. They too declined. It was a scary time, and all I could think was how I was going to protect my nontribal member family if push came to shove. During that time, Dominick had developed pneumonia, and we drove him in the middle of the night to the emergency room. They put him on oxygen and poked his little arm with a needle for his IV, and we waited. To this day, the sound of a heart monitor beeping slowly makes me cringe. After a few hours went by, Dominick was stable. He had steady oxygen levels and was resting. I told my girlfriend that I would go home, pack her a bag, and rent a room so she could shower and rest while I waited at the hospital with Dom. I hit the road and made the ninety-mile trip home. No sooner than I hit the town limits, my phone rang. I got the news that Dominick crashed, and he would be flown out to Albuquerque to the PICU, pediatric intensive care unit. My heart dropped, and all I could say was, "Call me when you get there!" I never shared this part of my story with anyone, but as I hung up the cell phone, I looked up into the night sky and said, "You are not taking him, Dad. You better look after your grandchild. You owe him!" I went inside the house and sat in my chair and tried not to overthink. The sun rose, and I went to work, told my colleagues what had happened, and that I was going to be out of the office for a while and was asked, "What about the impeachment?" I made no haste in heading for Albuquerque, and when I arrived at the hospital, I entered a large room where when I saw Dominick, lying down, hooked up to tubes and wires, so peaceful yet so lethargic. I almost felt weak and dropped to my knees. I remember tears filling my eyes but no need to cry out. I wanted to and maybe for my own ego, but deep down, I knew he was in great care at the hospital, and I just had a strong feeling he was being looked after. For the next two weeks, I would travel back and forth, making the six-hour round trip to be with my family sitting in the PICU for the later afternoon and evening and then back to then sit with my colleagues. I was grateful I traveled safe and sound and that my family was also safe and sound, and my son was receiving the best care ever, and I was traveling safe and sound to fulfill my obligations.

We went forward with the impeachment process and listed a statement of charges, and I often think back to that time and wonder if I made the right decision in casting a vote of yes. As I would learn so much more as to procedural and moral matters, I always come back to a resounding yes, my vote of yes was made unemotionally and without bias. And what I also have learned that I did not know a lot of back then was the ability of people to project blame as a way to distract from their own faults. This philosophy, although I had no idea then, would become my nemesis as I could never understand why a person would want to take a position to which they swore an oath, a promise to the constituents that they would do the very best, using logic, reasoning, and good judgment, to follow and apply all laws as both envoys and representatives. We held a tribunal and in a split vote removed the president from office. It created a rift, and within the community, there were varying opinions, and although I felt it very important to share the statement of charges, meeting minutes, and voting record with the general public, I was outnumbered as to not share because the act was done, and that was that, and there was no reason to distribute the information because it would only add to the angst that was already brewing. Even though I agreed, after all, I was the new guy and had not had a lot of experience with the dynamics of the community, with some internal disagreement, I went along with the group and found that my decision would some-what haunt me even to this day. I often think, Did I comply for fear of being the odd person out? Did I not give a good enough argument as to why it was important to share the information? If no one knew what and why, then speculation and conjecture would run rampant, and to me, there was no real justice in going through the motions of such a strong act like an impeachment if no one knew why and more importantly would have created a precedence to show the need to abide by the oath of office but to no avail, and to this day, I and my colleagues remain the bad guys who did not want a woman to succeed.

The impeachment and the bond financing along with the lack of shared information, in my opinion, led to the demise of me having a second term. Mind you, I was still green, but I was adapting and learning more than just theory. I was learning group dynamics and retaining information, and even when I voted no on some particular items, I would research as to why it might have been bad or good for that matter and just didn't have enough information to make a solid presentation. I was a sponge, and I made an internal commitment to myself to not sit idle and be complacent again like I was in my point of sharing the impeachment charges. After all, I was a repre-sentative and not a boss. I never considered myself a "leader," but I felt strongly that I was a giant cog that helped propel the machine that was the nation, and if I was not able to properly move in sync, then I was a problem and therefore not abiding by my own oath to do my very best.

It took a few months for things to calm down after the presi-dent was removed from office, and still yet, the matters of the Nation needed attention and planning. I took it upon myself to make a move and develop a personal goal. It was year 2 of my term, and so the clock began its countdown to the end of my four-year term. And even though I was still learning, I didn't want to just coast and be compensated to be a yes person. I needed to step up and out of my comfort zone, and so I learned the process of law creation.

I soon found out there were two types of law creation: emotional and proactive. I read many laws and in the first two years admittedly approved these types of laws, maybe because I did feel compelled to be a team player. But as I questioned more and more as to the reasons of why, I discovered that, in my opinion, there was a rush to try and appease the masses. In this hit-and-miss practice, most laws either punished the whole and in that created more moral issues than trying to empower through these laws. I felt laws were being treated like office memos. Although the subject matter was important, there were no specific details as to the need and reasoning of creating a law. For example, I now sit as a constituent, and in this pandemic, we have had two communal lockdowns. A decision was made to create roadblocks in and out of town to stop community members from traveling abroad. Now in concept, I agree with this tactic; however, my complaint was, with no permanent law that states in any declared emergency, the following rules will be implemented and in that would define sanctions or penalties for offenders. Now there would be a new ordinance that the court could then use as well as the police department now having a real statute that could be more formal as assessed in and when a citation is written. Not having the above only creates issues as to proper enforcement and the issue of—and I use this term loosely and only as a description as to the need to have proper laws in the books—a violation of member rights, not to mention any issues of jurisdiction for nonmembers living on or off the reservation and the general public who are traveling a state road. Simply passing a resolution, giving weak clauses as to nonspecific parts of other ordinances in an attempt to recreate some Frankenstein law again only creates more issues, which goes to my point of emotional reactionary lawmaking. In reading many resolutions that again in my opinion only added to more paper waste, these temporary laws were not only confusing but also hard to enforce and comply with. I felt it important to try and use a new approach, and through many drafts, most I shared with my mentor and closer colleagues and even legal representatives, trying to do so in way to minimalize billing but to make sure I tried to always honor the letter and spirit of new law and existing laws, I honed my self-taught skill and was able to write dozens of resolutions that were passed and could have been tweaked to accommodate the new year and new sitting officials all for the benefit of the membership.

One of the worst things I saw and in some regard was a part of since I sat as an elected official was the lack of shared information to the general membership. I would always get conflicting comments as to why there was no need to disseminate information. Most comments stated that people voted for us so in some weird way. There was an inherent duty to not ask because that was why we were there sitting as council members, an explanation I never could get behind but remains a perceived truth of all elected officials. I found myself at times feeling that if I did share information, that I was breaking some code of silence and that if I was discovered sharing information that I could face charges, so even though I shared limited information, I also kept in the back of my head the possibility that I would be caught and then chastised by my colleagues.

I felt there was a warped sense of understanding when it came to sitting officials, even newly elected ones. I was told countless times that the job was very hard, long hours, and people always wanting to talk to you and, in some cases, to always watch your back. It almost seemed like there was a brainwashing process that became part of some orientation to instill fear or dominance. I remember hearing this speech from those. New guys were now joining, and for a few moments, I did feel like all my wits, my core values, and my, although limited, experience vanished, and now I had to follow suit. My mentor would soon be a means to make sure there was empowerment, unity, team building, and accountability, and I would soon listen to what I categorized as bad advice—the watch your back comments—to trusting my instincts and reading and applying and interpreting the laws to really try and help.

It was an election year, and I was on the cusp of finishing my first term ever in public office. I remember thinking about how far I had come from my first day, sitting in the dark of the hallowed council chambers to now wrapping up some very progressive multimillion-dollar deals and also writing, presenting, and getting votes needed to enact new policies and laws. I also had a real feeling of accomplishment and in that some confidence that I would soon serve another term. That sense of confidence was assumption and cockiness that would be surprising and humbling. I use the term *cockiness* as a way to describe real tangible results; however, in the grand scheme of things, those matters were trivial. It didn't help that at that time, there was a lack of shared information, again a tactic I felt that created a facade to protect from people questioning and demanding but important, nonetheless, factor in the impeachment of a president and then a multimillion-dollar deal that was not understood and then used as a political platform as to questioning the roles of deal makers and council members who may not have ethically shared factual information, increasing disdain in an already controversial time of an election year.

I felt so dumbfounded as to the accusations that were being made, and those comments stung. I was reading unsigned letters stating I was having torrid affairs and that I was hoarding money and, the capper, I was only a half-breed and because I did not know the language or culture, that I was unable to properly serve as a representative of the membership. Many of these negative comments came from close family members, whom I held in very high regard, and boy did that sting. I felt confused and saddened before I got angry, and in retrospect, this was where I started to become cynical as to wanting to talk to people and then confused about my newly forming tactic because my job was to talk to people. I remained positive, but when the primary election came, I was the only one out of my group who made it to the general and then lost. I really did not have time to worry as I knew I needed to find employment to pay bills and feed the family, and deep down, maybe I repressed my emotions because I would soon discover that my personal priorities may have been backward. I would later ask the question of myself that made me stop and rethink what I inadvertently or even aversively did as a father, boyfriend, later husband, and all-around role model and supporter of my family.

It was at my concession speech that I looked out over the crowd, now gathered to part take in the installation of the newly elected officials, where I was overcome with disdain. But I kept my head together and represented myself and in that my family moniker with as much class as I could muster. My comments were, "I am thankful to you all for giving me an opportunity to serve. I had never considered myself a leader, but I did feel I was an important piece that helped move the nation forward, and I am proud of what I learned, done, and sacrificed. I had met some wonderful people who have the best interest of the Nation at heart, and for that, I and we should be grateful, and I will miss my colleagues of whom also taught me many things. I feel like I am talking to my son who is going to college, and I won't see him for a long while, so this is a little saddening, and I am going to do something right now that is not meant to be disrespectful but to show the utmost respect of our new governing officials. I am going to walk off the stage and wish well those now chosen to help us all." I turned to the row of officials sitting behind where I stood and turned in to shake their hands before walking off the stage. Truth be told, I wanted to run out of the auditorium as fast as I could but also as cool as I could, but I felt an arm reach out and grab my hand. It was an aunt of mine who hugged me and said thank you to me. I felt really good, and it was then that I sat down, her hand draped over mine where I had found a little peace and harmony.

I had finished my first full term as a member of the Jicarilla Apache Nation government, a long-standing tradition that was created in 1937 and evolved with a constitution and catalog of permanent laws. I was proud of what I had done and more so the peace I had made for myself with my father and the beauty that was safeguarded in the community and people of Dulce, and I had no regrets about making the decision to move back and now raise a family here so that they too could now discover the beautiful roots that kept me grounded and yet allowed me to replant elsewhere with the comfort of regrowing here. If that was the end of my political career, I may have been a little bit more at ease and would have been okay with a new career path, but I was addicted to politics and ideology of practicing empowerment, accountability, and team building, and even though these concepts are still foreign, I became good at doing just that, and I was ready for round 2, and it couldn't come soon enough. But for that moment, I had to wait and endure what I called the dismantling of the vetted business deals, the local hospital plan, and termination of anyone's associates who had helped us along the way, and it struck me as odd because in my mind, I had thought, Why wouldn't anyone want to know what was going on and why things had been done, simple questions that would now create emotional scarring?

The week after my term ended, I took a job as a marketing assistant with the Nation's casino enterprise. I was not sure what I was going to be doing, but the definition of marketing in and of itself told me it would be right up my ally, and I was committed to learning and doing my job in this new setting. The job was very boring. I had some ideas as to increasing advertising by voicing and editing our own radio commercials, and it garnered a slight response from the bosses but never took off. For the first six months, I literally sat in an office and was basically a floater to help out in what I thought were meniscal things, like cut postcards that showcased promotions and at times would stand around and help during giveaways. It was what I could only describe as being a lion, working as a protector but helper, and was responsible for working with and for the pride or community. But one day, I was shot in the behind with a dart and woke up and realized I was no longer in the jungle but in a very small cage, and not in some nice zoo like in San Diego but sitting in a cage at some gas station in the middle of some small town, growling for the one or two customers who either stopped for gas or the bathroom. Yeah, it made for a long day. It was on a guy's trip. My brothers and I had planned to Alaska, where I received a phone call from my supervisor telling me there was going to be some restructuring at the hands of the shareholder representatives, which were the council, who got it in their head that they needed to make changes. When I returned back into the office, the mood was tense, and it wasn't long before I also began to find out all the strategies that were put in place were now being picked apart. The joint venture with the Indian Health Service (IHS) Center Hospital had halted, and the

CEO and board were dismissed, and the ability to use what are called 638 money, which in essence are federal funds transferred to tribes, was declined, and the new state-of-the-art hospital was once again a shell of a building that was once again managed by the federals government under IHS. The other deal that had been put together was the gas and oil deal in which the Nation would have been partners with the company who had outbid the Nation in new lease acreage, but the Nation utilizing its own tribal corporation would have been able to partner, which would have allowed for more input and profit in, at that time, a booming industry. Since we settled on a hedge price rather than gambling on the volatility of the market, it now became an issue filled with contention because as newly elected officials sat in chairs vacant from prior knowledge, conjecture now became fact and without question felt that we had failed in our strategy to hedge especially since the market at that time was on an upswing. It was this new council that now unhedged the fund just about the time the market dropped. The Nation was now in an ebb-and-flow situation with a giant tide that was now rocking a ship with no working motor. It was a few months later that this sitting council also recanted as a partner with the company we had ventured with, and everything built was wiped away, and the Nation became status quo once again. The deal had a clause where if any party had severe changes, in this case the owner of the company had passed away, then there was right of first refusal, which allowed the Nation to take over all assets of land and minerals but to no avail.

I could hardly believe this news when I finally had heard. It was a one-of-a-kind deal for the Nation and way before its time for sure. It was also the first time I felt the mighty Nation, a small tribe who had been a giant as an owner of land that sat above one of the largest oil and gas reserves in the country, had merely been a landlord. Those elected officials who boasted that the Nation was an energy tribe were way off. The Nation had great power but only used a sliver and was not an energy tribe but only a lease and tax tribe. Sure, that was great, and it garnered a ton of money, but to me and my colleagues at that time, it was also settling and letting others take advantage of the Nation. And as much as I wanted to complain and chastise, I sat quiet and perplexed as to how and why only to learn the lesson, there is no how or why, its emotion, ego, and speculation.

I continued in the marketing department for the casino, and now that it too had been picked apart, I had to relearn and learn new things. I had to learn compliance and regulation to make sure any and all promotions were in compliance. I had to learn how to create print ads, so I taught myself photoshop, and I had to make sure our promotions were profitable. Luckily, I had a very bright and intelligent coworker who had been transferred to the marketing department, and together we did our best to represent in the most professional way.

Going into my second year with the casino's marketing department, I had heard there was going to be a change within the sitting president's administration. Somehow, my name was mentioned, and I was invited to meet with the president of the Nation, and it was a loose discussion, but I also knew it might be a long shot, so all of a sudden I blurted out, "I'll take the job and will do what needs to be done to showcase this office and the Nation." Weeks went by before I heard anything, and I even had to stop myself from calling and bugging, but out of the blue, I got the call, was confirmed by the tribal council, and then became the new public relations director of the Jicarilla Apache Nation.

I began my new appointed position as the public relations officer for the Nation in October of 2008, and I remember walking into the office of the president and asked what my duties were and what direction I should pursue in this administration. The president looked at me and said, "You will figure it out." I laughed and tried to respectfully pull out some direction but kept being told I knew what to do and I would figure it out. I left the office thinking, *What the hell did I get myself into?* I sat in my new office, looked around at old files, and wondered how I would get myself out of there. Thank goodness, it was only a thought as this new position would now be the catalyst to where I honed my skills as an envoy, diplomat, and politician.

I had pondered what I had learned in my past experience and thought what and where I can be of service to the Nation, the administration, and the membership, so I came up with a mission to provide information in all forms utilizing print, radio, and in person at general assemblies. Information in Indian country is hard to come by and held to the highest of confidentiality. The irony is that the rules allow information of the government to be disseminated for both knowledge and review, but somewhere along the way, the practice became to keep information clandestine. I still do not understand this logic and breach of law. I have to laugh because that is the better than shaking my head, trying to understand. I knew I still had to report to my supervisor who was the president, so I built up trust and was transparent in both my thoughts and actions. I knew that if I was rouge, then that would indeed ruffle feathers, and my job would now be a topic of discussion, and most of the time, when the government questions, it feels like you're facing a firing squad who already made their minds up that you were guilty. Another issue that still bugs me to this day, the lack of due process afforded to anyone deemed guilty even by suspicion. Once issues make it to the chambers, it becomes a trial of trying to defend oneself instead of being allowed any evidence of fact. I know I am digressing, but my point was to try and share information by making those who were titled look like they were doing a good job. After all, isn't that public relations?

One of my first tasks was to prepare for the upcoming state legislative session, which occurs in January for a sixty-day session and February for a thirty-day session, and during this time, the state had recognized one day to honor all tribes and pueblos of New Mexico dubbed Indian Day at the Roundhouse. This particular session was going to be a sixty-day session; it was typical to invite all twenty tribal and pueblo leadership to speak during a joint session of the house and senate. I was to prepare our agenda and make sure Jicarilla was properly represented in both seating and placement for comments. I had been through this effort before as a council member, but it was a totally different task altogether as my neck was on the line to make sure the council members and executives were satisfied with the day's events. I had not yet developed my network and was basically a new face in the old crowd of state government; nonetheless, the day came off without a hitch. Little did I know at that time that I would be exposed to a much larger world, and that world revolved around the busy bees of state government, not necessarily the elected officials but those hardworking staffers who were appointed or worked in state departments.

One day, I was called into the office of the president, and he told me I had to attend an upcoming meeting with the New Mexico Indian Affairs Department, and I asked what this was about but was told I would find out when I got there, and I knew what to do. I laugh now, but at that time, I was feeling like I was completely out of my element. But I did what I was told, and after all, it was my job. At least that was what I told myself on the two-hour drive to Santa Fe. I remember pulling up to the building and sitting in the car for a minute and thinking, okay, trying to convince myself I got this. And before I froze, in one giant leap, I jumped out of the driver's seat and hustled to the front entrance. I remember walking into the office and being greeted with, "Hey, Jicarilla's here." I have to say I felt proud, not at any personal recognition—after all, I was a new face—but at the regard for the Nation. I knew of its power and magnitude and its many, many possibilities, but to hear and see that recognition from others was a moment that stuck with me to this day.

I was invited to join the first ever New Mexico Indian Affairs Department Tribal Infrastructure Fund board. This new board had been created and adopted into state law in 2005 in which 5 percent of the state's revenue, derived from the New Mexico State's severance fund, would help address the many infrastructure issues tribal communities face to this day, challenges like running water or the proper disposal of waste and wastewater, unfathomable in this day and age of the future. The board was created to make sure funds were properly allocated and expensed to make sure not only all funds were audited but also projects were properly completed in a timely manner. This is where I learned of the criticism toward tribes because the assumption was that tribes didn't pay taxes, so why were we allowed to use tax money to fund "private" projects? I admit, I had thought the same thing, but what I began learning was that tribes in New Mexico were contributing approximately 20 percent to the state's coffers, and the reality was that tribal members do not pay state employment tax, but tribes as a whole contribute in large ways, for example, sales tax, gross receipts taxes, shopping in metro areas, employing residents in casinos or casino-related businesses. Jicarilla alone had contributed hundreds of millions of dollars since the 1950s via oil and gas exploration and even fought the rule of double taxation in the US Supreme Court and was successful. However, in a second case, the Nation lost the argument mainly because the Nation had not been given the courtesy to state its case as it did in *Merrion v. Jicarilla*, so the Nation lost in *Cotton Petroleum Corp v. Jicarilla*, but still millions of dollars went to many New Mexicans.

Sitting as a new board member, I was, well, lost. I sat there and just listened and observed and started to pick up on lingo and dialect that made me feel more and more comfortable each meeting and really feeling proud to give a vote of yes when it came to funding projects and then a sense of pride when a new building or new infrastructure was completed for a rural tribal community. I also found myself sitting on more and more state boards where tribal representation was needed, and this is where I began my network to now really push the major accomplishments of the Nation and at the same time help create strategies for other tribes to fight their good fights. I made acquaintances with tribal leaders and their staff as well as NM cabinet secretaries. It was a fantastic learning environment, and I was a sponge soaking up all the information and dynamics of working alongside very bright individuals. I soon found myself being more and more involved in state matters, serving as an envoy for the Nation, and not only rediscovered a new passion for the Nation and its political history but also rediscovered a new perspective in researching and promoting the laws of the Nation as points for debate in many of these new state appointments. One major accomplishment I was privileged to be part of was being appointed to a task force in which we were to debate why it was important to be heard when the state was going to reestablish new districts that would then create new boundaries for voting and representation. I really had no clue what to expect, and since most of my positions involved some baptism by fire, onward I went again sitting, observing, and asking a hundred questions. When you sit back and really observe from a different perspective, you see how tribes can be ruthless, in an indirect way, but agendas are still there. There was a lot of internal debate as to how the new boundary lines were to be accepted, and what I found ironic was lawyers representing tribes were most vocal in trying to get their clients the best area and, in that, best representation for Native issues. But the irony I speak of was it really didn't matter which tribe or pueblo won the debate; the point was tribal communities were not showing up to vote! Nonetheless, I did my part in representing the Nation, and since tribes were now promoting the prominence, we now had, with some proven tangibles, such as providing income to the state in the form of casino revenues and employment along with paying cigarette taxes, gasoline taxes, and severance tax, which was taxes that outside companies paid working on tribal land, so tribes were no longer being stereotyped as only looking for handouts. The task force finally agreed collectively that we had what we thought was fair and equitable to present to the state for approval. Voting is not only an important responsibility; it is a volatile and self-serving monster that can make those in the system fight to the death to preserve what they feel is right for themselves and with that had to go to district court to fight for the new districts we as a native caucus felt was in the best interest of all twenty-one tribes and pueblos that also needed fair representation.

In late August, early September of 2010, I had been invited to attend a meeting with the Native American Redistricting Workgroup. The NARWG, was established by the All Indian Pueblo Council to ensure that the Native American Voting Rights Act was followed during the 2011 redistricting process. What is redistricting? Redistricting is the process of drawing new electoral district boundaries in order to level district populations. Since the 1960s, redistricting has been done every ten years just after the US Census count. The overall purpose of redistricting is to review districts and, if necessary, redraw districts in order to address any changes in population. The numbers compiled from the 2010 count determine the state's growth, about 13.2 percent for New Mexico. Jicarilla now joined the NARWG, who had received several different maps from the state, some of the maps intended on redrawing existing districts. At the time, the NARWG saw some possible opportunities, for some of the lower Pueblos, to move around a bit to try and garner as much representation from the federal and state representatives as they could. You know, the best of both worlds, but on the flip side, some of the proposed maps were also going to severely alter those districts that already established minority majority. Minority majority basically means there are a lot of registered Native American voters in one specific district, like Jicarilla's district of 64 and 22. Here is a quick history lesson. Jicarilla together with the Navajo Nation went to court in 2002 because, at that time, Jicarilla was part of the District of San Juan County but were not receiving the proper representation we should have been receiving. Jicarilla wanted to be in a district that had over 50 percent Native American voters, and the only way to do that was to join the pueblos in large native populated counties. Long story short, we won the case. Jicarilla along with the pueblos established a minority majority district (64 percent) and since then had received plenty of positive representation from state leaders, with tons of meetings, input from tribal leadership and the legal beagles. The NARWG produced its own consensus maps and a set of principles that protected the tribe's interests and allowed tribes to promote the need and importance of our self-determination.

During the special legislative session in 2011, there were a series of meetings that were held throughout New Mexico by the *Legislative Redistricting Committee*. These meetings let the Legislative Redistricting Committee receive public input on the upcoming redistricting plans. The Legislative Committee would recommend new boundaries for the congressional districts within New Mexico as well as the state House of Representatives and Senate districts, the Public Regulation Commission districts, and the Public Education Commission districts. The committee hearings include the sharing of information about legal requirements of the redistricting process, sample maps of redrawn districts, and a block of time for public comment. The NARWG along with AIPC scheduled a hearing in Acoma, and Jicarilla came out in full force. The nation president addressed the state committee members, endorsing and explaining the importance of the NARWG's consensus maps and principals and reminding the Legislative Committee members they should honor the pueblos', Apaches', and Navajos' determinations as to what the majority Native American districts should look like because, after all, it is the tribes themselves that are in the best position to determine what their communities of interest should be, including each of the Native American districts. President Pesata would later address the Legislative Committee members one more time, this time in Santa Fe at a hearing held at the Roundhouse.

Court dates were set, and I wrote the speech for the president, who signed and submitted and, during his testimony, was questioned as to how he came up with his points and if he and, in that, Jicarilla had submitted these comments or if they were written by legal and given as a document for the Nation to pass off as our own. The president responded, "My public relations officer wrote this letter," and he is sitting right there, as he pointed to me sitting in the last seat in the upstairs gallery. I looked at the prosecutor representing the governor as he turned to the judge and said, "No more questions." I sat there quiet and at the same time stunned as to what just occurred. I thought, *Wow*, and didn't show any emotion. I did my job, and I was proud to have been able to do my part, and in that, new voter district lines were drawn, and our proposals were accepted! The letter read as follows:

> The Jicarilla Apache Nation has supported and taken the lead on the need to preserve the voting rights of Native Americans guaranteed under the Constitution and the Voting Rights Act. This support is reflected in the outcome of Jepsen v. Vigil Giron, No. D-0101-CV-02177, when the Jicarilla Apache Nation together with the Navajo Nation, fought for House District 65 and established the legal criteria for majority Native American districts in the 2002 district court proceeding.
>
> Jicarilla gave testimony at the hearing of the Legislative Redistricting Committee in Acoma

that any proposed maps must reflect the specific wishes of the individual tribes. The goal for tribes is to maintain the strength of the majority Native American districts in the NM House and Senate, and create additional influence districts in the Senate and the Public Regulatory Commission. The Jicarilla Apache Nation recognizes that we share communities of interest and political interests with our Pueblo and Navajo brethren in the redistricting process and see it as both a civil rights issue and an issue of tribal self-determination.

The Jicarilla Apache Nation endorses the Native American Work Groups efforts in fostering collaboration between the Pueblos, Apache, and Navajo Nations in New Mexico. The Principles and proposed maps submitted to the Legislative Redistricting Committee as drawn by Leonard Gorman, Executive Director of the Navajo Nation Human Rights Commission, honor the wishes of the Jicarilla Apache Nation and preserve the spirit of these new majority Native American districts with Native American percentages around 60% of Voting Age Population.

The Jicarilla Apache Nation is satisfied and concurs with the proposed maps as presented by the Native American Work Group for our Senate District 22, House District 65 and PRC District 4. Since the Nation helped establish the first majority Native American district, Jicarilla has benefited from Native American legislators elected in these districts who have historically carried the most important pro-sovereignty legislation adopted by the State and continue to fight off the attacks on tribal interests, taxing jurisdiction or cultural properties. It is also the wish of the Jicarilla Apache Nation that the Native

American Work Group maps and principles be
an agenda item at the Special Legislative Session.

Sincerely,
President of the Jicarilla Apache Nation

Welcome to litigation. This is where we end up when one side
goes against another and an agreement is not reached. Okay, this
isn't Law 101, but now we're in court, and in order to protect our
districts, we had to convince a judge that it was in our best interest
for the court to rule in favor of the NARWG's maps and consensus
plan. Unity needed to be shown so with an invite from the governor
of Laguna Pueblo. The Nation joined forces with Laguna, Acoma,
Zuni, Santa Ana, and Isleta to become the multitribal plaintiffs in
the *Pueblo of Laguna v. Dianna Duran*. The litigation process is a
slow, a costly process at that, literally hours of research on the other
maps. Some did not even make sense, hours of debating, witnesses'
galore, experts in political science and cartography, map drawers,
and tons of paper. The multitribal group persisted and fought back
on every argument thrown our way, through the House trial and
the Senate trial. Yours truly testified during the House trial, and let's
just say, I was so nervous I thought I was going to pass little green
apples. A very good friend used to use that metaphor to explain how
nervous or scared someone would get, and I'm just glad those little
green apples are little and smooth just in case I did, okay enough. As
nervous as I was, I took the stand, gave an oath, and did my part,
and I am glad to say I am now a part of history for Jicarilla. That's
a wonderful thing to say. Well, the House trial has since concluded,
and YES, we won! That's right, our fight from 2002 is secure, and our
minority majority district goes untouched. The judge approved all
our requests. He basically adopted all the NARWG's key findings
and approaches. The judge even reprimanded the executive plaintiffs
(governor of New Mexico's counsel) for failing to communicate with
the tribal leadership and to consider the tribal boundaries. The judge
recognized that tribes are in the best position to define what is in their
best interests, valued the extensive effort the Native American Native

94

American Workgroup and recognized the importance of respecting self-determination while complying with the Voting Rights Act, see history, pretty cool.

The multitribal plaintiffs did everything we could to protect what was created at the beginning of this process, and now as I type this letter to inform you about this tumultuous process, and then in a moment of light, I received an email that stated,

> The parties—all of the parties—have agreed to a settlement of the Senate map. The settlement includes the Unified Native American map in its entirety. All the other parties are making concessions, but not the Native Americans—since we had clearly won our case. Congratulations!

Congratulations indeed! I did speed through this story a little bit to cut out some of the more technical details, but I do have the court's opinion and the maps, which I would gladly share with you. However, this entire process was nothing but rushed. It was a long, tedious process that took a lot of work and effort from not only the Native American redistricting. This fight was once again a reminder that tribes were not being heard and in that treated as second-class citizens. It was not so long ago when Native Americans could not even vote, and now in this millennium, we still have to fight to be heard and recognized. Unfair, maybe, but to not get involved in the voting process makes it unjust, not to mention the message it sends to the state, county, and federal representation, the message that we don't care, so we do not get involved and exercise the reason most wars were fought, the protection of democracy. Let me tell you, throughout this process, there were comments made from representatives who are in office today that stated they know more what tribes need than the tribes do themselves and that tribal leadership are nothing more than ad hoc groups, harsh statements from people who create laws. Jicarilla remains a powerhouse that continues to receive plenty of accolades and respect throughout Indian country, and beyond, we are all a part of this victory. Preserve it by doing your part by voting.

We need to elect representatives who are going to be a benefit and not a burden, which should be true for all elections, but I digress.

I really found myself questioning the true nature of being a sovereign government and having to explain what those roles might be when dealing with other sovereign governments such as state government. There seemed to be a lack of understanding at least from the Nation as to the lack of trust responsibility the state was supposed to be doing for tribes in the state of New Mexico. What it really came down to was Nation tribal leadership trying to play a card in the game of sovereign relationships to which was not even from the same deck, nor was it is card designed to be used in one's hand. It was more like trying to use a playing card from a deck used in the game of Uno! The reoccurring argument that the state had to work with tribes was not only trite but also a shot in the dark. State government had no responsibility to work for tribes even when there were twenty-two tribes that make up the state of New Mexico. So how could we keep claiming foul, when the reality was, in the eyes of the state, tribes were just another community that should be treated like any other local municipality? Now to be fair, there was some state legislation that recognized tribes as sovereigns, and they have helped open the doors to engage in talks with sitting state governors as to how tribes can benefit for their own needs, but again, that is subject to change and opinion as to revolving administrations every four years. Case in point, during the voter redistricting for new election boundary lines, New Mexico had a republican governor, and there and of itself was already going to be a fight not only for the success of tribal representation and turnout in this case but also how tribes were going to be viewed and received with a republican governor.

In 2009, the state signed into law the State Tribal Collaboration Act. This law would now serve as the foundation in which the New Mexico State government would work with tribes to help serve the needs as well as the efforts tribes could do with their own economic development. There was even a clause that was built into the law that established an annual summit in which the sitting governor of the state would visit and discuss issues with all twenty-two tribal leaders in a round table format. I was proud to do my part participating as a representative for the Nation in the planning of said summits for five years, with all having some trials and tribulations but a strong opportunity to present vetted dialogue for the benefit of the citizens of New Mexico.

Two thousand and eight was probably the largest national, state, and county voter turnout we had seen in the community, and I was proud to help bridge the gaps of information that included candidates, bond issues, and other items placed on the ballot. I reached out to candidates and invited them to speak to both tribal leadership and community members and tracked carefully who showed up and what campaign promise was made. I'm not saying I got anyone elected, but those who showed up to our little community of Dulce are sitting in Washington, DC, and Santa Fe, New Mexico, now as elected representatives.

I had reached out extensively to the Republican candidate so that she could hear firsthand about the nation and its many contributions to the state as well as meet the growing number of registered Republicans in the community and maybe even ask for a political contribution from the Nation. I would write resolutions for both federal and state political contributions, and the Nation was benevolent in its check writing. Unfortunately, the initiation was never accepted, and the Republican candidate eventually won the seat, and in the nature of the beast of politics and elections, you work with what you have. Again, unfortunately, invitations to meet one-on-one with the newly elected New Mexico governor and the sitting Nation leadership never occurred. I was pretty upset as I believed a simple conversation would have allowed the Nation to take part in any dialogue dealing with oil and gas, the state's main contributor to the state coffers and other precedents the Nation was known for accomplishing. But never once did I get to the office to plant the seeds for discussion. It was then right around the time that the annual State Tribal Collaborative Summit was to take place, and there were a lot of grumblings from other tribes as to the absence of opportunity to sit one-on-one with the new governor, and some felt that the annual summit was just going to be a dog and pony show as the saying goes.

I had returned from Santa Fe after a planning meeting, and I put my Jicarilla hat back on and began to write the following speech for the Nation president. In my mind, I wanted to convey facts, not emotion, but it had to have a tone, still respecting the office and Nation, so I came up with this speech:

> On behalf of the Jicarilla Apache Nation I would like to read this letter as submitted by President Levi Pesata and concurred by the Jicarilla Apache Nation Legislative Council.
>
> Fellow Tribal Leaders, Governor Martinez, Cabinet Secretaries and all in attendance. Jicarilla is stating our disappointment at the low priority shown towards the tribes of New Mexico. Since the beginning of the campaign trail last year, Jicarilla made many attempts to contact Governor Martinez to visit Dulce to not only meet with but also hear about our Governor's Native American platform and possibly even make a campaign contribution, we received no response. Election time came, our district had quite a number of votes for Governor Martinez, and again an invitation was sent, from her new constituents to meet our new history making Governor, there was no response. Remaining hopeful, we thought we now have a chance to meet and finally speak with the Governor at this year's State, mandated, Tribal Collaborative Summit. Well, based on the amended shortened agenda, our plans for a productive meeting with Governor Martinez and her Cabinet Secretaries fell short, again another disappointing development from Governor Martinez, her Chief of Staff and her administration. Although there were visits to other areas in close proximity to Dulce it seemed that any attempt to bridge a rather large

gap between this new administration and Jicarilla was not to be. I would like to formally recognize the Summit planning committees work in formulating what seemed to be a strategic and positive two day event that would have included a pre-summit meeting but also a full day devoted to the tribal leaders and Governor Martinez in an executive meeting. Unfortunately, even though the Governor's staff approved the planning committee's recommendations, the strategy changed without any notice or tribal input. Jicarilla is not just some special interest group, we are part of the 22 New Mexico tribes who are as equal to any State Governor, Mayor or Diplomat. We have an innate ability to self-govern but have also successfully fulfilled a fiscal dependability as well as a fiduciary duty to our great State of New Mexico for many decades.

Furthermore, Jicarilla would like to express our disappointment that this administration has not abided by Senate Bill 196 (the State-Tribal Collaboration Act) specifically Section 4 (ANNUAL SUMMIT-TRAINING OF STATE EMPLOYEES) which states:

A. At least once a year, during the third quarter of the state's fiscal year, the governor shall meet with the leaders of Indian nations, tribes and pueblos in a state-tribal summit to address issues of mutual concern.

B. All state agency managers and employees who have ongoing communication with Indian nations, tribes or pueblos shall complete a training provided by the state personnel office with assistance from the

Indian affairs department, which training supports:

(1) the promotion of effective communication and collaboration between state agencies and Indian nations, tribes or pueblos;
(2) the development of positive state-tribal government-to-government relations; and
(3) Cultural competency in providing effective services to American Indians or Alaska Natives.

It is Jicarilla's opinion that none of the above policies have been accomplished much less attempted and we are left feeling frustrated at the lack of respect not only shown towards tribes but the Legislative Bill itself. It is imperative that you and your administration understand the importance of providing a better cooperative effort with your 22 New Mexico sovereign equals establishing a better government-to-government relationship.

For these reasons, Jicarilla has chosen not to participate in this years summit, it also seems I was scheduled to be a presenter for this summit, I feel that I should not be speaking on behalf of the other tribal leaders without their consent so therefore, I will not be presenting today. Although it seems that our relationship is off to a tumultuous start, Jicarilla remains optimistic, we look forward to working with you, your administration, and your Cabinet Secretaries in a concerted effort that will be positive during your tenure.

Respectfully,
President of the Jicarilla Apache Nation

The plan was for the president to read the letter during his comment time at the round table discussion; however, as the leadership caucused outside the event room, not one leader wanted to present the already agreed-upon statement! Fingers pointed back and forth, and all of a sudden, job descriptions were stated as to roles and responsibilities, but not a one stepped up. I then made the comment, "I can read it." Like a flash of light, everyone said yes, and they left the building or sat in silence in audience. I really can't remember as I was stunned not only by my comment of volunteering but at no one wanting to do their job as representatives of their constituents back home in Dulce. That moment for me was like pulling back the curtain on the mighty Oz and discovering that is was a facade and sound bite at best. A memory I vividly have to this day as to the lack of real accountability not only swearing to the oath of office but to the ability of what it means to be a leader.

With speech in hand, I went to the table where all tribal leadership sat and found the name tag for the president and sat down and gave a glance over the speech. I not only wrote but tried to find in my mind how I was going to present it, what tone of voice I would use, and when I would breathe in between sentences to avoid unnecessary distractions. The meeting began, and as luck would have it, the governor pointed to her left and said, "We will begin this way." I was in the second chair and thought, *Wow, of all the luck*. But I have always respected timing and the nature of timed events, even if I didn't agree, as things happened for a reason. The first tribal leader made his comments and sat down. I introduced myself and my position as public relations officer for the Jicarilla Apache Nation and began reading. I read every word as if I were reciting the Gettysburg Address, with timed breaths and smooth flowing deep but not too deep voice and out of the corner of my eye knew my words were being heard as I felt the governor and her staff eyeball me. I finished the speech to some light applause from some tribal leaders and audience members as well as murmurs coming from others sitting at the table. As I sat down, I would sound find out, other tribal leaders did not take the same approach and began commending the governor for her time and presence at the already delayed annual summit. It was a surreal experience, and I was to be the deliverer of the speech I had prepared, and I was glad I did it. But the lessons learned as to the dynamics of tribal leadership would forever resonate as a sham and breached responsibility in my mind. By the way, Jicarilla finally had a one-on-one face-to-face with the governor the following year, and I also wrote the letter highlighting the issues but thanking her for her time and consideration. You have to love politics; they do make strange bedfellows!

I loved my role as the public relations officer, and I really excelled as a student of both politics and reporter of information. I wrote dozens of articles for the local community newspaper as well as my continued writing of speeches and objection or endorsement letters for upcoming bills the state legislature would propose. I really found myself trying to find the best outcome of bills. I mean, sure, there were some confrontational ones that would really work against Indian country and the Nation, but there were some that may have required some light sacrifice for the greater good, and to be able to sit and listen and really gain an understanding and appreciation of the various types of legislation made me really open my mind and use a different perspective and not just pro-native just because we were native. It's a strange dynamic that has very little balance. It's either one or the other, and that can create further misunderstanding and assumptions of what this political relationship is or can be. There are many on both sides of the spectrum, native and nonnative, who view issues very black-and-white, and I saw things asking about the gray areas. That may have been around the time I started to fall in love with my new mistress, Little Miss Politics!

Once again, that time of year came around again. It was election time, and just like the opportunity it can provide to really help the community, political rhetoric can create biased opinions that can then spread like a brush fire. I am not sure if people really understand the magnitude rumor and hearsay have, both on a candidate, and someone who feels that all they can do is follow the crowd, and those who scream the loudest usually garner followers, which in turn can really skew the need for better, more accountable governance. As I stated, I absolutely loved my position as public relations officer and, quite frankly, was able to really propel things that were equitable for the membership, things as huge as input in political matters at the state or federal level, creating opportunities to bridge the community with the school district by having more meet and greets between teachers, staff, parents, and students; going to the local radio station to give reports as well as utilize the local newspaper to share information; creating more opportunities to highlight various departments in an attempt to help share protocols; as well as acknowledging hardworking employees. I was even able to negotiate hotel room rates with a large local hotel chain so that all tribal members could receive room discounts. I absolutely was proud of the possibilities the office was able to do for the greater good of membership information and opportunities.

I really debated running for office again. I had lost my last election as an incumbent, and that still stung, but I really felt I had a whole new outlook and would be able to really add quality as a voting member of the Nation's government. So out of the blue, a thought came to mind. Maybe I should consider running for an executive position. The Nation has staggered elections, during a four-year term. Timing-wise, every two years, there is an election either for four council seats or six seats that include two executive chairs, president and vice president, and four council seats. In this rotation, six seats were up for election. I really missed being in meetings and being able to offer debate that was both in line with laws and subjective to roles and responsibilities, and that was not too popular, but after all, that was the crux of the oath of office. I wondered if a council seat would be a good idea. I knew that the president's chair was not a good idea, nor was the timing right, and I would now come face-to-face with what I would now be forever known as and called behind my back, a half-breed. So I decided that campaigning for the vice president seat would be something more feasible, especially as to further capitalize on the need to help provide for and promote empowerment for both department directors and department employees. The norm to date has been to micromanage things to death and let titled opinions trump policy and, for that matter, moral. It has always been my thought that if there could be a clear understanding of empowerment, that could a create a more consistent effort of work rather than the perception to appease what feels like twelve bosses!

I went forth and paid my fee. By the way, in my first term, I had kept asking the question of what a seated "leader" is. Yes, I use air quotes, and I will explain why in a minute, but what is the determination deserving of a candidate to want to serve as a public servant, a term that I was only using to which may also be part of the misconception of serving in such a capacity? I had written an amendment in my first term pertaining to the candidate filing fee ordinance, which was a fee of $50 for a council seat and $100 for the two executive seats. It had been a running joke that people would even dare other people to run, and they would pay the filing fee, or some comments were, "It's only $50. I spend more than that at the casino." There were a lot of complaints about candidates, which was the basis of asking the question, "What is the caliber of character than the Nation deserves to run for public, tribal office, still public even, though that authority is abused? I met with the local election board office and received some info and buy-in and wrote the amendment stating that the filing fees were now $500 for a council candidacy and $1,000 for the two executive seats. Did it increase the caliber of candidates? That's a loaded question, and the fact that I will share points throughout the remainder of this story may answer that question inadvertently.

I did not know it or maybe blocked it from my mind as it ever being an issue, but this would now be the time where I was slapped in the face with a reality that would leave scars to even till this day. I hadn't campaigned in a while, and so I used merits from my last term in office as a council member as well as highlighted what my accomplishments were as the public relations officer, including all my board appointments and what was done as a representative of the Nation. I felt pretty confident in my new skill set and felt I really could enhance perspectives of what the office of the vice president could really do to help more than just sit idle and finger-point. I would soon find out the internal race card would rear its ugly head and be used against me. Now I'm all for calling out an opponent, but there was never a platform that would allow for public debate at that time, and word of mouth seemed to be the fastest way to attack one's character based on speculation and conjecture, again self-indulged as this was a choice to run for a public seat and therefore subject to the usual rhetoric and rumor. I had no problem speaking and even showing what was done in my career and in fact was quite proud to help create new ways to make the government more accountable and really earn the paycheck. Elected positions had earned a salary and were now viewed as full-time exempt employees—contradiction; well, that depends on the individual and how they perform their duties under the guises of a very ambiguous constitution. Nonetheless, there was enough substance in the constitution to create accountability for the greater good of the position, membership, and equitable growth of the community.

I really felt good about my choice to run for office again, and as I look back, I don't know if I ever believed in what I call pandering for votes. To me, there is a difference between quality and pretending there is a quality product. The irony I now feel is I should have known better, especially having a marketing background. People can be influenced, and that can mean job security in tricking consumers. In this case, consumers are members of the Nation, and I really still feel that using smoke and mirrors may get you the job, but it also then continues to play out the trick because political positions are many times used as on-the-job training, and by the time things are understood, the term is almost over. So many times, tactics like being clandestine or giving in to popular voting often keeps ethical and moral turpitude pushed into the shadows. All I wanted to do and still do know is to be able to showcase the law, the rules adopted as to allow accountability and in that empowerment so that moral and progress become a true team effort and not just a biased one forced by ten people who received the most votes. Yes, I am digressing, but if people were empowered to receive meeting minutes, the government would no longer be able to hide from those they swore to do good for. The fact that there are laws in the constitution and in ordinance that are selectively ignored, that specifically address the allowable dissemination of information to the membership, and that still not being done, in my humbled opinion, is what also keeps candidates comfortable in feeling they can run for a second term and sometimes win.

It was in my loose campaign that I had realized how bad internal segregation was in the community. I know there had always been jokes or comments that had a stronger tone of racism but always given with humor as to deflect from the direct comment. I look back, and I was either really blind to this fact or really ignorant that I could be a target. After all, I was an enrolled member, but I was not a full blood, a term that is very destructive in its pridefulness. I was working at my desk when people started stopping by the office and telling me what they heard about me and that I was not good and I was a half-breed who did not know the language and culture, and that made me feel bad because why should I be allowed to be a leader if I did not know what Jicarilla was all about? A reliable point, I must admit, but it is valid. Mind you, I was elected in 2002, and that seemed okay in being a half-breed, and I was back in the community as a member and parent who did whatever needed to be done for the betterment of the safety and well-being of the community. After all, isn't a leader someone who can help people see how things can be improved as to have a better outcome? I was blindsided by this conjecture and even more so to also eventually find out these half-breed comments came from people I sat across the table from as a council member. I even found out that there were some members of my family spreading hate about me, which was a much larger pill to swallow. I look back, and maybe there was a few minor moments I rested on some laurels but very short-term, and as humans, we can let our egos run rampant. The trick then becomes, how do you get the ego back in the cage and, in self-reflection, figure out how to do and be better?

I started thinking about these comments and actually had run into other types of comments such as starting a movement to lower the enrollable amount of blood mandated by the revised constitution, which was now three-eighths total Jicarilla blood to be eligible for enrollment. The rumor was that if I ever won a political seat, I would lower the blood quantum from three-eighths to one-quarter. It occurred to me that during the time when I ran as an incumbent in 2006, this was a mere seed, which grew into a gross display of ignorance for those "leaders," which is where I developed the use of air quotes when describing those who thought they were leaders and not just bumps on a log. But no real "leader" ever took the time to read the laws, much less try and understand as to help guide the membership toward these policies in an attempt to educate and create a whole new thought process rather than the usual political banter like "I stole money" and "I was having affairs," both I laughed off, but the half breed stuff was a whole other ball of wax. I dismissed a lot of these comments at first, but they started to become more reoccurring and from many different people who stated almost verbatim the same comments they heard or were now told. I remember getting angry but also felt a bit helpless as to try and address or confront. After all, I was getting hearsay comments, so out of the blue, my mind stated, "Write something." I thought, how could I write a political candidate commentary while addressing what was now becoming an elephant in every home? So I wrote the following and had it printed in the local newspaper and purposely titled the article as such—"Half-Breed: How I Learned to Love the Word."

I took a line out of a song by Cher that was quite popular in the '70s to headline this article. Although I did change the word hate to love, I promise I won't sing the song but if you are a Generation X'er (Born in the early 1960s to the early 1980s) you may know it. For those of you who may be a bit younger, Google the song and read the lyrics, there are somewhat germane to this article.

After some much needed soul searching and self-reflection, I am compelled to address a couple of issues that impacted me during the recent election process. Now, you may ask…why is this information being shared with us now? After all the election is over!

What's the point? So as a prelude to the concerns and questions that I will pose in this article, I have decided to share a little personal history, leadership experience and the principles for which I stand for. I come from a diverse family of productive, constructive, and well-respected members of the community of Dulce. My paternal grandparents were Wilson Green Reval and Secaria Muniz Reval; great maternal grandparents are Jack Muniz and Josepha Pesata Muniz all steeped in the Jicarilla Apache culture, tradition, and language. My parents are the late Kerino (Kimo) Reval and Abbie Segura; my maternal grandfather is the late Frank Segura Sr., (who was born and raised on the Segura ranch west of the old sawmill) and the late Mary Lynch Segura.

Due to my diverse family background and upbringing, I have been blessed to be the person I am today. I am also most indebted for the positive influences and guidance of individuals who reinforced and demonstrated valuable principals such as honesty, integrity; dedication; leadership, accountability, team-work; and most importantly genuineness and respect toward others, despite cultural or ethnic differences.

My educational experience provided me with the knowledge and understanding of national globalization and economics that directly impacts the Nation's financial progress and resources which we have entrusted to others outside the borders of the Nation. My professional experience has taught me the importance of effective communication, networking and adaptability which have allowed me to contribute to the many achievements of the Jicarilla Apache Nation.

My service to the Jicarilla Apache Nation includes: Enterprise Accountant for the Nation's Finance Department; served a four-year term as Legislative Tribal Council Member and Civil Servant for the Jicarilla Apache Nation; Marketing Associate for the Apache Nugget Corporation; Public Information Officer for the Jicarilla Apache Nation.

Some of the highlights as Public Information Officer for the Jicarilla Apache Nation include: Served as spokesperson and provided written and verbal Press Releases for the Nation. Appointed by Governor Bill Richardson to serve on the Tribal Infrastructure Board for the New Mexico Indian Affairs Department and The Tribal Economic Development Board, Appointed as key witness to testify on behalf of the Jicarilla Apache Nation in the Multi-Tribal Redistricting Lawsuit to ensure that the Native American Voting Rights Act was followed during the 2011 redistricting process, to which the tribes won, Appointed to serve as a Spokesperson and member of the New Mexico Indian Affairs Department Planning Committee for the State Tribal Collaborative Summit in 2010, 2011 and 2012 to which I was elected Committee Chairman, Served as active Tribal Infrastructure Voting Board Member, under Governor Susana Martinez's administration, that resulted in the approval of 19 million dollars to date for New Mexico tribes and Pueblos, Organized the third installment of the Apache Alliance Summit held in Dulce, in which eight Apache Tribes around the Country convened to establish an Apache Only Board for the purposes of protecting and reinforcing Tribal Self Determination and Tribal Sovereignty,

Networked with State Legislative Members at New Mexico State Legislative Hearings on behalf of the Nation. Organized meetings held in Dulce with US Dignitaries such as Congressman Ben Ray Lujan, Congressman Martin Heinrich, Congresswoman Heather Wilson and Jicarilla Apache Nation elected officials.

Authored the following proclamations:

Candidate Endorsements, To Promote Voting Within Our Community, Dads Take Your Kids To School, Teacher Appreciation Day, As Well As Many Press Releases For The Nation

Now that I have shared my background with you, I will address the issues of major concern that prompted me to write this article.

1) Article XXI (21) of the Jicarilla Apache Nation's Constitution states: amendments or referendums may only be modified when a minimum of 30% of the Jicarilla Apache Nation's eligible voters elect to amend a referendum. During the General Election process, it was alleged that, if elected, I was going to change the Nation's blood quantum from 3/8 (three-eighths) to 1/4 (one-quarter). Those who were circulating false information about the process of the Nation's Constitutional Amendments regarding changing the Nation's blood quantum from 3/8 (three-eighths) to 1/4 (one-quarter) dishonored and misrepresented the Nation's Constitution to the Jicarilla people.

The Nation's Constitution was written as directives to assure that our elected officials are accountable for honoring and representing each member of the Nation for the benefit of all enrolled members. It is our responsibility as eligible voters of the Jicarilla Apache Nation to

ensure that our elected civil servants unequivo-
cally demonstrate the highest integrity, honor,
consistency, and impartiality when conducting
business and making decisions that impact the
lives of every enrolled member of the Jicarilla
Apache Nation, as defined in the Jicarilla Apache
Nation Constitution.

2) Article III (3) and Article IV (4) of the
Jicarilla Apache Nation's Constitution states that
elected leaders are charged with providing equal
support and governance for all enrolled tribal
members despite blood quota. Discrimination,
exclusion and isolation should never be included
in any leader's agenda, whether you're campaigning or serving as an elected official. During the
General Election process, it was alleged that
because I was not a full-blood (4/4) Jicarilla, I
could not be an effective leader of the Jicarilla
Apache Nation, regardless of my credentials and
service to the Nation. This demeaning and dis-
torted point of view is very disturbing, especially
if this attitude was endorsed by our own elected
officials, as was alleged.

I'm proud of my lineage and I challenge
you to examine your own ancestry and the ancestry of your children, grandchildren, nieces and
nephews before you are quick to brand me or any
other member of the Jicarilla Apache Nation as
a "half breed." Show me where it is written that
being a "full-blood" automatically makes you
superior and competent in the business affairs of
the Nation? Is this the message we want to convey
to our young adults and children…that if you do
not meet the expectations of the status quo you
are unworthy, incompetent and undeserving?

Does this mean that if our children leave the boundaries of the reservation to pursue a college degree and familiarize themselves with mainstream America they will no longer be considered competent and effective leaders of our Nation? Will you love them any less? Should they be treated as second class members of the Jicarilla Apache Nation? Should they be considered less deserving of respect and entitlement to benefits and privileges available to other enrolled members?

There is no doubt that as a Nation that we must uphold the value of Jicarilla culture and tradition in order to preserve our heritage however, in order maintain a competitive edge in the ever-changing economy of the 21st Century, it is vital that as a elected leader, you acquire the necessary knowledge and experience that exists outside the boundaries of the Nation to properly service and protect the assets of the Nation.

In conclusion, I want to express my deepest gratitude to the voters who supported me in my candidacy for Vice-President of the Jicarilla Apache Nation. As a proud member of the Jicarilla Apache Nation, I am deeply honored and truly grateful for your reassurance, belief, guidance and confidence you placed in me.

In addition, I would like to express my gratitude for the honor of working with the current President and Vice-President as a Legislative Council Member and Public Relations Officer during their administration.

May all members of the Great Jicarilla Apache Nation work in unity so that we may continue to flourish and prosper as a strong and sovereign nation!

I thought I made a compelling argument, but I was in Utah visiting family when one of the kids decided to overeat and then had an accident in their pants. I won't tell you which kid, but needless to say, it took strength and courage to not fly off the handle as I must have scrubbed and scrubbed both behind and then clothes. This visit was during the summer, and I couldn't remember if Utah got so hot as it was in a mountain region and, at dusk, should have been cool. Well, thanks to climate change, I joke, the temperature stayed well into the nineties as I was sweating profusely in my daddy duties, cleaning up doodie! I knew it was around the time the election results were to be completed and posted. There was a part of me that was anxious aside from the divine intervention of cleanup duty to get my mind off the election and on the moment, which I still felt was debatable as to fate's reward. I had managed to get things cleaned up and with minimal cussing when the phone beeped, and a text message appeared from a cousin. It said simply, "Sorry, bro, maybe next time." My heart fell and, as I washed my hands, tried to act like it was not a big deal. But to me, it was, and I had to go back into the party, and if asked because I was going to be asked if the results were posted, I had to say I did not win and smile like it was okay and then hear comments like, "Well, it wasn't meant to be," and such. I felt all the air left my lungs, but I managed to make my rounds through the home, said my goodbyes, rallied up the kids, and went to the hotel and sat on the chair. My second loss, I never thought I would have four more in my tenure.

I buried myself in my work. After all, the election results produced a new president, vice president, and four council members, and I still had a job until September. I fulfilled my board obligations and wrote letters of resignation because I didn't know if I would still have a job since the PR position was appointed, but I also felt I needed to leave my office in order and as easy for the next person to walk into and understand what the position entailed. I was in the middle of writing an article about some legislation the state was considering for the upcoming legislative session in January when the president-elect came into my office. We had always been professional and cordial, exchanged jokes and other funny banter in his former role as vice president, so it was never a surprise when he would stop by my office. We joked and had some laughs and then asked me point-blank if I wanted to remain the public relations officer. He stated he felt I was a good person for the job and had been doing good work, and he wanted good things to continue in his administration. I shared my childhood earlier because I really wanted to say, "Nahhhh," even though deep down I was shouting "YES!" But in still trying to understand how I built my coping skills, spite and ego were flaring up because of my loss. I balked when I was asked, but I said, "I would be honored to serve in your administration," and my statement was genuine. I was extremely happy to remain. I did have one question. I asked, "What kind of independence or restriction will I have?" The answer, "Keep doing what you're doing." I said, "Thank you, sir," shook hands, and sat down and printed a copy of the article I was writing so he could use the information in his inauguration speech.

I continued to do my job and even gained a huge amount of confidence. Since I was to continue to serve as a representative of the Nation on all the state boards, I was able to hone my skill of observation in both group dynamics and protocol and policy. After all, anything related to the state was open and subject to the general public, so policy was of the utmost importance. I soon found myself more involved in my participation especially in talking about and promoting the Nation. Not only did I have to really know the history, but I had to present it and then make it sound so interesting that others would feel more engaged to want to know more about Jicarilla.

Having a broadcasting background was a fantastic benefit to add to my personal professional tool chest, and my skill served me and the Nation well. I would now be nominated to present at conferences and other events where a master of ceremonies was needed. I felt like I was the belle of the ball. I had gained knowledge of state-sanctioned organizations, and with those heavy hitters whom I sat next to and served with, it can be a very intimidating feeling of inadequacy when you're surrounded by people who hold doctorate and master's degrees with years of experience in their fields of expertise, and here I was, sitting at the table thinking about how I got here and sinking down in the chair a little. The positive that would soon blossom was the ability to watch, to observe mannerism, and then take some little pieces and apply them to my persona, not to mimic but to enhance my own set of skills that I felt I didn't have but would now be the catalyst for these heavy hitters to begin paying me compliments from my opinions and submissions of ideas and logic. It really inspired me and propelled me to realize that things always work out the way they should, a life lesson I may have said even in speeches to others but one I really never validated until I began chipping away at my own inner shields of false protection.

I began crafting all speeches for the Nation's leadership in ways that made them sound knowledgeable of current events and, in that, made the Nation be perceived as powerful. I would make the connections of state leadership and federal leadership but also provide any necessary information they needed to help add to their cause of either Indian country as a whole, specifically the Nation, when it came to matters of oil and gas, taxes, and other native legislation. It was a wonderful time, and I was grateful and humbled by being able to flow freely but also be able to reflect the quality of work. I even managed to set aside my anger at the guy who had campaigned against me with the half-breed crap as he now sat in the other executive chair, felt like a task, but after all, my job was to work for the Nation and on behalf of the Nation.

It was in mid-2013 where my career would change. There was an incident involving a siting council member who was arrested for driving under the influence. The details are sketchy as it was pretty hush-hush except for the rumors. I unfortunately was not able to ever give any outside press releases that dealt with anything political locally. I had written some press releases for surrounding area newspapers, but they were events that talked about joint political matters such as working with a large power conglomerate when the Nation agreed to a deal in which the Nation would become its own electrical power authority but nothing that involve internal government matters like this arrest. The actual event that led to aftermath of the arrest was also sketchy. Public opinion was a huge variable that could actually change how decision-makers would vote, and this unfortunate circumstance would give way to opinion rather than law. The arrest was an issue in the eyes of the infringement, and the arrest was also forthcoming as to the officers on the scene investigation. However, there was never any charges filed and no conviction. The Nation has a law that says any elected official who is convicted of a crime is subject to being removed from office, again no conviction, but from what I finally heard later, there was a split vote in which some argued the law and others argued their opinion. The opinions won, and the council member in question was removed from office. There was now a vacancy on the council, and because the law states that if any council member is removed for any reason by their peers and they have a less than a year left in their term of office, there does not have to be a special election. The president can appoint, and with council approval, the appointee can fill the vacancy, therefore fulfilling the term of that specific seat. I knew there would be names flying, and they usually were based again on opinion and the buddy system. I was at home when my cell phone rang, and it was the president. He told me that he needed to fill the vacancy and that he asked a dozen people, and they all declined. He then asked if I would do it; do it meant take the appointment. I was walking and talking, and I could feel my breaths get shorter and shorter, and I tried to take deep breaths as to sound like I was not freaked out by his question. I caught my breath and, in a firm, confident but ever so slight deep annunciated voice, said, "I will give you an answer at eight a.m. tomorrow morning." I asked if that would be acceptable, and he said, "Sure." I said, "Thank you for considering me," and wished a good night. I told my wife, "Guess what?" and asked her for her opinion. You know she was supportive, but in my haste of excitement—after all, I was upset I had not been considered up until that moment and I wanted the offer—failed to really ask if my decision would affect things positively or negatively. She after all had endured my moods, my travel, and my long absences away from home in my first term and was also caring for our firstborn and then Dominick and his health issues. I look back at that night and in retrospect should have really listened and asked for more input, but my ego got the best of me.

The second hand hit eight o'clock sharp, and I dialed the president's number. He answered, and I said, "I will take the appointment." He said all right in a happy voice and went on to say that he would begin the process of council confirmation. I went to my office soon after my call and began getting my affairs in order. It would be two weeks before I was summoned to the council chambers. I sat down in front of the presiding officials, mildly nervous. You never knew what you were in or when you had to go to the council chambers. I had two pieces of papers in my hand. I had a resolution that I prepared that stated if I was to not run for office in the 2014 election and I did my public service in leaving my public relations position to fill the vacancy of the council, I would be able to go back to my office after the term was officially up that year in September. I also held in my hand a resignation letter thanking the president for allowing me to serve in his administration as I would now be considered a public official again. The council was split and, before my resolution went to a vote, presented my letter of resignation and said, "I understand." I do not want my first request to keep a job deter from the spirit of the law or seem like I was asking for special circumstances, so I resigned my PR post, and I was unanimously confirmed. I was sworn in and, in one of the smallest ceremonies ever, took my oath of office. I thanked the three people in the gallery. One was the chief judge who swore me in, who by the way offered me a position at the court as an associate judge a few months earlier and said he would help me complete the classes I needed as well as the certification process, but I sent him a letter telling him of my intentions to run in the 2014 election and felt strongly that I did not want to have the court wait on me when someone else who was qualified could commit to a position especially in the off chance I may have won the election. But I was completely blown away at the thought and consideration, and here I was, taking the oath of office to finish someone else's term, but I didn't care. I was back at the table. After the photo ops, I went to the vacant chair at the council table, sat down, and looked at each and every one of my new colleagues and said, "Okay, let's get to work!" They looked at me like, *What the heck, who does this guy think he is!* It was quite comical as I thought about it after the fact, but I figured I was coming in as a new guy in a lame duck session, so I was determined to take a position of confidence, even arrogance, to show that even with eight months left to go in my new term of office, I was all business.

The very first agenda item was a request for special delegations, which was an ask of funds from the government. There was really no policy that governed the request for funds, so the ask could be for bill consolidation, new vehicle, travel funds to visit family who lived out of state, so it was basically an opportunity, if you could get on the agenda to get financial assistance. The individual who was requesting funds was approved, and the next person came into the chambers and had their own request for funds; however, this time, the vote was a vote of no. After the person left and I asked the president to give me a minute before the next agenda item was called so that I could ask a question, he gave me the floor. I asked, "How are financial assistance requests reviewed and then either granted or denied?" I went on to state that the first person who came in was not subject to scrutiny and was approved; the next person who came in and just left had a very similar request and was grilled and denied. I wanted to know what process was used to base these decisions on. There was not a process in place. In fact, one council member patted his heart in an attempt to show that these decisions were based on emotion. I said, "Okay, thank you. We can resume." I sat in some amazement. In my first term, we had developed a process in which there was a much fairer opportunity to help members in need, and it was to try and alleviate the process of emotional opinion, and it was working very well but here I now sat and couldn't help but think how opinions can really change the continuity of what the government should be and could be doing in a much fairer and equitable manner.

I fit right in with my new colleagues, and the plus was, they all already knew my persona and work ethic, so it was nice to be able to conduct business as usual with them. Sitting at the table and observing the group dynamics was also very interesting. After all, on day 1 of my new position, I had asked what about policies for assisting members with finances were and was taken aback as to the volatility of opinions and loose logic, and this time around, I seemed to have a much deeper insight along with my new perspective and would now question pretty much everything but not just question to challenge but ask questions to promote thought, dialogue, and possible clarity as to why and what the role of a Jicarilla Apache Nation council member really was and, in that, the limitations as to not encroach into other powers and their own responsibilities. With three levels of government, executive, legislative, and judicial, each branch had a major responsibility, and it was not the job of the legislators, council, to micromanage or add unnecessary input that would distract from protocol. Having a whole new appreciation of the sanctity of the government, some real-world experience and prior on-the-job experience, from my first term, made my insight much more liberated when it came to formulating thoughts and strategies for accountability and proactiveness, specifically dealing with the promotion of the laws and how to use this opportunity serving as a public servant to really help bring long-term goals for the benefit of any economic or other global surprises. Yes, in my first term all those years ago, I had some wherewithal and understanding, even in crafting legislation as a freshman official, but this time, sitting at the table brought on a whole new view of the world of politics and all the nuances contained in these approved rules and, if ignored, could infringe on these protocols contained in the oath of office we as elected officials swore to uphold, not just swearing to the Nation's constitution but also the United States Constitution, which I always questioned especially as a sovereign nation, in many regard but now more so in my new perspective, which would define more traits of irony in something as powerful and formal as the oath itself.

Working alongside the group that had inherited me was very positive. I may have disagreed with tactics and practices, but observing and then tactfully couching a point really honed another skill, the skill of diplomacy, not for the purposes of self-gain but to be able to articulate a point, reference the rules, and ask if that was what we, as elected officials, were charged to do. I actually did have an agenda. It began in my first term, and although there was quite a bit accomplished, there was so much more that needed to be addressed, vetted, and then done by law for the purposes of any new sitting council member to hopeful acknowledge and then advance. I had a huge issue with health care. Yes, we had almost finished the Indian Health Services joint venture with the purposes of creating the Nation-owned full-fledged hospital but was dissolved. There was a huge gap in receiving health care, and that to me never sat well. The Nation had worked with independent insurance agencies and managed to get employees pretty good health insurance, but even after the insurance covered a medical issue, there was still the lingering 10 percent co-pay, and that too was becoming an issue with people wanting to see the council for financial assistance to help cover some very large co-pays. I knew there could be a way to cover all head of household families and not just employees, but in the short time I had, I waited for the right time to gather information, data, and cost to properly give a factual presentation. The other issue I had was the lack of new housing development. Houses were built on the reservation, and many of them were now old and in need of rehab or replacement, but because of limited options, many of those homeowners just dealt with issues or waited for tribal departments to repair issues. The only other option was to leave the home and purchase a mobile home, and that became the norm for young adults who now needed their own homes for their families.

Since the majority of homes built on the reservation were funded federally, there were many stipulations. At first, in 2002, when I started learning about all the issues the Nation dealt with, I had felt that accountability was extremely necessary. At that time, we had tried some new approaches in home development. The first was a tax credit program in which low-income clients could apply for housing if their annual income was under $15,000 a year and, in utilizing this approach, created a whole new neighborhood, five miles outside the center of town, where lots were now spacious and could accommodate any new growth. We also started a separate traditional mortgage home program in which members who made significantly more than $15,000 a year could apply for a mortgage, and we partnered up with a modular home company in Albuquerque to build and transport new homes for qualified recipients. The plan was working. I am not saying it was perfect, but it was organic and could have been reviewed and nurtured to accommodate the changing times for more homes to be built, but because this plan was unorthodox for the Nation, new "leadership" felt these ideas were not very good and unfortunately never grew these programs for the benefit of new homes. And eventually, these home programs were dissolved and consolidated into other programs or departments and soon forgotten about, which all of a sudden created redundant home development programs that all had their own set of guidelines and standards. And as someone who personally had no place to move into because of the lack of homebuyership, when I first moved up to Dulce in 2001, I had always felt there could be much better options to provide quality homes to accommodate the growth of the community.

Eight months flew by, and it was once again election time. The election in 2014 was to fill four council seats, including the seat I sat in completing the term. I knew I was going to run for the seat, and I began a short campaign once again addressing the label of half-breed. Hearing this term was very daunting and demeaning. When I wrote the half-breed article, I had elders stop by my office and who would say my kids and grandkids are half-breeds, and I began wondering how such a label was to be of benefit to the culture and language of the Nation. I had heard wonderful stories of days past when the tribe would befriend and assimilate people of various races into the groups and live and thrive in prosperity. I thought had the "dorm mentality" somehow have a great negative impact on this boomer generation, that's where the push of internal segregation was coming from, and I even really tried to empathize with this philosophy. The "dorm mentality" as I called it was when tribal member children would be placed into the BIA care, by their parents, which I could only assume was a thought to try and improve their children's well-being but in turned led their children unknowingly into a place of horror. The heartfelt angered stories I had been told by people who had endured were to punish, tear down, and drive the savagery out of these children. If tradition language was spoken, boys were subject to having their hair chopped off as a sign that they were now normal. Kids would have to sit for hours with bars of lye soap in their mouth and kneel on hard floors with arms extended while dorm matrons would slap their arms with wooden rulers. Food had been tainted, and bread would be distributed with meals, and children would pick out mouse droppings that had baked right into the loaves. I could actually relate some. I did attend Catholic school after all, and that was relatable in some feelings and experiences, so I gave some credence, maybe some solace, from the rhetoric I was enduring but also found a huge amount of hypocrisy in the logic of finger-pointing when many tribal members had children and grandchildren who were half or not even eligible for tribal enrollment labeling me as unworthy.

Watching the various campaigns was extremely interesting. Most candidates started off their speeches by proclaiming being full-blooded and that because they were older, they knew more than all other candidates, and some of the crowd ate up this rhetoric. I say rhetoric because nowhere, in any laws, does it say all candidates vying for public office have to be fluent in both language and culture. Time and time again, I would witness sound bites to this effect but never was directly ridiculed or criticized by my colleagues when the subject would come up in some debates. I would listen but dismiss it as it was usually more of an "I'm taking my ball and going home" comment and, in that, a chest-bumping show as to who knew more than who. It still was, at least in my opinion, not a place for segregation. The Constitution was for all enrolled tribal members and not just those who were more than others. I started being more vocal as to the destruction such mindset was doing to the community, and if "leaders" were to lead, it was all not just some and that culture and language, as important as it was, should be given, not hoarded and held over people's heads, taunting. But what did I know? I knew I had my limitations and side from a few Jicarilla words, and some aspects of the culture was the outsider, and young outsider at that.

I was surprised that I had won the election and now was going to serve my official second term as a Jicarilla Apache Nation official, and winning by a large margin, over 50 percent of the votes, blew me away! Typically, elections in the community generate 30 percent turnout, which is a huge negative, not only in elections but also engagement of tribal affairs. So the majority are subject to conjecture derived from rumors, and others, what I continue to think, capitalize on the ignorance by continually feeding half-truths, and no information whatsoever and any that is shared for those irresponsible naysayers is shared for selfish agendas. Now having more experience, knowledge, and clearer logic and strategy and because of the large number of voters who sent the message, I was the person they felt was going to be of real service. I made a personal vow to do much better, have more transparency, create more ways to hold accountability and absolutely promote teamwork as to try and limit the mentality that the governing officials were the experts just because they now held a short-term title. I didn't think I could or even wanted to be a savior, but I had been able to prove an ability to perform well within the statues, had a large Rolodex for networking, and knew many of the issues that could be properly explained to tribal members or any other person the Nation did business with. My mentor from my first term had shared a comment with me that sticks with me to this day. He said the Nation has a bull's-eye on its back, and in that, people will come out of the woodwork to try and gain everything from themselves and leave the Nation holding the empty bag. I knew that this was a strong statement, but I also knew that if there was true accountability and shared knowledge of tribal affairs, there could be real transparency and buy-in all for a better outcome of the Nation's future both socially and economically. I was ready and tactful of my new approach, and it had begun in my last eight-month term where I questioned everything. It got to the point where in meetings, I would raise my hands, and you would hear "Ughh" or "Not Leon again." I laugh but would vouch my questions in a way that would be inviting and not threatening or belittling and that in turn would generate new positive dialogue. That didn't mean everything went positive. Despite great debate, I was outvoted, but the point was the practice of even creating debate to find the best outcome for that issue or moment, and it was not only wonderful to see minds working but to participate in such a wonderful exercise, all for the benefit of those you are serving but, unfortunately, not as consistent as I would have personally liked to have seen.

It was now becoming more evident that we as a group needed to find better solutions and then agreed to having retreats where we would literally lock ourselves in a room and discuss as a group what and where we felt individually Jicarilla came from and then where Jicarilla could go. It was a powerful practice and one where I saw real commitment and honesty. When we left the two-day retreat, we, at least I felt so, had become energized and willing to move together as a team. I was so excited I mentioned that we should have a general meeting to not only commit to ourselves but also try and inspire the membership so that they too buy in, and together we can hold all of us accountable. I was so excited I wrote this article for the newspaper: "The Nation's Governing Body Will Hold a General Assembly at the Dulce Athletic Complex at 10 a.m." by Leon K. Reval.

It is has been a long time coming since the governing body has properly updated the membership, not only on general information but also at full transparency. The time has come to blaze a new trail in how the leadership informs, becomes accountable and disseminates all info on strategic planning that will propel the Nation forward.

The Governing Body recently met and caucused for two days to develop a consistent way to plan for growth, the kind of growth one would expect from a group of professionals, economic growth and growth in the community. It was through this strategic working session that the governing body came up with a beginning on how to become as a group, more accountable, more informative, better prepared and most importantly become more empowering to the membership. The Primary deliverables from this strategic working session were Jicarilla Legislative Council Core Values, Development of a Vision & Mission Statement, Strength—Weaknesses—Opportunities—Threats (S.W.O.T.) analysis, Establishment of priorities, and a project implementation schedule. Although these may seem like very basic deliverables, they often get lost and forgotten but as you know, they are crucial elements to the future work and direction of the Governing Body, today and into the future.

One of the biggest reasons the Governing Body wanted to change directions now, was we have seen too many times how leadership gets caught up in the "What we do" and forgets or pays little attention to "Why we do it". The "Why" plays a crucial role in accomplishment, "Why" speaks of the values and the heart of everything the Governing Body needs and should do as leaders. Our core values, in the general sense of the word, serve as the corner stone and consciousness to the work. The Legislative Council put deep thought and intense dialog about what core values best represent the governing body as well as the membership of the Nation. In this soul-searching discussion, the following core values were identified and agreed upon, Respect/Love, Dignity, Family, Self-Confidence, Perseverance through Language & Culture. There was another question posed to the Governing Body, "If not now, When? "If not us, who?" Any dialog on change is difficult but values like these bring a different points of view to the conversation of change, when core values are understood and agreed upon, we all see desirable and sustainable results. Understanding that the reaffirmation of the Jicarilla core values, allowed for the Governing Body to then move forward in establishing, a Vision and Mission Statement.

The Nation's Governing Body has a deep and serious desire to see projects get started, with reasonable progress and of course project completion. This desire is critical to the leadership because successful projects benefit Jicarilla people. However, there have been many shortcomings and it was discovered and made very clear that in the grand scheme of things, there have been one to many issues that lead to poor project execution and accomplishment. Issues such as lack of policies, adhering to existing polices, outdated polices and or Ordinances, the role and function of the Legislative Council, lack of community communication and engagement and lack of due diligence for sound decisions. The leadership addressed the above mentioned issues that have led to the hindering of the Nation's critical steps to success. There was an understanding that the only way we could move forward was to acknowledge and correct these gaps that have also been recognized as "curable," this new thought process will keep the governing body away from any and all future inconsistent project execution and in some cases, project death.

The effort, in this strategic planning session, was nothing short of sincere and focused. As priorities are now established, the work can begin in a prudent manner. In this strategic working session, there was also significant time given to the concern and appreciation for the Jicarilla culture and language. Our language and culture will always continue to exist and never let anyone tell you that we will lose this precious gift. As someone wise once told me, "Jicarilla is the backbone of the universe, as the back of the universe, Jicarilla connects to the heavens and the earth and because of this deep rooted connection and Jicarilla will always be here, so never say that we will lose our identity." That was a powerful statement and I will never forget that message.

It is this reliance and acknowledgement of the Jicarilla "Way of doing things" that will give rise to success. The Governing Body acknowledged that faith in one another especially the people, will give strength to this new effort and style of government and we will all see measurable results ensuring a better quality of outcome for all Jicarilla people.

The PowerPoint presentation on Friday April 10, 2015 will go into further details, as well address other issues like rumors, priorities, benefits but for now, I wanted to give a brief description of how your Government wants to become more transparent, accountable and most importantly, amend title 20 to include this new philosophy for all future elected officials to follow. Good things are coming and with open minds and hope, we will achieve great things, as leaders, as employees and as Jicarilla people. (Iheeden Nzhogoo)

We presented to a handful of members, and it quickly reverted back to questions of worthiness of being paid a salary and other perks of the job, and I still felt it was a positive. The membership had become used to not receiving any information, and the only time they did get info was when they shouted and forced the government to comment, which was why the government rarely ever held general meetings, much less question-and-answer ones, which was a practice we actually did during my first term, and you talk about a baptism by fire. It's literally sink or swim, and to someone who has zero experience speaking in public, that will have you running for the hills. I actually loved it, but these meeting would soon be few and then null. It's a shame in my opinion but feeling so excited, and writing may have, for me, been my shortcoming. I still obsess about that point.

My diplomatic execution was now becoming honed as well as also a nice new strategy to be able to use in listening, really listening, offering a counterpoint backed up with logic and/or facts, such as a policy, and it helped in writing new legislation, all for the benefit of addressing communal social and economic issues. It was a bit enduring to be considered the go-to guy to be able to craft legislation and be asked of my opinion, and it was a very progressive time to serve in my new capacity. Most of the term was trying to really dust off and establish roles and responsibilities between the legislative and executive branch. There had been some weaving in and out of these boundaries, and the way I now viewed this method was to play politics. Finger-pointing ran rampant as legislators would "offer" what in many times was a forced opinion to the executive, and in that, the chairs would cave and then say, "Council said." Council said became scripture; it would become the wedge that kept the gap of progress inconsistent and, in that, failing. It was rare for even someone who gave their strong opinion to ever quote protocol or policy, and when quoting occurred, it was usually to highlight for the purposes of personal gain. Personnel issues became huge issues as employees were subject to scrutiny based on hearsay or maybe didn't jump if an official said jump. It created a huge palpable feeling that people hated being summoned to the council chambers. No one knew what to expect or what outcome might even go against them, which is why I was becoming more outspoken on such practices. My comments ranged from empowerment and allowability of being able to feel like employees were part of the bigger picture because they were. No official was going to be out removing snow or patrolling the streets. They might say they would, but day after day, shift after shift, I never saw that, which is why I used that comment in my points to make sure lines were drawn and encroachment could be recognized and stopped.

I really felt that talking about these very important issues and practices was something I wanted to do, the attempt to lift the veil of secrecy and offer a viewpoint from someone who was willing to share this experience and, in that, offer a discussion to the membership as to what they deserved or were not observing when it came to being represented by their government. I wrote this op-ed in a hope that it would generate some much-needed thinking as to how, where, and why the Nation would need to be going and was this something that the membership felt part of in supporting candidates to help. I saw myself speaking my two cents, and I also always felt that I was not ever trying to "right." I was trying to be kind, and yet nothing or, sporadically, things were done. However, at the same time, I also began thinking, *Am I trying to force an agenda, or am I really trying to create dialogue so that there can be more input to understood how important this position of council member really was?* My sincere hope was that opening up uncomfortable or even stand-alone dialogue would create more discussion to establish more mutual understanding and then more personal accountability. My mind would ping-pong back and forth. Was I doing the proper thing by writing and exposing things that the membership maybe never knew? I am still envious of those who can just exist, either block or have been able to coast. I could not do either of those, and so I would continue to feel like I was walking across a high wire between tall mountains and feeling that if I lean one way or the other, I would lose my balance and plummet to the ground. I still remain scared to fall to this day.

I received flak for using the word *I*. It was strange because elected officials had, in my opinion, brainwashed the membership and even freshman officials, that everything done was because they had a great group of governing officials who tirelessly never slept and worked day and night for the betterment of the Nation. I wish to this day, membership could have access to all meeting minutes, including a resolution registry, so that they themselves could see what was actually done, who made comments about what, who was attending meetings, and why legislation was passed. Membership couldn't even just sit in the gallery and watch. It was such a tyranny of justice, the justice the laws afforded to the government and membership but rarely occurs, and I still do not understand why. I can speculate, but there is a saying about assumption, if I do, then I am an ass, and you are and so on and so forth. But what I can say with confidence is that the record is my justification for all my *I*s.

I really took a huge interest in the economics of the Nation. Part of sitting in the chair at the table is to participate in many of the decisions dealing with the economics of the Nation. The Nation's constitution gives authority to the council to oversee all funds and nature of business dealings, but that can also be power that can be unwieldable and, in its swinging, can miss or hit and destroy. There has never been a real strategy to vet projects, separate politics from business, and it was because of the allowability of the Constitution that allowed a continuation of a very bad, unreliable practice, which was "Council said."

Oil and gas activity and the collection of taxes were the golden egg for the Nation for three decades, but I started thinking that this was also the only egg in the basket, and although it had served the Nation well, trends and other motivations started to change the political climate that had embraced fossil fuels and their developments. To be able to see things in a whole different light, to recognize, acknowledge, and understand how such changes could impact the long-term resources of the country and then nation was a scary realization, and if those who sat in seats for a short term of four years had no understanding of global macro- and microeconomics, well, you don't need a crystal ball to predict a possible outcome in which new paths are created to travel down for financial growth and preservation. Even if the opinion was that doing nothing and just remaining in some form status quo because the Nation had a portfolio playing the stock market, you would be much more proactive in financial growth if you fed the portfolio rather than just take surplus funds because it was a good year in the market. I felt that this was gambling, and since I am not a very good gambler, I also began feeling decision-makers needed new ways to develop better business concepts and structures and put into some policy rules for growing businesses outside the reservation so that there were more lucrative opportunities to grow money and, in that, provide new careers for students graduating. Unfortunately, there are very little opportunities for new employment, and employees who excel are very rarely, if ever, properly compensated, not to mention the shroud of feeling like there is no due process and an employee can be terminated for very little to no cause. This man-made glass ceiling that formed was done so over years, and it is in my opinion detrimental and irresponsible of the Nation's government to feel like they can abuse the privilege of having some authority. It drove me crazy to come in for a meeting and see personnel issues on the agenda. They had no business to be placed as items for action, and I became more vocal about this passing the buck practice, making the council continue to be scapegoats because executives, who were responsible for all employment measures, couldn't follow a very simple rule already spelled out in law practice. Therefore, the term "council said" became more and more of a practice that was becoming rampant.

I wasn't combative just trying to be diplomatic and redirect back to the protocols and policies already in place. It was challenging and frustrating, and to be honest, I am not sure if debating helped. I really think it just pushed these issues into the shadows, and the ideology was now, the president said, "I had to laugh. Otherwise, I think I would be crying." I strategized and thought maybe it was a good time to shine some light on the rules and activity of the government, how the government was proactively or reactively preparing for financial planning, contingencies, and growth of population. After all, if the Constitution gave certain allowabilities, at least in my mind, then there were also responsibilities to promote and exercise better ways to help all and in that build toward some five-, ten-, or twenty-year goal. During this time, I have reflected back and asked myself why I began writing op-eds. Maybe it was fate, or maybe it was frustration led by ego, but in retrospect, maybe not a good way to want to retain a position in local tribal government.

I had no intention of ever trying to be a hero or savior while I served in any of my council capacity. I just felt that the job had immense responsibility, and if I or others wanted the job, then why not see it as a privilege and not an entitlement? When the government does not follow its own rules, it leads not only blindly but also chaotically and in that sets the tone of its followers, those they lead, to impending doom. I'm not saying Armageddon, but I am saying that as an architect of building sustainability and possibility especially as a lawmaker, and to me, that came with certain expectations like using an opinion to create and build upon, not deject, destroy, and cater. Case in point, the Nation has exercised its right to establish section 17 corporations and in that approve charters for the purpose of allowing a for-profit corporate-style entity to flourish and in that help create consistent revenue streams and career opportunities. Each corporation had its own separate board of directors, and they too had responsibilities but were often stifled because the council also served as shareholder representatives; that meant the council were privy to corporate review at an annual shareholders' meeting established in each charter. To me, that meant at a meeting held once a year, I could ask questions of the organization, its goals, its objectives, and even ask of its finances, again for the benefit of creating a strong but separate business model so good things could continue and money could be generated. Well, unfortunately, shareholders' representative somehow had developed into. The council, being able to chime in when they heard something or when new bodies filled seats after winning an election, felt that they now had opportunities to question and make daily changes because they had been told from their colleagues that this is what the job of a council person was, and since they were voted in by the people, they were going to represent the people and get answers! I just felt that if you had the privilege of being titled a leader, then why waste time with little to no positive energy? This habitual practice of faking, to me, had to be challenged, overriding existing rules that were adopted to establish these powerful tools of section 17 corporations branches and at the same time separate such authority as to prevent overstepping boundaries. By doing so and allowing such practices to occur, to me, was an abuse of authority, hindering all profitable activity. That was when I decided to state my piece. I was a council member, yes. I was part of a team, but I was also responsible for my own thoughts, actions, and votes, and I was beginning to not trust the team.

It really bugged me that the council could impart their own ideas on everything and had these delusions of grandeur that they could fix whatever they touched. It was so the opposite of helping, and board of directors would cater and even pander for support. No matter how much I tried to grasp their concept of hands-on, I would just shake my head, offer my opposing views of involvement, quote a charter policy, and sit back and watch my comments dissolve into the air. A few months went by, and I had kept pushing the need for council to allow others to do their job, including the president, and finally there was some resolve. The council finally started to see that value of accountability and began promoting concepts such as creating a better avenue for financial requests of the people and keeping these issues from becoming political by not having these request placed on the agenda. Personnel issues were left to protocols, and if the question arose from the president asking what he should do, comments ranged from, "Do your job" to "Follow the process." We started to see a need to try and contract the best, most effective, yet reasonably priced representation such as outside legal counsel. The Nation had established an in-house counsel, but it unfortunately became tainted, and even though in-house had some really good young lawyers, they would always be met with disdain, maybe because they were women or maybe because they were young women. I could only surmise, but in my opinion, the ladies did very good work and toed the line when it came to giving their legal opinions as it pertained to the laws of the Nation. Nonetheless, we had agreed to start sending out request for proposal for legal matters that included finding law firms that had strong experience in economic development and a law firm that dealt specifically with oil and gas issues, including tax issues, and in this new process allowed the cream to rise to the top. We found two law firms that were both reasonably priced, and we contracted with them and began formulating new strategies. It was so comforting to see my colleagues, and not because they didn't know how to do good things, but they saw how good decision-making could help create new possibilities, and we all agreed to this approach, so I think that really helped.

What I really felt was that there could be a better way to try and create much more opportunities outside the boundaries of the reservation so that good things could flourish inside the boundaries. The biggest issue I saw firsthand and was a part of in my first term, to some small degree but more and more would speak out against, was how politics was killing business and, in that, any chance for consistent progress. In my first term, we had tried to do many things that would allow some life-enhancing benefits for the membership and had done quite a bit. We had created a plan that would rehabilitate homes that were built in the sixties. The Nation had finally litigated the majority of all its water rights, and when the water and wastewater facility was taken over by the Nation from the BIA, we allowed the use of water at no charge for the community. A plan was created from one of the Nation's section 17 corporations that would allow membership to only have to pay transportation costs for natural gas, which made their monthly bills around $20. We created a consistent monthly payment for each tribal member in which they now would receive $500 a month, and this new plan would now allow for the government to plan better in retaining this distribution with a better fiscal strategy for the purposes of increasing these awards annually. Again, the whole purpose, at least what I assumed was what a leader was supposed to do, was to create opportunities so that the next group could nurture, enhance, sustain, even alter if need be, for the time, these approvals for the benefit of continued growth and stability for members. Being here for the second time with a new mindset, understanding, and philosophy, I could no longer just sit idle. I needed to do more, and so I did.

I sat with the head of the new economic development law firm we just contracted, who was hired to represent the government with legal practices and matters and, in that, was to make sure any input, direction, and planning was done in a legal, proactive, responsible manner. I shared with him all my concerns and highlighted the issues of government encroachment in almost everything and that this practice, if continued, would not only be detrimental to the Nation's coffers but also prohibit any chance of creating real career opportunities for graduates and other members looking to work and feel like their efforts mattered. I had told him about the section 17 corporations and how they barely were squeaking by and had no real opportunity to break through their own glass ceilings. We had a very lengthy in-depth discussion. I felt I had to say that I was not just complaining. I shared success stories former councils had done in the seventies and eighties, but my concern was the plateauing and in some years declining that sitting governments did nothing about, and my biggest concern was the inability to use any economic benefit for the purposes of political gain or momentum at the state and even in Washington, DC. He took all my ideas, thoughts, concerns, and we began to craft a draft plan that was so unorthodox that it not only made me smile, but it also made me dream of a very limitless possibility. I was salivating because the new approach was a powerful tool to create so much benefit beyond what I call printing money, business ventures, that it could provide for tribal members' future and, in that, a much better strategy to preserve any and all aspects of growth for the Nation.

The Jicarilla Apache Nation Corporation (JANCO) was created. It was not a section 17; this would now be first tribally approved through permanent law, that could serve as a private holding company and didn't need congressional approval or disapproval, and it could no longer be subject to revolving governments who came into office with a biased mindset based on what they heard but never knew could not allow then to rescind the JANCO law. This new ordinance could only be rescinded by the tribal membership, which for me was the greatest use of tribal sovereignty and true self-determination. I was proud of this new company, and the best part about this new endeavor, it separated the government from getting directly involved in any daily matters and/or corporate decision-making. This job belonged to the board of directors and chief executive officer. The new law had a clause that established a seven-member board consisting of five independents who had real-life global experience and were able to understand the importance of a real corporate structure and ideology. Two of the board members were local, a sitting council member serving as decision-maker but also as a liaison to the council and a former and/or knowledgeable tribal member, again to bring some local insight and serve as an envoy to the government, board, and community. It was now ready to be presented and hopefully approved by the council. I had actually kept my colleagues involved with email updates, text messages, and in discussion at convened meetings, again to make sure the record captured my words verbatim and they were understanding and supportive. I even put together a bullet-point list, for my colleagues, and to also help explain to the membership. The need of its government to be visionaries and be responsible in creating sustainable resources for the benefit of their constituents and establishing a new company like JANCO would be vital for the future of the Nation. The JANCO talking points were as follows:

- With the recent oil and gas recession, the Nation has seen a significant drop in assets and wealth making the Nation unable to sustain current benefits for the People.
- In order to address the Nation's financial crisis, the Legislative Council created JANCO (Jicarilla Apache Nation Corporation) to immediately increase the amount of money available for the People; this also means the Nation will no longer be dependent only on oil and gas revenues.
- The Legislative Council created JANCO to protect the long-term viability of the Nation by ensuring the People will continue receiving benefits including increased dividends, shopping vouchers, and new credit programs.
- JANCO will expand the Nation's economy beyond oil and gas through other business opportunities such as operating e-commerce companies, developing technology and intellectual property, manufacturing and/or distributing goods, investing in real estate, and providing various services.
- JANCO is 100% owned and operated by the Nation; no other entity or person has an ownership interest in JANCO.
- JANCO is designed so that all revenues earned by profitable businesses will flow back to the Nation for the benefit of the People.

- JANCO will stop the Nation from "bailing out" companies that are losing money for the People.
- JANCO will hold managers of Nation businesses losing money accountable; this means managers will be fired if such businesses do not make profit for the People.
- JANCO will be operated by a seven-member Board of Directors and a Chief Executive Officer that will oversee day-to-day business operations.
- The Legislative Council still maintain control over JANCO because they maintain the power to appoint the JANCO Board of Directors and they also maintain the power to allocate, if any, Nation capital or assets to JANCO.
- The Nation will no longer miss opportunities (e.g.: Las Vegas Walgreens; Middle East coffee cream distribution, etc.) because JANCO is required to hire professionals to immediately conduct due diligence, properly assess, and take advantage of future business opportunities for the People.
- JANCO recognizes that the Nation predates the United States Constitution and JANCO protects all attributes of tribal sovereignty; therefore JANCO has been designed so it does not waive its sovereign immunity from suit to third parties and does not allow the State to assess taxes over the Nation.
- Most Nation departments will not be impacted by the creation of JANCO; accordingly, the purpose of JANCO is not to terminate employees or dissolve depart-

ments, but instead to create more jobs and better opportunities for the People.

- Furthermore, the Nation's laws have been amended to allow JANCO employees to opt into Nation benefits (e.g.: health care, 401k, etc.), on a case-by-case basis.

- Historically, the Nation has led all other tribes in protecting sovereignty (e.g.: the landmark Supreme Court victory, Merrion v. Jicarilla Apache Nation in the 1980s), and now JANCO will once again revive the Nation's reputation of being a trail blazer for all other tribes to follow; the JANCO Code is the first of its kind in the United States with features unique to the Nation and no other tribe.

- Harvard conducted a study that tribally-owned companies (such as JANCO) that separate business from politics are four hundred percent more likely to turn a profit.

- The Legislative Council has seen a need to have better due diligence on business proposals rather than the "Good Old Boy" system. Some people make the remark that in Indian Country there is usually "a bad deal" or "no deal" because the government is not equipped to properly assess business opportunities. JANCO will be ran and operated by a Board of Directors that will provide recommendations to the Tribal Council after conducting all of the required due diligence, Due diligence includes all factual and legal investigations, research, analysis, and financial projections. It will be one of the primary responsibilities of the JANCO Board of Directors to investigate new opportunities the Nation can invest in order to have a diversified investment portfolio which will be secure for future generations of the Nation's Members. Importantly, it can also advise deals that are bad for the Nation and result in a loss of wealth.

It was now time to present to the full government. It is always nerve-racking to give a presentation. There is a dynamic you have to be aware of: the flow, the tone, the content, and the body language. It was even around this time that we had decided that, as a group, we would hold retreats, not just sit around a campfire roasting marshmallows but sit down and hold real conversations about where the Nation came from, what might it look like in the future, what was working, what wasn't working, and whether we, the group of elected leaders sitting in the room, wanted to continue feeding the status quo mentality or embrace a new positive way and now be a part of some real viable, proactive change. It was a very powerful outcome. We all left the retreats feeling recharged and ready to make moves forward by discussing, vetting, and then agreeing, even disagreeing because our thoughts were now of the success of the Nation and not just egos. Since my method of operation was to share tons of information and ask questions, my colleagues had all firsthand information about JANCO and its details on how it would be structured and why it would be structed as a tribal ordinance. With a new vision, new sense of value of the job of a council member, and a desire to go into a new direction, they all felt JANCO was a very good opportunity and positive way to help the greater good, tribal membership, and along the way do something positive while still in office.

After I finished my presentation, I stood for questions and comments and then made the motion to approve the Jicarilla Apache Nation Corporation a.k.a. JANCO ordinance. There was a second and majority vote of yes; it was a great day! I mentioned to my colleagues that I was going to write an article for the local newspaper and congratulated the group for securing a new outcome for the Nation. In the back of my mind, I still felt something was off-putting. I couldn't figure it out then, and maybe I just didn't want to overthink and in that lose focus of what just happened and the amount of work still needed to get things up and running. After all, we needed capital to get company officers and an operational budget, and that was going to be a whole other issue that could also attempt to dismantle the newly approved ordinance. I was worried and needed to find ways to continue selling the idea of the JANCO holding company and in thinking sharing more happenings behind the scenes, and this would open a floodgate. I still felt this was the best approach, and I wrote this op-ed.

The State of the Nation
Editorial by Councilman Leon K. Reval
Uncertainty

What are your thoughts when someone asks, "What is the current State of the Nation?" Is this question being asked out of concern, uncertainty or dismay? Well I can tell you what my response would be when it comes to the current State of the Nation.

The State of the Nation is concerning and doubtful but not necessarily in disarray, which is good news. Yes good news! Since my tenure, the Legislative Council (LC) has strived to form a dynamic group of legislators who have come together for the greater good of the Nation, despite ambiguous administration practices the past eight years. The LC has made progressive strives and growth as far as changing the mentality of having the LC fix everything which I know for a fact has been heard throughout the community because some people are getting upset because the LC has not intervened by circumventing the system but for the most part these new philosophies have garnered positive responses.

140

What are these new philosophies?…
accountability, empowerment, team building!

1) Accountability

Webster's dictionary defines accountability as "the quality or state of being <u>accountable</u>; an obligation or willingness to accept responsibility; to <u>account</u> for one's actions; the quality or state of being <u>accountable</u>.

So when will the LC be held accountable you ask. Well, I will tell you that in the next few weeks, I plan to present a written document proposing that will commit the LC to adopting and mandating a simple Code of Conduct or Standard to define guidelines and responsibilities of Jicarilla Apache Nation Legislative Council Members, including the recommendation for use of a camera inside the chambers, in order for the Nation's members to view LC meetings, and the distribution of LC meeting minutes.

Well today's LC has taken a position on creating an environment of job accountability, for ourselves, executives, directors, supervisors, employees, committee and board members, including the office of the President and Vice President, to ensure that we are all working towards a more prosperous and effective goals on behalf of the Nation as a whole.

The LC has had lengthy but valuable debates on the role and responsibilities of the LC and sees no value when it comes to the micro-management of executive matters, as this has created angst, ill will, and inconsistency for all involved. Consequently, the LC has determined that directors, supervisors, employees, committee and board members, including the office of the President and Vice President are to be held to a higher standard of responsibility when it comes to determining and resolving specific management issues and decisions. The LC will no longer give specific directives regarding issues that could have been resolved internally within a department, committee or board, unless all alternative resolutions have been ineffective. Tough decisions are made daily to ensure fairness, consistency and longevity for all of our members. This method of accountability ensures that resolution and influence of specific management issues is done with impartiality and fairness as concluded within applicable management entities, rather than by a "select few" who indiscriminately and unambiguously determined how decisions were made and who would benefit.

Therefore, if you hear from management or administration that "The Council said"......, I am here to set the record straight! "Unless you see an official resolution or a document signed by the LC, the LC was NOT involved in making unambiguous decisions!"

2) Team Building

The LC's has established strong and effective leadership by relinquishing individual power and control in an effort to establish effective team effort to ensure that business transaction are efficiently negotiated in order to sustain the progress of the Nation as a whole. This step has been crucial to ensuring that vendors contracted by the Nation be accountable and liable for services they were hired to provide, i.e., repairing a diversion dam on Navajo River; Requesting for Proposals (RFP) to build much needed structures in the community, i.e.,

Community Center, Shopping Center; Waste Water Treatment Plant, which I'm proud to say will start construction in August 2016, thanks to our Progressive Construction Management for ensuring that we have well planned durable buildings; In-House Legal Counsel; Rosette Indian Law Firm; and other teams from the Nation's departments that have been involved in successful projects for the benefit of the Nation.

3)   Empowerment

The Legislative Council current strategy is to empower those who appear in the LC chambers. Rather than being ineffectively chastised, blindsided and blamed simply because a LC member thought they knew better how to resolve departmental issues without constructive solutions or direction given are a thing of the past.

The current philosophy of the LC is to empower directors, supervisors, employees, and members to become valuable and constructive resources in order to ensure a higher rate of success and achievement in their respective title for the good of the Nation. In order to achieve a greater sense of empowerment, departmental directors and supervisors have been instructed that they are the "person in charge" of the operation and productivity of their departments, NOT the LC, and in order to have departmental issues heard before the LC, supervisors and managers have been instructed to develop a viable "plan of action" that will be addressed by the LC and manager. To date, results have been very impressive! I mean, who doesn't want to come to the LC chambers and be told that they are in charge of their department and that their viewpoints and opinions are valued and respected.

More on Accountability!

Accountability needs to be a "**two way street**". If you demand accountability of your Government, you should also demand accountability from directors, supervisors, employees and all tribal members! Now let me clarify! There has been an incredibly ineffective practice of the LC telling everyone what and how to do things, which resulted in chaos and inconsistency!

Let's focus on how the LC has acted as the Nation's business developers without any due diligence or accountability for business transactions, i.e., making decisions for investments and purchases that have resulted in revenue loss, including continued funding of the Nation's corporations despite detrimental revenue loss.

In order to assess if these questionable business practices have worked, I asked for a past expenditure report going back ten years and according to this report, the LC has "loaned" over **$130,000,000 MILLION** to the Nation's three **for profit** Section 17 Corporations and Enterprises. Regrettably, **less than 1 percent has being returned to the Nation**.

The Nation currently has four Enterprises: The Sports Bar; Hawks Express; The Travel Center; Shopping Center; Laundry Mat; four Section 17 Corporations: JAECO (Jicarilla Apache Energy Corporation); ANC (Apache

Nugget Corporation); REC (Running Elk Corporation); JATUA (Jicarilla Apache Tribal Utility Authority). What is a Section 17 Corporation? A Section 17 Corporation allows tribes to create businesses that are **for profit** and designed to make money on for a tribe. However there has been a common misguided interpretation that the LC has the ultimate decision making authority over Section 17 corporations. In reality, that is not the case due to the separation of powers that is created with the establishment of Boards of Directors by the LC, and that the LC is only to act in the capacity of **shareholder representatives**. As a shareholder, the LC has the responsibility for selecting/terminating board members, approval of major corporate transactions, authorizing the charter, protecting the assets but is not responsible for day-to-day operations, management of company affairs, etc.)

JATUA (Jicarilla Apache Tribal Utility Authority)

Wait, I thought that JATUA was a tribal department? **No!** A former Administration said that they fixed the issues by simply halting the corporate shell and absorbed the employees, equipment and other costs that now made JATUA a department but did nothing to hold any kind of standard of accountability from the Board or operation.

Consequently, the LC dissolved the JATUA Board in order to avoid any dispute or obligatory restitution which resulted in the absorption of a **$3.5 million a year** budget thus increasing the Nations budget by **$23 Million to date**.

145

ANC (Apache Nugget Corporation)

What about ANC (Apache Nugget Corporation)! Why did the LC terminate the CEO of the Casino? Well, let me set the record straight. The LC did NOT terminate anyone at the Apache Nugget Corporation! The LC, in the capacity of Shareholders Representatives requested an audit report and discovered that there were delinquent business debit; delinquent IRS payments; irregular reconciliation to the general ledger (over a year in some cases); major declining cash flow. The audit showed that during the last four years, the Apache Nugget Corporation has had operating losses totaling **$4.7 million through the end of 2015!** Despite operating at a **$4.7 million** loss the LC absolved a **$15 million** loan the Apache Nugget Corporation had borrowed to build the Casino/Travel Center down south, which is currently operating at a loss of **$1.4 million** and a cash balance decreased of **$103,462** that has lead to delays in making payments to many vendors.

During 2015, ANC had a **$1.4 million** operating loss. During 2014, ANC had a **$693,000** operating loss. More recently, the audit information also showed that ANC's management incurred approximately **$140,000** of credit card charges, the majority on the Chief Executive Officer and General Manager's corporate credit cards and was noted that several meals charged did not include IRS required information, such as purpose of meals, who were in attendance for meals etc. In certain instances, there were no documentation to explain the business purpose of charges or a secondary review to ensure the purchase was a legitimate business expense.

JAECO (Jicarilla Apache Energy Corporation)

Ok so I heard the LC fired people at JAECO (Jicarilla Apache Energy Corporation). No! JAECO was supposed to be the Nation's Cash Cow or savior but has yet to generate any profit. Although the Nation created the Reduced Gas Program using JAECO as a vehicle to do so for the past 10 years has resulted in JAECO management and board members to use the Reduced Gas Program as leverage to justify the need for the LC to continue hurling money to JAECO. However, that has now ceased!

Based on audit reports, the condition of JAECO is very somber, due to the declining oil & gas market, the lack of strategic diversification, the need for assets, and the lack of management restructure initiatives. JAECO has had net operating losses of **$4,148,000** for the last three years, and are uncertain as to any future capital resources by the Nation or other financial sources. So basically JAECO is saying that without the LC giving them more money, JAECO will go bankrupt! The consecutive net operating losses are attributable to price declines in oil and natural gas. JAECO's ability to continue operating is dependent upon the success of management to find additional sources of cash revenue to meet operational needs, so that means they should have been beating the brush to find their own source of capital and not rely on the LC to fund them annually.

JAECO's Board of Directors has given several suggestions that were presented to the Shareholder's and were intended to aid the process of generating revenue, reducing cost and contributing to the re-strengthening of JAECO. However, other than lip service, it was ambiguous that the suggested solutions would be in the best interest of the Nation and to date have not presented any viable recommendations to the Nation. In fact over the last five years, the Nation has given almost **$9,000,000.00** to JAECO to which the Nation has NEVER seen any significant return.

REC (Running Elk Corporation)

So what about the Running Elk Corporation or what is more commonly known as the Chama Lodge? Well there is a bit of good news. REC has actually given the Nation an annual dividend of **$100,000** but in the past year that number has grown to **$250.000.00**. Not bad huh! Well let's look at the facts and I will say that this last Shareholders meeting drew concern. Running Elk has reflected a total asset amount of over **$44 million** in revenue but only about **$4 million** in cash has been returned to the Nation. The reality of this 44 million number is that you run the numbers, the Nation has received less than a **1%** return on its investment. The shareholders had great concern with a concept REC had been using called a "Bill of Sale", which in essence would authorize the Board of Directors to assign corporate assets to the Nation which can only be explained as a practice that reflects a cash value on inventory like equipment, glasses, towels, furniture and other used daily items and then adds that number to the total dividend claiming that they paid the Nation more than just a cash value of two hundred and fifty thousand dollars, appearing to try and over value the true financial condition of the corporation. This practice was glossed over by former LC members and since the last shareholders meeting held two months ago, we created much issue and concern, but without key financial information, this topic could not be well flushed out, yet. The major issue was that REC had never had an external audit done. So the Shareholders directed the Nation's CFO to contact an auditing firm and request an updated audit. It is imperative that the audit be completed and presented to the shareholders, however, shareholders have not yet received the requested audit.

JANPA (Jicarilla Apache Nation Power Authority)

What's JANPA, it's the Jicarilla Apache Nation Power Authority, the electric company that has a price tag of over **$30 million** to date. According to records there is a 20% delinquency rate, which means some members are not paying their electric bills.

So my question to all tribal members is, where's your accountability? We currently have over **30 benefits** that all tribal members receive in order to provide a better way of life! I hear complaints and murmurs about the lack of service we all get but let's be fair-minded, every tribal member receives these benefits but in order to continue provided these perks to our members, it is imperative that guidelines and policies govern these programs and be effectively utilized, in order to avoid abuse and exploitation of these valuable resources. We have so much abuse of tribal property, homes etc. and unfortunately there members that have an attitude of entitlement simply because they are Jicarilla and demand more from the Nation without regard on how their greed and lack of accountability impacts fellow members. Sadly, we have a high rate of delinquency, people not paying their bills, for resources that are provided to our members.

The following reflects a list of programs, the number of people who are delinquent on their payments, the total amount in arrears to Jicarilla Apache Nation Power Authority:

1)	Dulce Direct TV	37	**$17,537**
2)	JANPA	523	**$57,069**
3)	Mundo Ranch LP Tax Credit Program	16	**$33,259**
4)	Southridge	05	**$53,983**
5)	Mundo Phase III Rental	01	**$1,600**
6)	Home II Program	05	**$41,141**
7)	Home I Program	01	**$10,254**
8)	JAN Home Loan(Refi)	14	**$24,889**
9)	Mundo Ranch Phase III Mortgage	10	**$38,438**
10)	Mundo Family Homes	10	**$16,828**
		Total Arrears:	**$294,998.00**

What about the Credit program? I have those numbers as well and yes people are not paying back their loans. Why share this information?

Accountability! As a Nation we ALL need to contribute our fair share to our resources! Nowhere
else would you receive these luxuries that many
take for granted! For the most part many of us
are responsible and do our part by having a job,
managing our resources in order to pay our bills,
and rarely go to the Nation to request financial
assistance, which by the way has been come to an
end by the LC because when the numbers were
crunched the numbers reflected an amount of
over **$1.6 million** of assistance which was given
just over a six month period! Consequently, that
defective practice needed to stop. There were a
few hundred tribal members who went to the LC
and screamed, threatened and cried in order to
continue receiving assistance to pay their bills,
get vehicles worked on, pay for their trips, etc.
Sadly, most requests for financial assistance were
from individuals who had received assistance
then came back demanding additional assistance
after their money ran out without any sense of
accountability or regard to the Nation's resources.
I am saying, if there is going to be a program
that distributes "free" money then either make it
fair and available to ALL members or stop it all
together as to avoid picking and choosing which
members receive assistance. That being said, I
understand there are times we all need assistance
and there are still procedures in place that allow
members to visit the Treasurer's or Executive
offices to request funding, however, the LC
chambers is not unavailable to disperse financial assistance. In addition, all tribal member
perks will continue to be budgeted for and more
importantly be properly planned and funded
on an annually basis to ensure these services are

available to ALL members. Currently, there are just under 4000 enrolled members of the Jicarilla Apache Nation and every one of these members are able to equally enjoy all benefits from these programs. The Nation's government is happy to provide the following services to our members and we are proud to help make our community a better place to live.

1. Revamped Credit Program Per Capita advancement loan, short and long term loans for Home Rehab/Renovation
2. Elite Benefit Package for Nation Employees/ Workman's Compensation
3. Higher Education Scholarship's to Regionally Accredited Schools within the US
4. 100% Medical Assistance (Dental, Vision, hearing, travel, etc.)
5. Free Water/Free Sewer
6. Free Wood
7. Free Trash Pickup
8. Home Maintenance
9. Snow removal/Road Grading
10. Free DNA testing for Enrollment
11. Minors Trust Fund
12. Monthly Per Capita distribution
13. Monthly Senior Fund
14. Burial/Funeral Assistance
15. Survivors Benefit
16. College Student Medical Benefits
17. Hardship/Financial Assistance
18. Vehicle repair/Vehicle Hauling
19. Administrative Leave
20. Tribal Jobs/Job Training
21. Moving/Other Public Service Assistance
22. Reduced Home Mortgages

23. Mobile Homes Refinancing
24. Free Check Cashing
25. Discounted Natural Gas Program
26. Groceries Home Site Development
27. Cattle Hauling
28. Cattle Feed
29. Water Hauling (assist's cattle growers)
30. Free Fishing/ Reduced Hunting License

So let's recap. The LC, acting as business developers instead of Government Legislators (Law Makers) has "lent" over **$130 Million** to the Nation's businesses and in turn has only received **less than one million dollars**. We are going through the worst economic down turn we have ever seen in the Oil and Gas industry and yet we sit idly waiting for the "boom" to come back! Well ok, we have money in investments, Capital Reserve, so yes we are not destitute, but how long can bad decision making go on using the Nation's funds feeding good money into inferior business deals with substandard companies, including our own? With financial losses as indicated above, this sort of business performance will surely trigger future financial distress and devastation that would impact future benefits that our Nation's members.

Leon, you didn't even win the election and now you're crying foul! No, I'm not crying foul, I greatly appreciate those individuals who took the time to exercised our most valued inherent right and showed up to vote and especially those few hundred people who filled in the arrow for me. I do wish my colleague, friend and confidant, President elect Wainwright Velarde the very best and will work alongside him to secure and protect what we have already done.

Separation between the Executive and the Legislative branches is vital and I know President elect Velarde not only knows that but will reinforce it.

So enough with the gloom and doom! Let's take a look at some proactive alternatives for generating revenue for the Nation. It all begins with creating a more diverse plan for economic development which creates a strategic model related to specific projects or development initiatives. I strongly believe that without creating a tribal economic development environment with the following elements, the Nation's likelihood for long-term success is extremely limited. What are they?

1. Government Continuity
2. Separation of Business and Politics
3. Proper Strategy

Let's talk about element number one. It is absolutely imperative that the Nation's government establish continuity by establishing a stable political environment by electing Individuals who have proven record in supporting innovative standards and practices that have been established. It has been proven over and over that political leaders who are elected in a negative campaign against a previous government seldom continue with those same goals and objectives. This cycle of "perpetually starting over" in political, administrative and business strategies has resulted in major losses for the nation as reflected in the money lost in the Nation's

154

corporations. This learned behavior desperately needs to change and former ideals, challenges and successes should evolve incrementally. Such incremental developments are possible within a long-term stable political environment as newly elected officials come to an understanding that to ensure continuity and success that they are open to innovative and proven business practices that provides the Nation with financial revenue and stability, rather than reinventing a wheel that has produced unacceptable business practices and lack of monetary profits. Reinventing the wheel greatly increases the likelihood of radical short-term decision making resulting in a "No Deal" or ineffective transactions which we have experienced far too many times.

The second element for success is to have a true Separation of Business and Politics! Tribal governments like all governments are terrible at running businesses as per the Nation's 130-million-dollar loss in revenue. Political agendas have influenced all aspects of the decision making process regarding the Nation's business ventures, thereby interfering with all long-term prospects and business operations. Harvard conducted a study that proved tribally-owned companies that have separated business from politics are 400% more likely to turn a profit. Ok so if the LC is taken out developing and managing business endeavor then what is your brilliant plan?

Well let me introduce to you an innovative business prospect called Title 26, JANCO (Jicarilla Apache Nation Corporation) a holding company not only developed to have a true separation of politics and business development but have strategies, due diligence, and a body of vetted professionals who can make hard business decisions like any other successful Fortune 500 company in the United States. JANCO needed to be developed, more than ever with the recent oil and gas recession, the Nation significant drop in assets and capital, making it challenging for the Nation to sustain a steady flow of income for current resources for its members. To date the plan has just been to take funds from accounts and shift them around with no valid plan of filling the Nation's coffers. In order to address the Nation's financial crisis, yes I use the term crisis, the Legislative Council created JANCO to immediately begin making a turnaround of profits in a declined market and look for lucrative business ventures that will create a steady revenue stream for the Nation. The creation of JANCO also means that the Nation will no longer be dependent only on oil and gas revenues and having "all of our eggs in one basket". The Legislative Council created JANCO to protect the long-term viability of the Nation by ensuring the People will continue receiving benefits including increased per capita, homes, entrepreneurial opportunities, the 30 perks, and new credit programs. JANCO will expand the Nation's economy beyond oil and gas through other business opportunities such as operating e-commerce companies, developing technology and intellectual property, manufacturing and/or distributing goods, investing in real estate, and providing various good and services through manufacturing. JANCO is designed so that all revenues earned by profitable businesses will flow back to the Nation for the benefit of the People and will immediately stop the Nation from "bailing out" our own companies that are bleeding money. JANCO will hold managers of the Nation corporations and enterprises more accountable and will not tolerate losing money, meaning managers can be fired if such businesses do not make profit for the Nation! Yes JANCO will make those hard decisions that the LC or Shareholders could not do. JANCO will be operated by a seven-member Board of Directors and a Chief Executive Officer that will oversee day-to-day business operations. JANCO is 100% owned and operated by the Nation. Does JANCO possess too much power over the Nation's business practices and ventures you may ask? The answer is NO! The LC still maintains control over JANCO because the LC has the authority to approve the JANCO Board of Directors, after a series of stringent interviews and background checks on all candidates. The LC also maintains the power to allocate the Nation capital or assets to JANCO. JANCO means that the Nation will no longer miss opportunities (e.g.: Las Vegas Walgreens; Middle East coffee cream distribution, oil and gas opportunities etc.) because JANCO is required to hire professionals to immediately conduct due diligence, properly assess, and take advantage of future business opportunities for the Nation. JANCO protects all attributes of tribal sovereignty, therefore, JANCO has been designed so it does not waive its sovereign immunity from suit to third parties and does not allow the State to assess taxes over the Nation. Most Nation departments will not be impacted by the creation of JANCO; accordingly, the purpose of JANCO is not to terminate employees or dissolve departments, but instead to create more jobs and better opportunities for our members, and to a large degree, tribal departments serve a social function related to improving the lives of tribal members and JANCO will grow capital to fuel the nation's budget ensuring these services continue well into the future.

Historically, The Jicarilla Apache Nation has stood as the leader in protecting sovereignty, i.e., the Landmark Supreme Court Victory, Merrion vs. the Jicarilla Apache Nation in the 1980s. and Now JANCO will once again revive the Nation's reputation of being a trail blazer for all other tribes to follow. Title 26 (JANCO) is the first of its kind in the United States with features unique to the Nation that no other tribe has ventured.

Okay, what about element number three, Proper Strategy? This particular element needs Trust, trust that this new endeavor although completely unorthodox from what the Nation has even done, is completely necessary. Trust in allowing JANCO to go to work using the values of empowerment, accountability and team building. I know in my heart JANCO will work and it will generate wealth for the Nation that in turn will permeate down to all of our members. We have never planned for the future, and yes it took a brave group of leaders who took all the money out of the BIA and invested it in the Stock Market which created a robust financial portfolio in spite of the horror stories and rumors, that this business venture was the worst thing to happen to the Nation, that it will fail and the Tribe would go broke! But look at how that pioneering business venture turned out because of trust! So I ask you for that trust once again, trusting that the people you elected will continue to honor the oath of equal rights to life, liberty, industrial pursuits and the economic resources and activities of the Nation. There is a ton of work the LC needs to do to maintain and ensure that Legislative business will be our priority as the LC will no longer be involved with business development and ventures of the Nation. JANCO will not only protect the current assets of the Nation but will feed it like never before. I ask you to give us a chance and allow JANCO to work, all the pieces are in place and JANCO is ready to be launched, we have a domain name, JANCO.net, we have a CEO and we have a Strong Independent Board of Directors with the honor of me sitting as the Chairman of the Board. I know that you will hear chatter about JANCO some true and some false but please feel free to ask me any questions you may have regarding JANCO. I will share information every step of the way as we move forward and you will see that the pace of JANCO is steady, consistent, and worthwhile.

This op-ed was not only the first of its kind but was, I think, a real shock to the public and some of my colleagues. I had not given this story a second thought because I had shared everything in this article with all my colleagues either in messages or discussion at the table and for the record, so to me it was what we even agreed upon in the retreats as to establishing the utmost transparency, but all I can do is assume it only raised more questions of the membership and questions that could not be properly answered, and in that, survival instincts took over that made some feel that if they finger-pointed and claimed ignorance, they had a shot of winning a second term or avoid accountability altogether because maybe they didn't know how to provide answers. To me, that answers were all there; it just took some work and wherewithal to see that government was its own worst enemy, and numbers never lie. So much money was wasted, and I still say to this day that this is inexcusable. Word got back to me that some of my colleagues took offense to the article and that I didn't get permission. I made comments that they all knew, but I was also banking on the character of a person who looked you in the eye and shook their head and nodded yes, painful lesson that would only get worse.

Things had actually cooled off, and it turned out not all my colleagues were upset with the op-ed, but we still needed to fill the board member seats and then find a CEO. It was decided that since JANCO was new, that new approaches also needed to be done, so we sent out request for proposals in search of qualified candidates who were interested but proven to add their value as a board of director member in Jicarilla's newest venture. Jicarilla had been very instrumental in opening many doors across Indian country, and it was really cool to see how many résumés we received. We asked our colleagues who wanted to be on a screening committee in this search, and the four newest elected members of the class of 2014 were nominated to spearhead this process. I said, "Of course, I would do my very best," and knew that I would make it a point to keep them all informed along the way.

We sat down, agreed that we needed ten strong questions to ask each invited candidate, and screened the group down to eight strong candidates who would be interviewed. We even had a tribal member interview, but we also agreed that nothing was a given. This was about creating a solid corpus for the benefit of the holding company and about not relationships, respectfully speaking. The pool of candidates ranged from lawyers in both the Native world and real world, former tribal chairmen who had done many positive proven business ventures in their own communities, to former board members who sat on other Fortune 500-type boards but also had vast proven experience in Native American organizations. To see this be acknowledged as a positive and then see it grow and then come to fruition was incredible; to see the caliber of people who wanted to be part of such a limitless possibility was phenomenal. The outside world knew Jicarilla was a giant, and for whatever reason, this giant going into hibernation was unfortunate, but it was time to wake this sleeping giant again! The screening board conducted the interviews and even made sure all candidates went through a rigorous background, selected five board members who would now sit and represent the Nation in their new role, and because of their vast tribal and world experiences, knew how to deal with the nuances of tribal government. Out of this selection, we even found a candidate who was perfect for the CEO position, and we entered into an agreement. The JANCO structure for officers was complete, and we felt like we were part of history. It was a very profound and proud moment to see how good governance was going to do great things.

This was right around the time that President Barrack Obama was finishing his second term, and word had spread that President Obama wanted to hold strong to his commitment to Indian country and was going to do all he could to finally settle all breach of trust lawsuits. I had mentioned that the Nation was in litigation over bad accounting and mismanagement of trust funds in assessing and collecting income derived from oil and gas and timber revenue. The lawsuit that we had voted to enter into in 2002 had been bouncing around the courts for a decade and, before the news of settlement, would have not been positive for the Nation. And at what cost was the Nation willing to pay to continue to hold accountability of the federal government and prove that point when any restitution would be lower than any actual calculations of a judgment award? I had first received the news that was buzzing in Washington and had some great connections, one who had been contracted for the Nation in legal matters, who had even bigger connections, who told me what might be happening. I had issues on the lawsuit, not about giving a yes vote, but when we left office in 2006, the new group came in and never asked why we began but fired the law firm we started with back then and almost every other key knowledgeable person who could have been an asset but instead decided to go a whole route with new people. We had lost the oil and gas arguments, and it was still pending, but the ruling against the Nation had some unfortunate precedents for Indian country, and we still had the timber issue. Either way, to me, if there was a way to recoup past legal fees in excess of $20 million and settle on a vast amount that proved the point and generated funds for the Nation, I was all over hearing more and creating a plan to finalize this historical act of these breach of settlements.

Before I did anything or made any commitments to even create dialogue, I felt it best to inform my colleagues on the news I had heard and if I could continue to ask questions, create a strategy, and then based on the validity of this information, discuss and consider steps on moving forward on these settlements. I was put in direct contact with former Department of Interior Ken Salazar and was direct in my questions, and he began to share what he knew and the possibilities of any outcome. Ken had firsthand knowledge since his role was instrumental in dealing with tribes and also being the moderator for trust responsibility issues for all 550 tribes in the United States. He told me he was coming to the Southwest, and he wanted to meet in person. I said, "If you come to Dulce, I will cook for you." I received a call and a time, and we set up a dinner meeting. I felt it would be more beneficial to have Ken drive through town and to my house so that he could see the scenery, the town, and get a feeling of how important it was to receive what was owed for the benefit of the community.

While in public relations, I came into contact with a company out of Texas that just purchased a food distributing company in Albuquerque. They sold name-brand products and processed meats to hotels, restaurants, and they had created a program in which they were purchasing cattle from Native American cattle growers. The company found that native beef had a whole different taste, being in the high desert and mountains, but more importantly, Native cattle growers would get the best price and value for their cows when they sold directly to the company who also had their own in-house FDA-approved processing plant for butchering, packaging, and distributing of beef. As soon as I saw this presentation, while I was sitting on a planning board with the Indian Affairs department, we actually asked for a donation, and this was when I learned of this company and their new cattle development plan. I was blown away and made the connections I needed to so that I could see if tribal member cattle growers saw the vison I saw and that they too could benefit from the family linage they chose as local cattle growers. There was mild interest, more pessimism than optimism, but I knew of one family who had a strong, reputable cattle-growing business model, and I felt if I could engage the patriarch in seeing this was a good opportunity, I knew he could do great things. The short of this story was that he did, and he and this food distribution company worked together, and there was a finished product that was superb. As a token of appreciation, I received a small box of some locally sourced Jicarilla beef, and that was the meal I prepared for my visitor. I wanted to share the story and product of how the Nation had so many opportunities and if there was a shared vision of the government and membership; the sky was not even close to being the limit. We ate, we talked, and we left with a plan that I could share with my colleagues, and I then began setting up a formal meeting during a convened meeting to make introductions and then allow Ken to share his insight and strategy.

The council listened, stated their concerns, asked questions, and we decided to move forward. My question was geared toward legal fees and even gave an approximation of what had been spent to date on legal fees and why we would want to change law firms again and run the risk of paying redundant costs. It was then we agreed to a 3 percent commission of total funds received, 3 percent that was usually one cost for an email. Three percent was not only a responsible cost, but because we had created a new way to control costs with the request for proposal process, we had inadvertently but already in my mind as to even utilizing the process, set the tone as to limiting costs, and still receive the highest quality of service. Four months went by, and during the updates of the settlement procedures, you know, the volleying back and forth, the feds started off with the offer of $20 million. We had a long meeting about how valuable $20 million would be especially if we were fiscally strategic and grew that money exponentially. In ten years, we could have quadrupled it, but we felt that twenty million was not acceptable and countered. Some weeks went by, and the second offer came down to $80 million. We all grinned and head-nodded to ourselves but said, "No, we won't settle for that amount." The last offer came in, $124 million. We had been told that this was the most that the Interior office and Tax and

Revenue Department were able to do, not a penny more; we smiled and took the deal. The Nation would be awarded $124 million for the breach of trust accounting issues the Bureau of Indian Affairs was responsible in managing properly. This amount received some criticism especially by those former council members who may have been privy to some smaller details and even been responsible for changing the players and the additional costs that incurred, but I knew because of the long history, day 1 when we talked and talked and went back and forth as to why and how much it would cost, I knew that the settlement amount is what experts calculated as to the viable cost of what would be fair to fight for so many years ago, and to now be able to see this come to a positive end, well, one of many proud moments to smile again and say, "I love this job!"

It would be some time before the Nation would be able to get a multimillion-dollar check, so in the meantime, there was still business to conduct, and now once again, another election was coming up. There were issues with the then-sitting president; there was even an attempt to recall his seat for reason that may have been reliable, not doing the job, failing to abide by policy, even some rumors of questionable behavior, but in my mind, nothing solid that would make these accusations viable. But the attempt was made. It only created waves and finger-pointing and maybe even some bruised feelings, but we reverted back to the agreements we all made during our retreat, and that was the solidarity I promoted. After all, it was a group effort that brought us to this point, and the comradery was joyful and inviting but also the most open-minded I had ever witnessed in my tenure. By this time, JANCO had a partial board selected, the independent board members had all accepted the offer to serve, and all the board needed now were the two Nation board members. Since the election was right around the corner, I made the pitch that it would be a good idea for one of the seats who were termed out consider being the next board member for JANCO. It was pretty quiet and becoming a hard sell. For some reason, I got chills and for a moment wondered if they still felt as energized as I did in this new concept. I then turned my pitch to the sitting council member who could sit as a board member in their current capacity as a council member, again not a lot of discussion. I asked each member and at the end said, "Well, I can do it." There was concurrence, and it was done. I was now the sixth member of the Nation's newest tribal-approved corporation called JANCO. The ordinance allowed for six members to conduct meetings and act on behalf of the holding company. The very first meeting was scheduled, and I was traveling to Arizona for a meeting and had to pull over the side of the road so that I could participate in the meeting. The meeting was called, and I thanked my new board colleagues and reiterated how we got to this point, and as we began, the first order was to establish board officers. A treasurer was selected, a secretary, then a cochair. The only thing left was chairman of the board. There was a nomination made, and I heard my name. I immediately got tunnel vision. Motion was made, seconded, and I was now chairman of the board of JANCO. I thought, *What the hell did I get myself into?* This had felt like my child, and I had no problem birthing and nurturing, but parenting? What the hell. But I accepted in my bravest voice to say, "Thank you for your trust." The rest of the drive, well, I don't remember the drive too much as all of a sudden, I was at my hotel. I was very excited. The possibility of being able to be part of the biggest thing to hit Jicarilla since oil and gas was upon us, and it had every opportunity to be a billion-dollar private, Nation-owned company that could generate so much income that there could be a dozen golden eggs. Thinking about it now is making smile; the power this newly designed model had was ginormous.

With the holding company moving forward with a board and now a hired CEO, we proceeded to have meetings. When JANCO was presented, there was opportunity but no capital, so the ask was to help fund the Nation's newest corporation just like other for-profit corporations had been given capital, except this time, the plan was to create short-term ventures to produce income and not only pay back the Nation but begin to grow JANCO's operational budget in an aggressive but low-risk way. A total of $1.6 million was approved by the council, and this time, the vote was split. At the meeting, there were only seven council members in attendance, and after another update and presentation presenting an approximate operational budget, a motion was made to fund the one point six million helpful to kick-start JANCO, and the vote was now five in favor of the motion and one opposed. It was very interesting, and my intuition began to make my body flushed with a cold feeling, but I dismissed the feeling because the motion was approved, and now JANCO had some funds to pay the salaries of the CEO and his staff, which would include a chief operational officer and in-house controller and a chief financial officer, which may have seemed redundant having extra accounting measures. But it was thought that having a controller and CFO, it would eliminate excuses and issues when having to present the balance sheet at an annual shareholders' meeting. The world was bright and shiny, and JANCO was ready to blast off. I was so proud of everything and everyone who came together and supported this new concept.

The election grew closer, and I began hearing comments that some campaigns were mentioning JANCO, but like most soap boxing, facts were rarely made, and sound bites were often used to get crowds excited, but to be honest, I did not hear anything. I think back, and maybe I was too high in the clouds and choose not to hear. I don't know, but hindsight is and can be a hard thing to understand and accept. Since the rumors were flying and my senses were tingling from the split vote, I wanted to create a short document that the council could also use to help explain why they supported this concept and more importantly why they voted to approve some funding, not to mention allow the one vote of no to also be able to show why he was not in support rather than just saying, "I didn't like it," another comment phrase the government loved using. So I titled the document simple. I titled it JANCO 101 and used the following bullet points to help provide quick reasoning and engage in good debate:

- With the recent oil and gas recession, the Nation has seen a significant drop in assets and wealth making the Nation unable to sustain current benefits for the People.

- In order to address the Nation's financial crisis, the Legislative Council created JANCO (Jicarilla Apache Nation Corporation) to immediately increase the amount of money available for the People; this also means the Nation will no longer be dependent only on oil and gas revenues.
- The Legislative Council created JANCO to protect the long-term viability of the Nation by ensuring the People will continue receiving benefits including increased dividends, shopping vouchers, and new credit programs.
- JANCO will expand the Nation's economy beyond oil and gas through other business opportunities such as operating e-commerce companies, developing technology and intellectual property, manufacturing and/or distributing goods, investing in real estate, and providing various services.
- JANCO is 100% owned and operated by the Nation; no other entity or person has an ownership interest in JANCO.
- JANCO is designed so that all revenues earned by profitable businesses will flow back to the Nation for the benefit of the People.
- JANCO will stop the Nation from "bailing out" companies that are losing money for the People.
- JANCO will hold managers of Nation businesses losing money accountable; this means managers will be fired if such businesses do not make profit for the People.
- JANCO will be operated by a seven-member Board of Directors and a Chief Executive

Officer that will oversee day-to-day business operations.

- The Legislative Council still maintain control over JANCO because they maintain the power to appoint the JANCO Board of Directors and they also maintain the power to allocate, if any, Nation capital or assets to JANCO.
- The Nation will no longer miss opportunities (e.g.: Las Vegas Walgreens; Middle East coffee cream distribution, etc.) because JANCO is required to hire professionals to immediately conduct due diligence, properly assess, and take advantage of future business opportunities for the People.
- JANCO recognizes that the Nation predates the United States Constitution and JANCO protects all attributes of tribal sovereignty; therefore JANCO has been designed so it does not waive its sovereign immunity from suit to third parties and does not allow the State to assess taxes over the Nation.
- Most Nation departments will not be impacted by the creation of JANCO; accordingly, the purpose of JANCO is not to terminate employees or dissolve departments, but instead to create more jobs and better opportunities for the People.
- Furthermore, the Nation's laws have been amended to allow JANCO employees to opt into Nation benefits (e.g.: health care, 401k, etc.), on a case-by-case basis.
- Historically, the Nation has led all other tribes in protecting sovereignty (e.g.: the

landmark Supreme Court victory, Merrion v. Jicarilla Apache
- Nation in the 1980s), and now JANCO will once again revive the Nation's reputation of being a trail blazer for all other tribes to follow; the JANCO Code is the first of its kind in the United States with features unique to the Nation and no other tribe.
- Harvard conducted a study that tribally-owned companies (such as JANCO) that separate business from politics are **four hundred percent** more likely to turn a profit.
- The Legislative Council has seen a need to have better due diligence on business proposals rather than the "Good Old Boy" system. Some people make the remark that in Indian Country there is usually "a bad deal" or "no deal" because the government is not equipped to properly assess business opportunities. JANCO will be ran and operated by a Board of Directors that will provide recommendations to the Tribal Council after conducting all of the required due diligence, Due diligence includes all factual and legal investigations, research, analysis, and financial projections. It will be one of the primary responsibilities of the JANCO Board of Directors to investigate new opportunities the Nation can invest in order to have a diversified investment portfolio which will be secure for future generations of the Nation's Members. Importantly, it can also advise deals that are bad for the Nation and result in a loss of wealth.

What was another election year, there was buzz about who would be running for president and who would run for the council seats. There were two incumbents, and that was a good feeling as a colleague because if they won their reelections, then they already knew all the intimate details of what was done to date, the retreats, JANCO, and other matters that were very positive and adopted for long-term strategies. I heard comments from colleagues that they had no intention of running for the office of president, and I kept thinking about that and felt that not having anyone with an open mind and some real experience could prove to be disastrous. After all, there was almost an impeachment, and that would have been my second one I had to go through. I thought about it a lot and decided I would try. After all, nothing precluded me from running for the office of presidency sitting as a council member, and if I won, I could have really made some huge efforts to continue the promotion and execution of empowerment, accountability, and teamwork. It was working with the council, and if it was working in the chambers, there was a good chance it would work in all departments given time. Just then, a colleague whom I had developed a real connection with declared his candidacy. I thought, *Okay, well, he is much older. I am pretty young. At the very least, we could campaign on the same principles and ideas.* We had approved almost all since we were elected in 2014. This could be a great thing no matter who won. After all, together, we had all created and agreed to this new agenda in continuing to move forward, or so I thought.

I campaigned on the laurels and brought forth in my capacity as a council member, and with all the op-eds and other information I was sharing with membership, I really felt this time might be the time I might sit as the executive of the Jicarilla Apache Nation. I was still nervous, thinking, what if I did win? Was I ready? Was I capable? I took the role of elected official to heart and, with every major move, made sure there was a paper trail and proof of what I said and did by saving all text messages and emails. I had to share what I had said verbatim with some who came to me and said they had heard I was defrauding the Nation, and all I wanted to do was, again, lower the blood quantum. This was still a comment that still annoys me.

I served with pride and dignity, and every law I crafted was for the benefit of all enrolled tribal member, and that also meant driving my own children further and further away from ever benefiting as an enrolled member had been. So rather than go on the defensive, I went on the offensive and created this letter for the local newspaper and the voting public:

Community in Motion By Leon K. Reval, Candidate for President of the Jicarilla Apache Nation

As a candidate for the Jicarilla Apache Nation President and a current member of the Legislative Council, it is my belief that it is not advantageous to simply and passively observe, scrutinize or criticize, but collaborate in a manner that will inspire and utilize our community to become an active contributor of solutions that will propel our **COMMUNITY IN MOTION**.

As in any other community, the election process is a time that community members exercise their right to vote by consciously and thoughtfully weigh the virtues, competences, leadership and intentions that each candidate brings. This process should be done with the best interest of our community in mind, and with the type of future we envision for our children and those that are yet to come. Unfortunately, this blessed process inspired by clear thought, contemplation and support can also be tainted by divisiveness, destructive accusations, and short-sightedness.

As a candidate for the Jicarilla Apache Nation President, I would like to share with you some insight into my view of our obligations as leaders and why I feel it is vitally important to incorporate our community as a whole in the effort to move the Nation abundantly forward.

171

The illustration below identifies some key points I feel we must consider when electing our Nation's leaders:

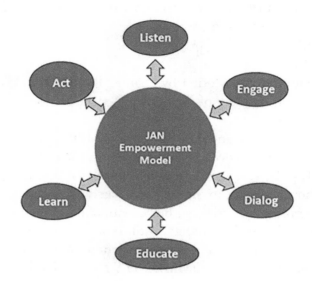

First and foremost, the President, Vice President, Legislative Council, tribal employees, advisors, consultants, attorneys, etc. work for the sake of our Nation, period!

The framework in which this work takes place is for the purpose of protecting our lands and natural resources; preserving our language, traditions and culture; creating a quality of life for all our JAN citizens that includes, health, education, safety, housing, infrastructure, etc. and creating a future that ensures our young ones will have something to work with when they are in leadership roles for our community. This is the foundation of our work and the core of the JAN Empowerment Model.

Listen: Whether expressing a pleasant comment or conveying a concern, it is imperative that those in leadership positions give a genuine ear to the voice of our people. Likewise, it is imperative that community members interact with leaders and one another in a way that is mutually beneficial to all regardless of our differences, as listening is a two-way street. Effective and clear communication may be established by hosting structured community meetings where we can share council actions and seek community involvement and feedback.

Engage: Being passive, complaining with no solutions to offer is not conducive in advancing our community together. It is essential to promote constructive community engagement and proactive legislative partnerships with our community members that focus on revenue generation for our nation, the stewardship of our resources, restructuring and rethinking how we can best govern and advance as a progressive Tribal Nation. By utilizing tools of communication such as community programs, tribal entities, advisors, consultants, tribal departments, and other tools like social media to create new opportunities and platforms for broader and deeper community engagement.

Dialog: Even the simplest opportunities to dialog have escaped us in the recent years. I have seen instances where we walk by each other without even offering a simple "hello". We will achieve this by asking everyone to re-engage in dialog with each other, especially if you don't know one another, take a minute to introduce yourself. This is something that does not require tribal government involvement, but as community members, it should be something we all do for one another.

Educate: Often times the unknown breeds rumors and assumptions when it comes to decisions made by the Executive and/or Legislative Council. As our nation's Leaders, engaging, educating, and communicating with our community members on how major decisions and resolutions regarding of the Nation's monetary and natural resources is imperative, as we all have a vested interest in our Nation's advancement into the 21st Century.

Learn: There is a belief that if one is part of government leadership, remedies are abundant and elected leaders should have all the answers. I say with all humbleness and humility that I do not know everything, nor do I have all of the answers, but I am willing to learn, look for remedies, and be duly reminded and reprimanded where necessary. I also recognize that our community is sometimes faced with the inter-workings of our differences in our position regarding culture, language, government, community affairs, etc., I propose, that we provide inspiration and encouragement to one another and capitalize on the values, wisdom, and knowledge that we bring as community in order to flourish as a Nation.

Act: The catalyst for achieving results is for the Executive and Legislative Leaders to ACT collaboratively with our members in order to become a **"Community in Motion"**.

As you can clearly see, sustainable progress and opportunity for our Nation can be effectively achieved when we work together. I realize that we will not always be in 100% agreement in every position and that is fine.

With that said, as future President of JAN, I pledge to bring leadership and governance that

honors the aspirations, principles, beliefs of the
Great Jicarilla Apache Nation and respectfully
ask for your endorsement and support.

I was proud of my campaign concept and really tried to inspire
some positive direction, what I had felt was a hope for understanding
that if we had good governance that allowed the promotion of hard
work, dedication, accountability, and empowerment, the community could finally feel like that could have some buy-in and some
worthiness to come to work, knowing that what they did absolutely
mattered and be compensated based on accomplishments. I was on
cloud nine with how my colleagues seemed to be firing on all cyl-
inders and that things were actually being done in a proper manner and by the book. It was a gratifying feeling to know that my
comments and information sharing was being received extremely
well by the membership and that, as a government, we were on a
path to be more progressive, a feeling I had not felt since my first
term. It was about two weeks until the primary election, and in that
time of reaching the agreement with the federal government on the
settlement of the $124 million, it was at one JANCO board meet-
ing that a strategy was presented. I had made a lot of connections
in my tenure. I worked alongside and even brought to the table to
meet the council to showcase their expertise as to be a possible fit to
help move the Nation forward, and let me say, there were some very
proven and effective individuals and some that were okay but ended
up not being a good fit. My process was to open the door and never
push or coerce anyone. This was about introductions, my opinions,
and then up to the council and individual presenting as to any next
steps, I did not care if I was introducing my best friend. This was
always about business and transparency for me. It was a gentleman
I had met in 2004, and he was bright and was doing great things in
Indian country. I even asked him if he would be interested in submitting his résumé for the JANCO board. He graciously declined
but said he is always willing to help if the team was strong so that
there was no politics muddying up the waters. I said, "Well, let me
introduce you to the CEO, and you guys can talk, and then he can

175

give you more information on the JANCO concept." Turns out, they did speak, and he saw real potential. The new strategy was this. Since the Nation was going to get a check from the federal government, if the council invested $100 million into their own company, just like they did with the section 17 corporations, JANCO could leverage that $100 million and in turn get use the funds to increase JANCO's financial position and therefore have the availability to have a new cash balance close enough to the $100 million, all while keeping the principal investment visible and making money. I say visible because the council or members could be able to see that the principal would always be there. JANCO would be using the money it received in the leverage to begin investing, loaning, building, anything it took to create strong-vetted, even vested, business deals. What I needed to do was present to the council and then get a vote on a huge possible can of worms for some. I mean, I was asking for the settlement funds to be used for the holding company they all had approved and, in that, gave $1.6 million to for the budget. I handed out the materials, and there were some surprised looks. There was even very good discussion and then an agreement to procure a place in Jicarilla's financial future. I made the motion, there was a second, and with a vote of six for and one against, the motion passed. That was a very surreal moment. I was even more freaked and determined to make sure JANCO was so stringent, transparent, and successful I got tunnel vision.

The election came and went, and although I made it to the top 2 candidates, I was once again unsuccessful and had loss number 3 under my belt. I won't say that didn't sting, but as I mentioned earlier, my colleague had been very vocal and even an advocate in what had transpired during the council time, including pushing JANCO. All of a sudden, things did a 180-degree turn, and everything that was tied together in a nice strong bow was now being picked at with dull scissors. I hadn't really had a chance to process yet another loss. Now there was a new president with four new council members, all whom I tried to personally invite so that I could share what we, as the remaining members, had done and even committed to as far as new understandings made clear during the retreats as well as share an opportunity to continue this kind of teamwork, but to no avail. Two sat in on a meeting as council-elect, and their body language said it all. There was no interest to continue with this new approach in creating a new and different way to create some economic development. There was no chance of sitting this new group down so that we could as a group discuss the hows and whys so that they could have a chance to see and even add comments on what they were inheriting now as officials charged to protect, promote, and create a better way of life for all tribal members as to show and prove that this new style of creating better accountability for better chances of success was crucial. Business and politics had a bad track record of ever working for the greater good, and any success was short-term and subject to change when new elected members sat in chairs. This was not about who was smart or who was not; this was about creating consistencies in which the government could focus on the many things they needed to do for the equity of the Nation and the members. There were no political strategies; there were very little opportunities to develop more retail establishments, much less create any form of entrepreneurialism, all these being the basis of some economics to help individuals, in turn, then helping others. The days of the government acting like they are helping their people were not supporting this present day and for not going to properly and responsibly help in an uncertain future.

Despite the many scheduled meetings, despite the many attempts to engage in dialogue to try and promote the need to ask questions and even hear from others rather than feeling like I was pushing, that went by the wayside. Then the new president, all of a sudden, forgot all about his comments, endorsements, and votes in the creation and funding of JANCO. That was when the foundation started to succumb to the jackhammers trying to tear down JANCO. JANCO's foundation was built so well that because the ordinance included many forms of checks and balances, again all created from all the shortcomings of the section 17 companies, I wanted to make sure that even I could not take one dime without being caught and then made sure I was held liable. That was how strong just the accounting was. The other components had their own steel barriers again to make certain nothing was even out of compliance. All of a sudden, there was selective memory loss. I had three colleagues who stood by what they said and why they voted for this new way of financial independence, but we would soon be outvoted.

There was even an attempt to challenge our own laws. The Nation has a law that states how ordinances are officially approved. Permanent laws are not valid when they get the majority votes. Despite a very bad practice of the council, laws had to be signed by the president before they could be enacted. In the case of permanent laws, ordinances that are approved at a duly called meeting are then subject to review and approval within the BIA and, once approved, can now be added to the other existing codes. The new argument questioning JANCO's authenticity claiming it had never received BIA approval created a momentum to attempt to rescind the ordinance that was approved and now titled title 26. Turns out, all action of the prior council and the validity of their votes to approve JANCO were valid and had become effective per the provisions of Nation law. The law of the Nation states that once an ordinance is approved, it has ten days to go to the local BIA agency, after being signed by the Nation president. In that time, the BIA regional office, located in Albuquerque, has 120 days to reviews and respond. If there is no response and the 120 days has exceeded even by one minute, the presented ordinance is automatically approved to serve as new Jicarilla law, and in the case of JANCO, since the ordinance also had a clause that stated no sitting council could EVER rescind title 26, only the membership would be allowed such desire, and if they would have really listened and participated in some dialogue, they would have known this huge fact, but I digress.

Things were off to a bad start with the newly elected officials. I tried to really be optimistic and a team player, but wall after wall would now come up, and there was no discussion. Very little allowed input, and decisions would be made in nonofficial meetings that now took place in offices, almost now serving more like speakeasy joints. No matter how hard I tried to provide opportunity to hear about JANCO and even her from the board separately, JANCO was now in their sites, and they were going to dismantle this holding company regardless of fallout. All of a sudden, the bull's-eye turned to me personally. The sights tried to target me as someone who was breaking the law because I was the chairman of the board of JANCO. I was met with, "I don't agree," or "I don't like it" comments but never anything factual to back up such extreme slander. The laws of the Nation state that no sitting council member can ever hold a second full-time or half-time position, serving on committees and boards, which most other council members never did, which I thought was a huge negative. They assumed the law and then tried to use the clause of being on the JANCO against me. Yes, the charter of JANCO allowed board members to receive a board stipend of $500 per meeting, and meetings ranged from once a month to twice depending on issues brought forth by the CEO. There was never a second full-time or even half-time employee position, and that was also legally proven just like the BIA approval process, but that was still not satisfactory. All of a sudden, someone thought they had a bright idea and thought it would be a good idea to audit JANCO, a point that could have been made and was always the case since the council were acting as shareholder representatives and had every right to see the books. I even welcomed any review. I did make the comment that they didn't need to spend thousands of dollars on an audit firm. The JANCO board and JANCO itself had a CFO and controller who had been keeping track of all funds of JANCO. That fell on deaf ears, and at a duly called meeting, a motion was made to hire an auditing firm and check the books of JANCO. I was excited. I knew there would be no findings because I helped build a solid, secure, and highly accountable company. I called JANCO's legal representative, and we both spoke to the CEO, and then I emailed the board, letting them know what was going to transpire. We all felt confident, feeling that this would be a great way to show how strong the standards of JANCO were and that this might be an avenue to create some understanding as to the need of such a holding company. The controller and CFO of JANCO gave all information to the newly contracted auditing firm, and they went to work.

A couple of weeks went by, and on that day's agenda was the presentation of the audit of JANCO by the auditing firm. The mood was tense, and as I looked at the new group, all I felt was like salivating dogs ready to bite and tear into flesh, my flesh to be exact, as I was solely to be named in the audit by my new colleagues. The auditing firm presented to the council, handed out their materials, and it was quiet. I glossed through the auditing firm's pages. I already knew that there would be no issues, so I sat back and was quiet. The audit firm went through the line items, and a question was asked whether the auditing firm agreed to the practices and initial setups of JANCO. The presenter stated it was a good concept. We thought the salaries were a bit high. Just then, I spoke up and said, "Mr. President, I have a question," interrupting the presenter on purpose. I usually waited for people to finish their comments, but I felt I needed to intervene. I asked the gentleman, "What is the purpose of conduct-ing an audit?" He said to look for issues or discrepancies in money. I remarked, "So you look for something that is unaccounted for when it comes to funds or budgets or anything dealing with money that cannot be counted for?" He said yes. I went on to add, "Well, then your opinion should be moot as far as how a company is set up, and that included salaries or other approved budget items, so you all", referring to the audit firm staff, "were contracted to look at numbers, not one who was hired, and why?" The spokesperson said, "Yes, you are right. I apologize for my opinion." I then asked, "So can you tell me, as I am not very smart, did you find any issues?" The presenter responded with, "No, we found nothing that was out of place." I said, "Excuse, sir, you just said you found NO issues with the funds of JANCO," looking at my colleagues who all held their heads down in disappointment. I said, "Thank you for your time," and then as I began to sit back into my chair, I said, "I knew you wouldn't find anything. It was created to not have any issues." The president, who also chairs the meetings, asked if there were any questions. It was silent. The audit firm was excused, and we moved on. The issue was done, or so I thought.

During the scuttlebutt of new government members trying to unravel JANCO, my two other colleagues and I also bore witness to many other attempts to dismantle what was set up despite very informative presentations as to the why. All of a sudden, things that were more prudent and responsible, like the request for proposal process was a bad thing, despite saving money and creating better oversight and communication as to being in the loop of things along the way. Going from group debates, discussion, and even laughter, things began to feel like the only agenda was to dismantle based on what I could only surmise, hearsay, and rumor that clouded this new group, and based on their mindset, they were determined to undo and "fix" everything! I sat shocked in many meetings and, for the longest time, continued to be the diplomat and encourage just open dialogue back up and read what was done and then be able to provide input and further solutions, but nothing occurred that would create a team feeling, much less feel like there was trust. It was a turbulent time, and yet I continued to provide invitations to create more communication, but nothing still. The agenda was agreed to by five, and their attempts to control were prevalent as they continued holding secret meetings and boasting their experience. I actually was extremely happy at some of the newly elected personnel experience. One member came from BIA, another from the private sector of the oil and gas industry, and all I ever heard was, "I have forty years of experience" or "I worked for a company for many years, and I learned it all." It was a delusion of grandeur of the highest form.

Having experience, I felt, was very beneficial, but as an elected leader, there are also protocols that need to be consistent, like laws, policies, and practices. Having an opinion is great, but if your opinion is skewed based on hearsay, rumor, or emotion, then you are infringing on the sanctity of the government and stepping over lines that are established by permanent law, but yet, this bad practice of speculation, assumption, and spite continues this very day. I could never understand how this was acceptable by sitting members and the general membership at large. I guess that's why no information was ever shared. If you keep people in the dark and you're the only one holding a flashlight, I guess they feel like they have to follow and not question.

Case in point, the new president was all over the place. he made a grand speech at the inauguration and told those in attendance that he was going to show the people that we are going this way and pointed to the skies like he was Babe Ruth calling the world-famous home run shot. It was a total change of character from the person I laughed with, shared positive discussions with, kept in the loop on all things, and helped basically create his political platform, lest the cultural things. He had been a historian of sorts and, although quite knowledgeable, was also quite comfortable calling out those he felt were beneath him in his cultural and linguistic prowess, but he never told me anything negative to my face. Quite the contrary, he shared many wonderful stories and even was teaching me words to use in Jicarilla. I took great pride in this friendship. It was he who came running into the office carrying a piece of paper saying that he had no idea what this was and that he was not going to sign anything because he was now responsible for following all rules of the office. I asked to see the paper, and it was a bank statement from JANCO's budget and operational account from the Bank of America. You see, we had huge issues with a principal bank the Nation had dealt with for years, even when there were mergers. The Nation never strayed but in that had never really questioned the details such as fees. We had, in 2014, created a team of financial experts, including in-house legal, to backtrack and review all bank statements. What they found was there were excessive fees that the Nation was being charged and in the neighborhood of a $200,000 over the years. We set up a meeting and stated our case. I made my comments as I knew some background info and even new information that was collected and asked the simple question, "What is the difference between a fiduciary and nonfiduciary, during the audit of statements?" It was determined that the Nation was being charged higher fees when the bank felt that they were doing more as custodians of the accounts and acted in a fiduciary manner when they really had no real authority and were only nonfiduciary representatives of the Nations accounts. Maybe they were told by a sitting executive like the present, but it was never official and now a practice no longer tolerated; needless to say, we received a refund.

That is why I felt having JANCO's funds would be a better idea to spread around as to avoid a possible monopoly with the Nation's bank. I also felt that it was very important to allow the Nation's money to be in a separate bank from the Nation so that it had a better opportunity to diversify the bank's position to then help other business such as business loans. I felt strongly that showcasing the Nation's potential to be able to help other neighboring communities in further promoting the prominence of the Nation's success and then to also become a much larger blip on the state and federal political radar, again all for the benefit of the Nation.

So to now try and put out a fire that was set by someone who had a negative agenda with the document that was being waved around like it was a set of planes that were being sold to the Russians was now even more ridiculous because if the bank statement would have been looked at, there would have seen a breakdown of the account, including the balance of the principal, which again was open to the government per their role as shareholders' representative. I made the comment that since we were free that day, why don't we all go and sit down and have a work session to discuss, ask questions, and find some clarity as to the "why" rather than remain in the dark because of the "I heard." And that was what we did, but only for a few minutes until listening turning to not and more critiquing. At this point, I was getting really tired, and it felt no matter how professional I was trying to be by promoting communication, it would be all for naught.

I knew this more and more, and then the facade came crumbling down during a convened meeting of the council. There was a committee I had presented some years ago while I was in the PR office to a former chief of police, and it was attempting to try and create a better way to help protect both the police department and the community. It was a communal action committee designed to be a five-person panel, consisting of three or more who had knowledge in law enforcement and other related background and one of two community members who had some proven open-mindedness so that the whole point of this committee was to hear grievances filed against peace officers during their shift. There was not any opportunity to have due process of an employee as I mentioned earlier. If issues landed on the council table, there was a fifty-fifty chance the person in question was out of a job, and that to me never solved any possible issues, including false reports, so the communal action committee was an opportunity to empower others for the benefit of real solutions, and the individuals had to have some experience, or else anything less would be a redundant abuse and misunderstanding of authority. Eventually, it did pass; however, I was not in office but was still glad to know that this was created to help all vested parties in serving and protecting and even being rogue. Needless to say, when the new president came into office, he was presenting to the council a new group of committee members he selected personally. I read the law and began asking questions as to why he was not following the law. The law was specific as to who could sit a committee member, and as I began asking more questions and getting more frustrated as to why the law was being ignored, I was greeted with a banging of the gavel and the comment, "I am the president, I am in charge, and what I say goes!" I kept stating my point as the attempt to drown me out with the gavel became louder, when one of the new colleagues looked at me and said, "Just be quiet." I looked through her and said, "You know, I am just quoting the law, the laws we all swore to uphold in our oath of office, and I hope the gavel will not be a way to censure comments in the chambers." The room was quiet, and then the typical comment of "We will table this item" was stated. The term *table the item* was yet another tactic to try and circumvent the system to push again, a personal agenda. The gavel never came back down on any comments after that day. That was because the newly elected president found himself the center of controversy with a huge personnel issue.

It was close to the completion of first one hundred days of the president's new term, when all of a sudden, an issue arose when an appointed staffer claimed quid pro quo harassment and hostile work environment against the president. I will not go into details as to the charges, but what I did advocate for and push was to make sure that the council was not the primary investigators. As the track record extremely bad, I mentioned the council member I replaced in 2013 who succumb to emotions from legislators whose job it was to legislate, not be judge and jury. I knew that if this would continue to be the protocol, there would never be any fairness and proper punishment of the innocent and guilty, so I pushed for allowing in-house general counsel to request for proposal of an outside investigator and then an outside legal firm so that there was complete independence based on the facts, not emotions. The investigator did his job along with the special legal counsel, and there was enough evidence discovered that reflected negatively against the president to warrant an abuse of power charge. Based on the investigators' report and then legal advice, which came from the Nation's own laws, the council now had to make a determination as to whether or not the president would be deemed guilty by voting to be removed from office immediately. I had gone through an impeachment before, and everything had a solid process, even on the former president who had a petition by the people to be removed from office. In that case, it was determined that the process to submit charges was not followed, and although the petitioners felt that justice was not served, the laws were followed, and it was unfortunate how quickly people forget things. The president I served with in his administration and then sat by as a governing official would soon bad-mouth me, and I don't know if he knew that I actually advocated to let the laws prevail, and he actually completed his term and is now subject to be in good standing.

Once again, Jicarilla had a vacancy, and now, there needed to be a special election. I pondered as to once again trying for the chair, again feeling confident that I could serve in the highest of standards as well as promote the need for real substance for proper buy-in and understanding. I never thought I was a shoe-in, but based on my experience to date, my practice of enforcing the law, and the ability to build bridges for empowerment and consistency, I was more confident.

It was the days in between the special election where, once again, my credentials and Jicarilla blood would once again be the platform and called into question, but I felt strong enough to once again put my name in as a candidate for the president of the Jicarilla Apache Nation, and this was the letter I crafted for the newspaper and voting members:

> Recently I was sitting in a Legislative Council meeting, wondering what the future has in store for the Nation. Are we in a tailspin? Are

we headed for the iceberg? I used to think that we would be ok. But now, I have to be honest, I have serious doubts regarding the short and long term progress of our Nation.

I also ask myself, why do I want to be President of this Nation? I have been in the public sector as a public Servant for 16 years and could show what I have done. I have written resolutions, Ordinances, Proclamations, speeches for Presidents, Presentations that were adopted and approved. I am proud to say that my work is still positively advancing today. I continue to speak publicly locally, in Santa Fe, in Washington D.C. and anywhere and everywhere I get a chance, to promote the Nation.

Yet, the substance of work is never witnessed or acknowledged because the Nation's bureaucracy afraid to allow the people to come into the Legislative Council Chambers to witness meetings and the Nation's bureaucracy is afraid to have questions asked at general assemblies of the People.

I must question why our Nation's elected leaders are reluctant to share such critical information with the People. In fact, why become a public servant if you do not want to have transparency and accountability to our people but yet get to walk away with a government vehicle and a stipend even after creating destruction. I know some of you have heard rumors about me and I look forward to speaking with you directly as well as showing you what I have proudly done.

I work earnestly to make laws, enforce laws and promote laws that segregate my own children, whom are not Tribal Members and I also know that there are many of you who can relate.

I know that I am an easy target because I do not speak the language fluently, nor am I an expert on various cultural intricacies, but yet I work harder than anybody to ensure the long term preservation of our Nation's language and culture, and I am a protector of our Nation's rich history and will always hold my head high as a Tribal Member. I was given a gift from the Creator to speak articulately but command respect. There might have been a time where I was embarrassed to recognize this gift but I have come to embrace it because my voice get things done in the Legislative Council Chambers, in Santa Fe and in Washington D.C.

On a personal level, I was in a relationship that is now dissolved because of bad choices but rather than blame or chastise or fall, I have risen and learned from my own shortcomings and mistakes and can look in the mirror and strive to be better father, a stronger professional and a much better advocate on behalf of those I want to protect, you the People.

I come from a strong family. My Father, the late Kimo Reval and my Mother Abbie Segura, my brothers Audie and Jamon and my many Aunts, Uncles and Cousins have instilled in me the strongest values of our community. There may have been a time that I had forgotten but I have also reflected in remembrance the fighting Apache spirit and core values they gave me and still give to me this day. These values are not new, nor are they from somewhere else. These strong core values came from my roots, Dulce. Dulce has produced many great memories and even in those negative times, I have been able to learn and apply for the better. I have learned that our

Apache spirit is not only strong, but it is also loving and caring. And while at times we quarrel or hold grudges, we also have a sense of forgiveness and kindness and love towards each other.

I have seen past Legislative Council's vote on laws that provide fairness and strength and I have seen past Legislative Councils approve resolutions that act as glorified memos and worse, unraveled good work that has wasted time, energy and money. I have also seen Presidents become ineffective and sit back and not debate or address issues. I have also seen President's sign documents without knowing what they were signing and then blame the Legislative Council after the fact. For me, the time has come to have someone sit in the Office of the President that will truly lead the General Council and maintain an agenda that is progressive and constructive.

We need a President to guide the Legislative Council so that good business decisions can be made for the benefit of the People, and not because they've become emotionally charged on an issue that becomes a purely political decision out of spite. It's those emotional spiteful resolutions that never get vetoed by a strong President. A strong President can keep the Legislative Council away from department issues, can make sure laws are remembered and then followed and most importantly share all information on resolutions. These simple acts will change the structure of government which will then be truly for the people. Any President who allows laws to be signed off on that are less than for the benefit of responsible law, is feeding into the stereotype that the Legislative Council has all the power. A responsible government should be creating laws that have structure, longevity and strategies, not changing laws because there was an impasse or someone heard. That type of leadership is irresponsible and destroys the sanctity of such a privilege of being an elected leader. I ask again, why sit at the top if you are not doing the very best?

However, it is too easy to blame the Legislative Council when the needs of Tribal Members are not addressed fairly and equitably. Very candidly, I must ask the People to recognize some facts. The People only have a thirty percent (30%) voter turnout for our elections. That means that out of two thousand and eight hundred eligible Tribal voters, less than eight hundred cast a vote! That's very low and I ask, is that being responsible as a Jicarilla Nation Member? We as a Nation have so many valuable resources and tools other tribes wished they had and yet we coast and just survive. Our Nation have so many valuable resources and tools that other tribes wished they had and yet we coast and just survive.

Now my statement about the lack of Tribal Member voting participation may have ruffled a few feathers but ask, does anyone really know what the worth of the Nation is? Does anyone care? Strong leadership educates and shares responsibility but at the same time, we have to be responsible with the information we receive. We as tribal members all have a stake in our past, our present and our future. We should never forget that we all need to respect our land, our laws and of course our most precious resource, the People.

In fact, I think we may have forgotten some of our past, the first Constitution, August 4, 1937, identifies respect as a core component of our government. For example, Article III—

Membership, states the blood quantum in that approved constitution was one fourth or more Indian Blood. Article IV Rights Of Members states ALL members shall enjoy equal rights to life, liberty, industrial pursuit and NO person shall be denied the right to worship as he pleases, to speak and write his opinions. When and why did we get away from those original beautiful words? Always remember, the People change the Constitution, never elected officials!

My final question, why do we continue to accept the status quo and allow our Tribal leaders to leave their elected office adding no value but yet we reelect the same recycled politicians? We have the privilege of democracy again from the 1937 document and yet were still stuck in the rut in 2017. Always remember, our laws are solid but there may be times when the government is just not properly enforcing these laws or may also be picking and choosing what laws to enforce.

There is a loud cry for sovereignty and we often say, we don't need the United States government, we don't need BIA, we know how to do our own thing on our own land But I have to ask, do we really know what is best for our tribe? That may be a loaded question but the answers rests in our Tribal leaders, if they are not stepping up and challenging themselves or those other leaders, we become complacent. I know I do not want that. We have had that long enough. I say no more just getting by! We, you, the Government need to prove our value, our strength and ability to wake up from our sleep and be the giant Jicarilla Apache has always been. We need to fight for better federal legislation not just demand money and not follow the rules, when that happens, we all lose, not only our rules but our word and then we have compliance issues with grants and the answer should never be, just absorb these costs under the Nation's budget. The golden goose of Oil and Gas may have flown, we can no longer just sit idle and wish for the best and we sure as heck cannot continue to absorb more costs under this current budget. We have the wherewithal to diversify and rebuild our economic development but for some reason never execute because of rumors and speculation. Is it not the job of a leader to build upon, promote and empower for such betterment?

There are hundreds of communities and groups that are simply present in DC and more importantly turn out large voter numbers and even if possible donate money to campaign contributions. Whether we agree, like it or dislike it, that's the way the game is played. Going to DC and giving grand ideas with no substance or tangible plans and simply saying we need, is, to me, an outdated concept that does little to nothing accept waste time. I would never say that the government should NOT enforce nor respect its trust responsibility. I'm saying that we take that and enhance and prove that the Jicarilla Apache can not only provide for our own, but the Jicarilla Apache are mighty, and they can provide for many others surrounding our reservation, county, state and neighboring states. We have the wherewithal be a regional and national economic and political powerhouse, but for some reason the Nation never executes because of rumors and bad personal agendas that control our bureaucracy.

The biggest issue, in my opinion, is that we have a massive power struggle within the Council and the other two branches of government. To date there have been a lot of encroachment on territories rather than respecting and enforcing. We desperately need a strong President, a visionary that recognizes the true unharnessed potential of our Nation. This same person could be courteous and professional in order to keep politics at bay. I recognize we need Legislative Council to vote on laws as they should, but there is a difference between approving law and not allowing political maneuvering to paralyze our Nation's progress. I have seen my fair share of laws be approved or even rescinded because of emotional votes that were not seriously debated or discussed or based on sound policy. This bad practice has resulted in a picking and choosing of personal agendas which have resulted in inconstancies and failings and usually at a tremendous cost, and yet those laws were never vetoed! Case in point, a resolution I wrote that would transcribe and disseminate ALL Legislative Council meeting minutes. The Vote was five to three, which passed the Legislative Council, but then the next day was vetoed by the President! Don't worry, I wrote another one which highlights Article X, Title 15 Chapter 2(3)(a) and Title 19 Chapter 1(8) & Title 19 Chapter 3(2)(3) which basically states that ALL information needs to be shared to the public.

Here is another fact. Ninety percent of the Legislative Council's agenda is dealing with Administrative matters. People are frustrated because they feel there is no structure and when they utilize the system, they still fall short because of no accountability in the Presidents or Vice Presidents office. Take a look at the Court system or the Human Resources Department, the

Police Department, no that's not a jab but we have allowed politics to intrude when it should have complete immunity. We all deserve equality and fairness and most importantly movement forward.

I leave you with a quote from famed Author Ernest Agyemang Yeboah "We yearn for opportunities, we pray for opportunities and we seek for opportunities. The good news is that we meet opportunities. The bad news is that we miss the opportunities only to come to a later realization of missed opportunities."

Help me leave our footprints in rock, not sand. Vote and encourage all eligible voters to vote. The job of the President is to stand up and create unity while also being a barrier between the Legislative Council. Simplicity better yet transparency can hold us ALL accountable which will then hit those positive results rather than miss!

Since the office of the president's term had more than a year to complete, the constitution stated the need for a special election; however, there was no primary or general. All special elections take place, and most votes wins the seat or, in this case, the chair. Once again, I lost another election. The sting of losing feels a little less painful, and don't get me wrong, there is a tingle of ego that tries to surface, but I still had a job to do and was going to continue to toe the line in an ethical and moral manner. I actually felt that this was good thing as it was a possible opportunity to promote the already challenged JANCO issue and could have been a great opportunity for a new president to learn of its value and the why and then also help promote how positive this approach really was. Unfortunately, that didn't happen. It would be long before there was yet another attempt to attack my character and JANCO. The topic would resurface, and although JANCO had been making huge strides with new ventures and other vetted business opportunities, the opinions of "I don't like" reared their ugly heads. It was in a duly called meeting where cries of "We need another audit" were almost chanted. I made the rebuttal that we just had an audit and that the ordinance was so strong that there were no issues, but that was not good enough because the new bunch, as they would be referred to now, were adamant that I had every intention of stealing money, millions to be exact, and they were responsible to make sure nothing of the sort happened because the people put them in office to help and protect. I laugh now because that was never the reason. If it was, then in my opinion, they would have done everything in their power to learn about not only JANCO but also the many other things that were on the table ready to help support the Nation's advances and especially the financial status.

The new group was so convinced that JANCO was bad and that the players associated with JANCO, including the Nation's newest legal counsel, the board, and officers, including myself and two of my colleagues, were all guilty of illegal practices. No matter how many times I tried to show, invite, and extend every opportunity to gain buy-in, I would receive further disdain. The time came where I had to tell the board that we needed to terminate the officers of JANCO, and when I was signing the resolutions and termination documents, my heart was in the pit of my stomach. I felt so beaten because I also felt it was my fault that we had failed, and now I created such huge negative impacts in the lives of the people who take a chance on what they had felt was positive, made a commitment, and were now cut loose with nothing at all! I would soon find myself on the cusp of depression.

Even though JANCO was a shell, there was still pressure to find me guilty of any infraction, and the new bunch were going to find a way to show that JANCO was wrong. It was during a meeting that I would hear the chants of another audit, and I just shook my head, not at the attempt to hide from accountability but at the continued attempt to disparage. I tried to once again explain and referred back to the first audit, but my comments fell on deaf ears, so I went on to state, "If you really want to spend another $16,000 on another audit to find out, again, how strong the ordinance of JANCO is, then as your colleague and out of the need to ensure accountability of all,

I will support the request, and I know that there will be no issues because of how strong the standards of JANCO are, and hopefully we can put this issue to rest and begin to let it do what it needs to do," and, with that, made the motion for another audit. This time, unknowingly, the audit was now going to be a forensic audit. Audits are crucial and not always bad; they can be a good thing to also help create better ways of oversight and proper accounting principles, and I knew that which is why the JANCO charter had clear, stringent accounting measures, not to mention again the two roles of the controller and CFO who were both proven strong gatekeepers. The forensic audit would target the specific funds of the initial investment of $1.6 million, and the $100 million investment was never given to JANCO despite the approval, but I still wasn't surprised or worried, but I was growing more and more concerned as to how many more times JANCO and Leon were going to be thrown back under the microscope or a much larger lack of support would ensue because, once again, the majority of my colleagues "knew" I was stealing money and the whole idea of JANCO, my baby, was a bad idea, and they didn't like it. It was also unfortunate that the newly elected president also went along with the group and never once asked about the how or why, and I even served with him and worked for him, and that was tough for me to personally accept, but I kept my head held high and knew there were no issues with the concept, practice, and philosophy of JANCO.

It was time for the meeting, and the auditors came back in to present their report. This time, there was a milder feeling of the "gotcha" and, upon presentation, no questions and no findings! I asked the audit spokesperson again if there were any findings; the comment was no. The report produced that there were some receipts that were unaccounted for, but that was common as these findings were for purchases like dinner meetings, gasoline purchases to travel to meetings, and other small business-related purchases. And even though the purchases were valid based on bank statements and credit card summaries, the actual paper receipts were still pending, and since now the JANCO officers were placed on furlough pending the audits, business had stopped for three weeks. It was a great feeling to know that my thoughts and ideas and experience created such a powerful tool that would help the Nation find a new way in its economic development and economic stability, and I wanted to show this more especially since JANCO's charter was steel-tough, and no matter how much cynicism and spitefulness, some thought this was a great plan. I wanted to share the findings with everyone, so I asked the JANCO CFO to write a breakdown in laymen's terms so that people could see for themselves and then hopefully also question why their government has a habit of allowing their opinions to crush everything they heard was bad, feel was bad, or are ignorant as to what is really good for the people they are supposed to help. The CFO letter stated,

Chairman,

The following is a summary of my analysis of the Forensic Investigation audit performed by Moss Adams and presented to the Nation's new legal rep; Strategy on August 30, 2017.

The audit performed by Moss Adams reviewed all transactions and related authorizations of JANCO for the period August 4, 2016 through June 30, 2017. JANCO provided all available documentation to Moss Adams requested for this investigation and worked closely with them in the performance of this audit.

The audit findings are as follows:

1. All financial transactions concerning the $1,600,000 funds controlled by JANCO were documented and authorized by the Board of Directors. This encompassed the transactions in all three JANCO bank accounts. All bank accounts were reconciled on a regular basis and there are no other bank accounts controlled by JANCO.

2. The audit listed potential financial obligations of JANCO as of June 30, 2017. These obligations are:

a. Allen Mosley employment agreement
b. Potential $6,661 Bank of Albuquerque amount for legal work on a line of credit.
c. Potential $4,084 to Sedona Wellness for contract never initiated.
d. Valid accounts payable amounts for legal and tech services in the amount of $5,684.

These amounts have been paid.

3. The audit identified other issues documented in the report. I will give my input on each of these items:

a. Health insurance premiums for employees was paid totally by JANCO with no employee contribution. This issue was brought to the attention of the Board in Sept 2016 and after an analysis was performed, the Board made the determination to not collect the back portion from the employees. In November 2016 all employees except myself were terminated. All employee health insurance was cancelled in Dec 2016 and I now provide my own insurance, at no cost to JANCO. The Board of Directors of JANCO was aware of the insurance issue and a valid Board decision was made.
b. The audit found $25,960.22 of payments that did not have actual receipts attached. Most of these items were payments made

on expense accounts where receipts were not attached or had been lost in the transfer of documents from Mr. Becker to myself. Most of these expenditures were for trips by management which was approved by the Board. The majority of the expenses were from the final expense reports from management which were approved by the Board for payment after termination of the management team. Note: Each of the terminated employees had in their employment contracts substantial severance payments that they could have tried to collect through a legal process. The Boards decision to pay the final expense reports even though all documentation was not presented, may have prevented employees from bringing a legal suit against JANCO. There were a couple of items concerning payments to Board members for expense reimbursement that I believe adequate documentation was provided.

c. The audit found that all assets of JANCO were accounted for and available to be transferred back to the Tribe.

My thoughts on this issue are as follows:

Total disbursements for JANCO for this period amounted to $827,002.50. Unsupported amounts were $25,960.22 of which $17,403.37 were final payments to terminated employees, leaving $8,516.85, or 1% of total expenditures without proper documentation. All expenses should have adequate documentation to justify payment and there were some that did not meet the bar set by Moss Adams in this forensic audit. However, any financial audit conducted, probably would not find that the amount, or substance, of these payments would meet the threshold of an audit finding.

Chairman, in my experience, the purpose of any forensic audit is to determine misappropriation of funds or malfeasance of management, including the Board of Directors. Nowhere in this audit is any indication that either of these exist. This audit does in fact state that all assets are accounted for and available to be transferred to the Tribe. The Board of Directors set in place policies and procedures to assure that all funds were secure and all disbursements and transfers were approved by the Board.

Nowhere in the audit is there a mention of any actions taken that were not in the scope of approvals given by the Board. It appears to me that all Board actions were documented and codified by Legal representation and documentation.

In my opinion, every action taken by the JANCO Board of Directors has been made in the best interest of JANCO and the Jicarilla Tribe. I am honored to work with such a distinguished and dedicated group.

Thank you.

Unfortunately, by the end of the second audit, JANCO was only a name. The new bunch had got what they wanted and killed the Nation's first and only true Jicarilla-owned corporation, and while dismantling not only crippled the true nature of sovereignty and self-determination but also breached the laws of the Nation by allowing their votes to rescind title 26, the Jicarilla Apache Nation Corporation—because the only way JANCO could have been rescinded was by a vote of the tribal membership and that point was raised and shouted by the only thing that changed—was my voice as I grew more hoarse and tired, but I wanted to try one more time to showcase the value of JANCO and the concept of separating politics from business. I wrote this letter to the membership:

Dear Members,

You may recall that in the February 2, 2018 edition of the **Chieftain**, I related to you a brief history of the Legislative Council's and the President's enactment of the ordinance creating the Nation's economic development entity, JANCO. As a follow-up to that letter, I want to report to you that the JANCO Board, on February 5, 2018, sent to the Nation's Treasury a check for $585,000.00 which the first of several checks that will be sent to the Treasury. A second check in the amount of $60,153 will be sent to the Treasury as soon as the bank completes its paperwork and another check will be sent to the Treasury from the return of a fidelity insurance policy premium which the Board cancelled, as soon as it is received from the insurance company.

As I mentioned in my February 2 letter, JANCO had only one share of stock, owned by only one shareholder—**you the citizens of our Nation**. This one share of stock was voted by majority vote of the Council and when the Council determined that it didn't want to proceed with the various economic development projects that JANCO had proposed, the Board took the prudent action to conserve the Nation's funds and authorized the return of all assets to the Nation and to resign their positions.

A complete forensic audit was conducted of JANCO with my full support by the national accounting firm of Moss Adams and the audit confirmed that all financial records were in perfect order and that not one penny was misspent. I have always advocated as your Council member for financial transparency and accountability and I believe that you—Jicarilla citizens—the owners and beneficiaries of our natural resources and assets are entitled to it.

You should demand that all Jicarilla entities and departments likewise be audited and indeed they should welcome forensic audits to establish their transparency and accountability. Unfortunately, in Indian Country, there are too many instances of mismanagement or worse where the assets of tribes are unproductive, lost or stolen. I call upon you—Jicarilla Apache citizens—to demand of your representatives and President that forensic audits of all tribal entities and departments be conducted so that we can all have confidence in them.

I pledge to you that as your elected representative, I will dedicate myself to accountability and to uncover underperforming assets or mismanagement and report back to you.

Thank you. LEON K. REVAL

By this time, I was exhausted and extremely hurt by the attempted cuts to my reputation and character even by those whom I had held in very high regard. I could not understand why. It was a tough time trying to get answers to my questions, and I had finally, for the first time in my career, felt defeated and weathered. I did have some drive, and I knew that I needed to stay focused as I was coming up on the completion of my second term of office, and if I wanted to run as an incumbent, then I needed to get my head right.

It was also during this time of fighting daily at the office that I would now find out my marriage was crumbling. I had a gut feeling that there was something not right, and I played it off as it was work and the accusations, but this feeling never subsided and would only get stronger. I couldn't quite put my finger on this feeling, but it was like an iron cloud floating overhead but so heavy that it made me feel extremely vulnerable. I finally got to the point that I need to ask my wife directly if something was going on, but I also felt I had to ask in a way that was not confronting and accusing without some proof. I just asked, "Is everything okay? Are you doing something that you would frown upon if you found out or felt I was doing something that was questionable?" the answer was "no" with a lower tone than a more resounding higher forceful pitch of expressing an answerer of no. I wanted to cry because my feeling became palpable, and crying was a better way for me to release my angst rather than bottling up and doing something crazy. All that I did ask was to let me know so that I would not be played. I was assured nothing was happening, and I was stewing for nothing. My intuition was confirmed when I found messages being exchanged, and although I was not going to get in the car and track down any shenanigans, I had read enough messages and seen pictures to know that I was being lied to. Two things occurred. I actually had two choices to make—one, I could react, let my emotions rage, and then run the risk of doing something very stupid, or two, I can see this for what it is. I could reflect on my attitudes and behaviors, my lack of support, and all the things I may have contributed to choices. I took the high road. As much as I felt I wanted to explode, I let my mind remain clear and did my best to reevaluate my role as dad, husband, and even public servant. I wore a smile to work and endured the continued challenges of spite and continued rumor and at the same time deal with how I would enter the house when I came home. I felt I needed to do more as the head of house, and I decided I needed to step up and do better. I would now listen more than ever when I would talk to the kids, I would cook, I would try and be a much better domestic partner because I may not have been, and I did take things like my marriage and the kids for granted, and this was my way of making amends not only to my wife and kids but to me as well. I still wasn't sure if my new approach was based out of necessity or survival. I was unable to sleep, eat, think, and already being labeled a thief and half-breed and every other thing that is thrown at you when you are in the political spotlight. I kept thinking, *Don't do anything that will give anyone ammunition to use against you*, and so I just went through the motions and didn't say anything at home and work. I felt I was on a high wire, and I was walking to find either side of the mountain for some security and stability, but I just continued to slowly creep along, trying not to look down or think how thin the wire really was.

Out of the blue, I went to see a therapist. In retrospect, I should have seen a psychiatrist so that I could have asked for some prescription meds, but speaking to the therapist did help and helped me understand that my coping skills were completely off, and in that, all the repressed feelings from my youth started to come back, not in a scary way but in way that made me face them more, and then that allowed other emotions to start surfacing. I kept thinking, what the hell, everything I knew or felt or said was all wrong or felt wrong, and now with all the issues weighing on me, I didn't feel like I wanted to snap, but I did feel like I was being tested, and my biggest issue was I didn't know what the test was about, and I had no idea what to study or feel that I could even pass.

I went through the motions of life and, aside from doing a better job as a dad, felt myself wanting to stand tall but also wanting to quit, quit being nice and professional and understanding. Everyone else had no qualms about what they said to me, so why should I care about being nice? That was tough talk, tough feelings. I started to realize that I had let my ego lead me all these years and that my coping skills or lack thereof were not all wrong, just blurry. I was surviving, and my skill of deducing and being compassionate was how I was designed to cope. It sounds strange because even though I felt confused by acts by my parents, nuns, colleagues, membership, and even my children, my initial reaction when I felt slighted was to ignore and then treat those closest to me like pariahs, and those whom I should have not cared what they thought, I embraced and lived my life as a pleasure, making sure that I did not react or confront, which only invited people to feel like they could become even more confrontational and demanding, and I would just smile and then go home and release.

Being labeled a thief and accused of fraud and defrauding the Nation and then having to face the embarrassing issue of emotional infidelity, I did not prove physical, and I didn't want to. I knew enough parts of the puzzle that made up the picture, and I started reciting the adage of careful what questions you ask. I may not like the answers, and even though I felt so strongly that I needed to know the truth, after some deep thought, my quest to find discovery was only to feed my ego, and I was determined to find better ways to cope and accept things I couldn't change.

In my introspection, I was at war in my mind. I knew that I needed to adapt. I also knew that things happen to everyone, and I was not special, but I kept thinking, *How is all this stuff happening to me?* What I also began to learn about myself is I am a literal person. I need to see things, touch, feel, inspect, and then I can begin to formulate a thought, then action. I also came to the conclusion that I am unable to have a discussion, where two people or a group of people can present viewpoints so that there can be an attempt to reach some understanding, not expectations—another issue I discovered about myself during this self-reflection but understandings so that there could be agreements moving away from impasses. This is a very hard thing for some people to do and can be tricky as they may feel that yelling, being forward, and/or crude is communication.

With my personal life feeling like it was unraveling, I took a step back from feeling I needed to be a part of everything at work. I had dumped myself into work that I felt I had to attend every meeting so that I could chime in and help keep things on par. I would sit in a meeting in town and then take off to Santa Fe, two and a half or three hours away and then, even in the same day, travel to Albuquerque to attend another meeting. I would travel to Washington, DC, sometimes alone, to make sure that the Nation had a representative at the table, not to talk for the Nation but to share the strong economic history of the Nation and its ability to continue to do so. That part I may have been wishing for, but to be at any table, in my opinion, was a wonderful opportunity for the Nation to show up on all these radars. I had been traveling so much that on one trip back home, I was driving and found myself being startled by the highway rumble strips that indicate to drivers they are not on the road, and it was so surreal that in another two seconds, I could have run into a guardrail head-on. I may not have even been in any danger as I corrected, but the thought did occur that things could have been catastrophic. The rest of the drive, all I could think about was, *What the hell am I doing? Why do I feel like I have to be at every meeting? Why do I have to act like what I am doing mattered to people?* These were tough questions to answer. I took my job very seriously, and I may have compromised in my tenure, but I did so to try and not only give great respect to the sanctity of the Nation's governance but did everything by the book.

I was always being told that "I was doing it wrong" or that I didn't know the Jicarilla people; those were so strange for me to hear. What I did know day 1 or felt instinctually was that politics was separate from everything else. That didn't mean it was not to apply some skill, wherewithal, learned knowledge, logic, and simple common sense, but it did mean that the Nation had rules and laws that were to be upheld to the highest of standards, despite blood quantum, culture, and/or language. And it takes a strong person to see through the facade to know what is black and white and what is gray, all for the benefit of helping one another, especially as a tribe, who are all deserving of the same, equal, equitable outcomes, especially when it came to serving as a member of government.

My term was coming up fast, and I had a strong feeling that I was not going to be victorious in my incumbency, but I was determined to keep moving forward despite the attempts of slander and libel. I actually had presented a draft law to now make slander and libel a much stronger civil issue. It wasn't not a mechanism to try and sue people because they yelled at you or called you name, but this was a draft that gave the court more teeth to be able to hear and make a determination as to making sure the plaintiff could prove and then be compensated accordingly, but unfortunately, it was tabled, and then I received a comment that this was my attempt to stop people from criticizing and questioning the government. I explained there are no specific laws or opportunities to hold someone accountable for their words and actions. I said, "Quite frankly, this draft law arose from witnessing time and time again the attack on people's character by their own 'leadership.' If people were allowed, by law, to get copies of all meeting minutes and comments, they would hear how disgusting officials charged to serve their people, start up the bus, and run them over at the same time, with zero recourse." I explained that my draft was not protecting the government. It made a much larger opportunity to hold the government most accountable and that no sitting official could cry foul because a constituent yelled at them or cussed at them. The law was designed to protect all membership and make the government produce more of a case than the membership. It never made back to the table while I was there. I had heard through the grapevine that there was a similar, if not the same, draft that was approved, but it had more barriers in it to protect the government rather than the membership at large, but I never saw a tangible copy.

At this point, I felt I had nothing to lose to keep sharing and spouting facts that I felt strong about and felt that if I was unsuccessful in my bid for another term, well, I did everything I could to help shine the light on giant issues that occurred and would continue to challenge the growth of the Nation as a whole. I wrote this statement:

Hear any good rumors?

Well let's begin with me, who is Leon K. Reval? I am a single father of three, three non-tribal members. In fact I create, enforce and promote laws that keep my own children segregated from the many luxuries we as enrolled tribal members enjoy. I unfortunately went through a tough separation of someone I loved very much and have managed to learn from my own shortcomings as a husband to whom I am able to teach my children the value of principals and morals of staying on the high road despite life's harsh lessons. I am a still considered a half-breed who runs for office to change the Nation's blood quantum. First and foremost, NO ELECTED OFFICIAL can change or alter the Nation's Constitution! Only you, the membership can make amendments to our Constitution. That is an immense amount of power and that will always belong to the people!

No, I do not speak the language or claim to know our beautiful culture or traditions and yet that seems to make you and you others who do not speak the language, an easy target of ridicule and bullying. It would be easy to blame but yet we do not, the desire is there and I have had many good people stop and respectfully teach me words that I really try to retain. The attempt for us remains and please do not give up on us, we are and will always be eager students. I have been blessed with the gift of language, call it the "White man's" language but I have no problem standing up promoting the Nation and even calling out the Government if need be. I have been to Santa Fe and stood up and lead the dissatisfaction of our current Governor, Susana Martinez, I have been a witness in trials protecting what is called the "Indian District" which is a voting area that encompasses Native Leadership in the State and I have been to Washington DC to express and promote just how strong the Nation is and that we will continue to protect our sovereignty and self-determination even when other tribes rally against us.

My gift of communication may seem like it is ego driven, I have some Councilmembers who have told me that the Council is a team effort and there should be no "I" well ask the question, show me what you have done and how have you done it. Councilmember's are individual positions where one should be accountable to not only what they say but accountable to their vote. I hear present and former councilmembers say, "I didn't know what I voted for even though I voted yes." That is Ludacris in my opinion, I wrote a draft resolution stating that All Legislative Council meetings should be transcribed and disseminating to not only the Council but to all membership including being printed in outline form in the Chieftain. It passed five to three and then later was vetoed! Well I have not personally seen the reason for the veto but I heard it was because of confidentiality. Well I have written another version highlighting already approved parts of the Nation's code like Article Ten of the Constitution, Title 15 and multiple sections of Title 19 which covers confidentiality but also under Title 19 Chapter 3 Section 2 and 3 state and I paraphrase, info should be shared with the Nation's membership as well as also being shared in the Chieftain or other news sources. 1 but know that passion and confidence sometimes gets confused with ego and a personal agenda but you all have heard me speak and you know that my passion is and will always be for our Nation and No, I have not stolen any money nor have I ever discredited my name aside from the many rumors and dare I say slanderous remarks.

The Legislative Council has one job, to amend, rescind and or make laws. Every Council member has that ability to do their job and earn their check. If all that one does is complain and pick apart ideas and never provide solutions, then how about just stepping back and being honest by saying you don't know and you don't care.

Trust is a word that unfortunately has lost a lot of its power but not all is lost. Trust can also be a resurgence that is reflected by action. I know good things can happen with good leadership but we still wait for that one person to come forth and show that empowerment, accountability, team building and clear communication can do wonders, not only in the workforce but at the State and on the Hill in Washington D.C.

I have asked, why do elected officials fear giving information? Whether it's sharing or whether it's receiving updates about the government or even at the department level. There is a lot of responsibility in giving information; I say that because sometimes information is shared only at the gain of a personal agenda or to talk bad about somebody. I think the role of the Chieftain is vital, unfortunately in my opinion no one really went up to bat or fight as hard as they should have and maybe that even solidifies my point about the fear of sharing any vital information. I also think that the recent article about the unfortunate circumstances for removing an elected official is crucial to what the Chieftain should be and has been in the past. I think it time to get the Chieftain back to what it should be, a source for factual news!

It is long overdue and time that the government be reminded that they don't control the media, whether it's the Chieftain or even in social media but at the same time, it is the responsibility of all the membership and the community to not only receive the information but ask follow up questions about the information being received and if that follow up is not happening, maybe we all guilty of not sharing, not receiving and not taking the information responsibly to properly mull it over and discuss it. The most cherished rights of being a citizen, not only of the Jicarilla Apache Nation but of the United States, that is freedom of press and freedom of speech.

Are the Legislative Council meetings open to the members?

People are under the impression that they are not allowed to attend meetings because of the security guards that are at the door.

I'll tell you this, you know this is interesting, there was a comment made about me that said, "Leon says I, I, I." and we as the Council are a team. I don't think I do but if I do, I apologize. However, for this part there was a statement made and I believe it was for the record. I simply asked we hear these sound bites at public forums, general assemblies come see the council, come sit in the chambers and I ask well, I have people texting me asking if they can come in. You got five departments waiting out there, why not bring them into the chambers so they can not only witness the great comments that are being said, but the accountability of, to your point, who they voted for. The answer I got was, well you know, ranged from silence to well it still hasn't been done yet. I understand that there is a need to hear and it is loud outside in this huge hollow hall. A simple request take down the big wooden doors and put up some glass doors, so they can see the council and actually be waved in. However, the response I got was silent to well we can do it, well let's do it. I want people to see what's going on in those chambers because there are many good comments. It is unfortunate that even if you and I were just having this discussion and it wasn't for some sort of public record and you leave here and maybe you didn't hear what you wanted or maybe you had a request well I am sorry I can't help you because maybe it's not in line, it's not my role or it's not in the rules and you go well that Leon he is just the worst, he is not here for his people. Well that is a pretty broad statement too because as a public servant you do the best you can you have two things you have to stand by and yeah ethics and morals are huge, but you have two things to stand by an understanding and willingness and your gut. If you vote yes or no, and this is just my opinion, you better have a reason why you voted yes or no and it better be valid in your mind and you better be able to prove it because if it is yes or no based on well I really don't know umm but maybe everybody voted for it and I didn't want to be the odd man out and then vote yes and come back and complain that it was the wrong thing to do will shame on you. That has been going on, has gone on, and has been going on for a long time. Where is the personal responsibility of an elected official? That is why I am saying yeah it is a collaborative team but it is still an individual who makes a vote but a strong vote that has a responsibility of either saying yes or no for almost 4,000 members of this tribe. Now you get comments well I am here for my people, well that is great we all are, that's great. However, if you have to remind yourself daily, umm maybe not so great, again this is just my opinion. I'll tell you this if less or just slightly over 30% of our voters turn out, to your point, if you don't vote or do your research then you can't complain, well you can and you should but really you had every opportunity to cast your vote and someone says well I am here for my people well ok even at 30% or even 40% we are still missing that other 30–40% and that is still a huge amount of responsibility. It might be a sound bite because the proof is in the pudding. And if the people are not seeing that, they are not seeing how the council operates then you're going to have a bunch of rumors and the biggest rumor and again since I am talking oh Leon is this and Leon is that. Well maybe because it is my job and secondly maybe because at that moment it was the right thing to do, the right thing to say and everything that I say I have no problem with anybody reading the record back or having it played back and hearing my voice and my comments. Yeah, for me I say open it and it should be open and we should have access to the records of the meetings. Every other municipally, county, city, state release information and meeting minutes. Now I did put a resolution on the table for meeting minutes, dissemination and transcribing and there was some concern about it because it was verbatim, to be honest they are already verbatim, they are already being transcribed, they are just not being disseminated. So, it got vetoed, I'll tell you what it is coming back again and I will fix those little clauses in there that state what is maybe confidential and again they are all in the rules of what can be released and what can't. As an editor you're responsible too, you know what the people want to hear and what they need to hear. The Nation's secretary, the same way, that role is a mince because of the responsibility of sharing information. I'll even go one step further what's confidential I don't know because maybe the personnel issues, ok fine, but the personnel issues should not be going to the council anyway. Keep everything out of the council to the executive duty. What else is confidential? Well money ok well maybe but anybody can go online and find what audits because we do an annual audit. So, is it because the mindset is to protect or the other side of the coin, the mind set to hide. There is power in information and the more information we share the less likely we will have bad rumors happening, now they will always be there, people are going to complain which is find. Complain against your government, challenge your government, I would encourage you to challenge your government but if you don't ask and you don't get a couple of stories. Then figure out for yourself and you're taking one bad piece of information at full face value and spreading that, shame on you, that is not, that is not being responsible of information. Now I don't want to sound like I'm coming off as oh I'm speaking down to people, it's true. Information is power and we all need to understand it well all need to try and understand it and if you don't know come ask. I was told it's open meetings, GO TO THE MEETINGS. I hope that you will have an ability to see what actions were placed on the agenda. Therefore, now you know how people voted now you know what comments were stated; now you will know if Leon is a ringleader. Let's go to the source and find out. Not just, because someone got mad or someone had every opportunity to say something and he or she didn't and now they are complaining cause that happens too. Be responsible to your job, whether it's a council member, whether it's this whether it's that we all have a role here and we all work for the Nation, we all work for our community and we have to do it responsibly, regardless. I get lazy, I get upset, I get angry but you know what coming to work and trying not to smile is difficult for me because I like to laugh, I like to smile, I like to joke but we all have our days. Let's just remember that we all on the same team and I do I expect people to hold me responsibly and I will hold everybody else responsible just as much as they will hold me responsible because that is how we will function not only as our society, our community but as Jicarilla people. A little sound body but that is the truth. When you talk about it that is the truth.

What is this rumor stuff about Jicarilla Apache Nation Corporation (JANCO)?

Good question. Therefore, JANCO evolved from many bad deals now going back to the sharing of information. There was an opt(?) written from me that shared a lot of information. I got a lot of praise I got a lot of brow beating. But, information is power, now the information I shared in that article were not confidential, again those were corporate numbers, entities designed to make a profit for the Nation to create revenue strings to help us provide the services that the Nation's government do. Well to that article, I think we failed. 300 million dollars in ten years and less than maybe one percent return in our investment how is that acceptable. There were many deals brought to the table some good some bad. My opinion, that's just my opinion. You look at the numbers, were they lucrative did they produce some return on an investment, No. There was one deal in 2003–2004 the government I had served with at that time was privileged to serve with, in my opinion beyond it's time but it wasn't

just a government we had a great team create a
deal. Three initials CDX oh that was the worst
deal ever well let me just try to summarize what
the CDX deal was. There was a company that
was selling a lot of acreage a lot of leases on the
Nation and at that time the council said this was
a chance to buy back our leases and do what we
wanted to do for a very long time so the decision
range from no we don't want to do this to yes,
yes, finally we reached understanding we created
a team of individuals who not only veted the deal
but we also did a huge survey to what is under-
neath the ground we're going to spend a lot of
money then we need to know what the return on
the investment is going to be on oil and gas so we
did, we did a reserve study, we hired a team, we
had the utility authority at that time as a section
17 on board helping. We wanted to create a team
it was not about the council. We got the numbers
we were prepared I think at that time we should
maybe go 30–40 million dollars and the Nation
was like ok that's a lot of money but let's see what
happens. Started betting more, more, more well
the land went for over 100 million it was like
ok, put your change away because this is the big
boys stuff. So, it was discussed through the team
well maybe we can joint venture with CDX.
Therefore, now we become a partnership and
not just rely on royalty like rental payments now
we're actually producing, now we're having a lot
of skin in the game we have a stake we're putting
our corporations to work. Well the long short of
it is, we knew we needed to reach an amount of
money, not only a return on our investment but
to really get the things moving with the revenue
string. So, we went to the market, we looked

at the market and the market as you know is vault, up and down who knows what going to happen based on a motion a lot of money can change today and you can make a little bit of money tomorrow. So, we decided ok look, we are looking for certain amount of money. Let's just say if we can do 40 million annual, we are good. So, we decided to hedge which is basically pick a price and regardless if the market went high or low that was our price, we are still getting that amount of money. It worked because we had a margin that we wanted to reach. So, we went to market sold it, got our bonds, our bonds through our triple A rating, the first of its kind for any tribe at that time in the early 2000s. A great amount of credit to all our staff and team for accounting because they looked at that and said you guys have the same credit rating as the city of Las Angles had. Wow! Therefore, we went to market sold the bonds. Now the bonds paid for the Administration building, paid for the Supermarket at that time, the infrastructure down to the east side of town, the Mundo Ranch area, to the joint venture of the Jicarilla Service Unit, it did a lot. We wanted to do that, now we could go to the coffers of the Nation's money, why not use other people's money and make a small payment back to the bond and we did that and it was working. Well in 2006, I did not get voted in, new council comes in got bad information, CDX is bad look at what they did the market is way up here, they basically set the price here and we are losing out on money. So, was that veted at that time after, maybe not. I'll tell you why after they unhedged, we don't want that anymore, because the market is really high, the

216

market fell not only did we lose our safety net we fell to what the market was not only did we lose a lot of money in the deal. Events happen and it was a down ward spiral. Now I am not saying or trying to be negative about the government, the role of a government official in my opinion if they are charged to do business they had had had better create a way to do business that is responsible. Not because I didn't agree, I don't like, or what did they know, No it is about business. We missed a lot of money; we missed getting back that acreage, we lost back on reclaiming wells that could be for the Nation and producing now. Again all proven, I'll make sure you get that information, the team was chastised. Oh yeah they are taking money, we had the Nordhaus Firm and they were labeled, their thieves they are taking money we can prove it, I have yet to see anything that proved that council including me did anything wrong, stole any money, nor did the Nord House steal any money. Therefore, at that time Nord House was working on a breach of trust lawsuit. Took it all away, council took it all away, we are firing Nordhaus. Some firm out of DC was hired. At that time, when I came back in 2013 I was like how do I protect us from ourselves. Because I am not saying the council is dumb, I am not saying that at all. I am simply saying the council has four years to tackle a thousand and one issues and do it right, from laws, current policies, structure, our court structure is failing us and what happens balancing business and laws four years comes and goes just like that who suffers, well not the councilman, but the people and that is wrong.

JANCO was a novel idea and not novel first of its kind and unorthodox. Started out as that idea, we had RFP because we wanted to look at having some outside specialty with legal so we RFP for two types of law firms, oil and gas expertise, taxes and all that and an economic development firm, so we threw out a large net, in house counsel Darlene Gomez did a great job and Paul Holfman on compiling all those set interviews did our homework, did the RPS, did the meeting. We hired a firm called the Rosette Firm. Now it is interesting because here unfortunately the turn gets ugly because not only this outside firm does their job but also JANCO was created. Eight council people voted for it. It started with the vote it was a new ordnance that simply said a couple of things this is the structure of a new holding company that can acquire the assets of the Nation like our section 17s and the government doesn't have to worry about it anymore if they wanted to if not fine. This holding company was designed not only to work with the Nation but with the outside. Buy commercial property use through a capital investment, not Nation's money, but through a capital investment give to the holding company, now they can go after land, after deals. The reason, to provide revenue to the Nation. JANCO was approved we had hired a board through a vetted process again. Large net cased out for experts. We wanted five independence on that board. Why? Because we wanted five people with no ties who had knowledge, but no ties to the Nation. So it would not be emotional, old council people coming in saying oh I don't agree because I didn't do that. It was about people that came in and did their job; we kept two council members on the board for continuity a sitting councilman and a former councilman. However, even at that were the two council members were completely crazy, we still had a majority to keep things moving and it worked. We hired a CEO, the CEO hired people, there was a request from the Nation ok look holding company, everybody voted for, everybody sees the value can we get money. We need an investment, we invested in everything else, what about we invest in something that we finally see as lucrative, we got a 1.6 million dollar investment just for the budget, that's a lot of money, I understand that. Remember this is not a department, this was a skilled group of individuals CEO's, CFO's people who have proven themselves in other business dealings who were able to go out and look at many projects and it was working. Let's bring in the settlement again through accolades, not only through the Rosette Firm because they had connections in DC but being able to hear that. President Obama before he leaves office wants to leave a legacy with the tribes and he wants to settle all breach of trust suits, some tribes got a lot of money. Osage for instance was the largest; they got like 300 million dollars. Their lawsuit was for over a billion dollars. 700 to a billion dollars, they only got like maybe less than a third back, most of the tribes who were in the breach of trust got like a third back. We reached out and said ok, let's find out. Long short of it is and that is another conversation, through a former cabinet secretary under Obama, who left said we could probably get this amount. We got 124 million dollars given to the Nation. Now it is a drop in the bucket for the breech sure but at that time JANCO ran the numbers, and said well it is kind of, like here is a bone Jicarilla. Well that bone if invested properly in a holding company could have had leverage, and it wasn't about using the money, it was about using the money as collateral keeping it in an account and the council could have still seen it still there still shiny. We could have leveraged that and turned investment of 100 million dollars into 200 hundred million dollars instantly and go out and start doing these projects. This is going to sound completely bias and it is not only do I sit on the board and I still sit on the board. The projects that we were doing that are being voted, not me but the experts, I am not an expert but the experts who were doing this that were working for the Jicarilla Apache Corporation and the Jicarilla Apache people were already looking at projects we could have already had a revenue string, proven and I can share that information with you, of at least, on one project a million dollars a month. The responsibility of receiving information and hearing information and I chose my words very carefully on this. New council comes in, they here a story all of a sudden it is bad. All of a sudden, Leon is stealing, accusations made against me, me. Ok sure I get it, part of the game, we had one individual that was completely creating lies and that was an appointed official under this administration that has yet to prove anything. I understand that I know it is new, JANCO did two things and this is where the contention comes in, it separated business and politics. Council you can't tell JANCO what to do. The only thing you can ask is where are your financials and why are you not making a profit. No more oh I need to see your receipts I need to see your mileage. Those little things and I am not saying that are not important, but one may consider that as telling you how to do your job. Simply said this is a mechanism to build wealth, council you as a council member can work on other things so we don't have to worry about building wealth. Another thing, the biggest contention that I have received the only way because of the CDX deal and how council came and killed it, literally killed it and said it was a good thing and turned out to be bad and have never talked about it since. The only way to kill JANCO is through a referendum vote and that means the people kill it. JANCO up and running, a million dollars on just one and there was 30 projects that were on the to do list, that have been clear and vetted. JANCO has been approved by BIA and you are going to heat that it has not been approved by BIA. There are two rules for approval by BIA on an ordinance, BIA approval or 120 days. 120 days came and went, it is a law. It is a Law. JANCO has the ability to be a billion-dollar organization, creating a revenue string to the Nation that could be in the hundreds of millions of dollars. It still has to make money for itself, the reason why it has to keep going after money; it is a business, a fortune 500 company. That is how it is set up. A caliber of people working, including the board. Why do the people get to kill it because if new council comes in or any council comes in, says well I don't agree, and destroys it, we have lost our nest egg. It was not taking any money away from anything it was what I call a gift and investing that gift. Put it in the market, oh we don't want that, give it to the Nation. Put it in the stock market, stock market goes up and down, we probably lost a hundred million dollars yesterday and maybe well gain it back tomorrow, that's the volatility. At least if we kept it here it would have been safe and we could have leveraged on it. The contention why can the people kill it, we are the council, why can't we kill it. We need to know, you will still know, I am just not telling them how to do their job. I will still complain and complain to Leon (me) because I am a board member and a council member, why are you not making money. That should be the only reason to complain. JANCO is on highatouse right now, it's not dead but we have had unfortunately have had to write those letters, my signature is on those letters to fire the corporate officers and say you know what if we don't have any money, the board and I feel it's in the best interest to protect the Nation's assists and of that budget only money and say we have to let you go and we did. The board is stagnate we are still meeting on some stuff, cleaning up the things that were created so we can try and shut down any more money. I have proved numbers showed financials, we hired a CFO for JANCO on purpose the CFO's role is to protect the board and the money. Not work for the board or JANCO, he is almost an independent. He showed numbers, that wasn't good enough. Now Leon is this, why are you on the board, why are you this and this. That's the law, well you be on the board, well no. Ok fine. It is still a struggle and I chose my comments carefully, to me if I made an opinion, shame on me I don't think I threw anybody under the bus those are the discussions, to me the council has a lot more responsibility. You have four years to deal with 1001 things. Our laws our courts are in serious jeopardy, I will say that, "serious jeopardy." The council is still trying to figure out their role. Are we supposed to build wealth, build businesses, are we supposed to work on laws. All of a sudden, four years comes and goes, no one is re-elected or they don't speak a good political game and they don't get whatever and know they are mad. Oh, well that's stupid the council is the worse. We have to be account- able for our vote as well and 30% of people com- ing out and voting is unacceptable. We need everybody to vote and I understand it is tough. I understand people disassociating themselves but why. I don't care, my opinion doesn't matter, and oh, the council is going to do whatever they want. That is only a perception, the council may have seemingly done whatever they wanted but they can't do whatever they want. There is struc- ture and rules in place. There was a resolution approved and for the first time ever if they have done it but it was a team, effort and I credit my colleagues, now and from the past. Especially Lillian and Adrian, but we put a law on the table, what is called council policy. There are some rules a little bit more than title 20. There are things in there that show there is accountability to the gov- ernment. The next thing is meeting minutes. To me that is a no brainer and if I say something out of context, you should come and see me when you read that. You ask me why I voted no; you ask me why I voted yes that is a role of a public servant. That will be forth coming. JANCO is the redeeming feature, everybody who sees it from the outside and even the inside say that sep- arating politics from business is the best way to do it. We have a capitol reserve, a portfolio the

Nation has back in the early '80s, I can imagine the council at that time saying you know what, BIA you're the trustee you are holding our money, no way, we are going to take it and put it in the stock market. That is, I applaud that, that is progressive thinking and scared to death thinking. It is not because Leon wants it; I think we are in preservation mode. All our eggs were in that basket of oil. What are we doing now to build wealth. We have to versify, it has nothing to do with the capitol reserve or the portfolio but have to have 5 or 6 of those portfolios revolving around so we are not just worried about one portfolio. We don't have one treasure chest we need to build through a holding company that is responsible like tribes are doing across the country. Seminoles have taken politics out of business and are doing well. You have many tribes doing things different other than casinos. You have tribes that don't have natural resources like Jicarilla kicking and scraping and they are doing it. Making money, so when somebody says something negative ask them where is the proof show me some the documentation. The corpse the structure of the law, the beauty of separating business and politics. The council not worrying about how to build a buck, but worrying about our failing court system, behavioral health, that needs help for our people who are struggling to survive. Let the council worry about that and let the others take care of business. Is it wrong to create laws where the people are in charge to say we want it or we don't want it. Is it wrong to separate politics and business or was that negative. Did I say anything negative, other than the council needs to work on these laws to support our community and not worry about the dollar.

Why are our entities are they making a profit, or are they supposed to be making a profit. If they are section 17 and JANCO is not a section 17. It is a tribal charter so we can put rules in it. These section 17s were amended and put council is supposed to stay out of the business, it might work. Look at the casino yeah it is in the middle of now where, it provides entertainment but it should still be profitable at least to pay for itself. JACO, look at JACO was our cash cow but what happen to it and the only reason it is surviving because they come to the council and ask for money, they are a section 17 corporations. They should be out there building their own wealth but we have failed because governments have allowed this mentality of we is going to fix it. They can't but for four years if think you're going to fix everything you're fooling yourself and more importantly you are letting down the constituency. You have people who were board members for JACO that may have been on council. Who have given away lots of money to maybe former CEO's who have done not a whole lot for profit and that is acceptable and I am a thief.

JANCO is the redeeming feature and has nothing to do with Leon. Has nothing to do with council, has everything to do with the sustainability, the financial stability the needed, the direness of creating wealth rather than having the council do it, that's it. Let the council work on these section 17, fine but don't get involved with the big things, let the people have it, build wealth, sure we want more per-capita that helps. Let's build more homes, infrastructure, communities; jobs things were are falling short on. Falling short on.

We have a Vision statement, it is as follows, Jicarilla—A Sovereign Nation under the Indian Reorganization Act of 1934, desiring to assume more responsibility to govern our own well-being, protecting the resources of the Nation and creating equal rights to life, liberty and culture where families and businesses thrive.

The Mission statement is, The Jicarilla Apache Nation, in partnership and communication with residents, businesses, and schools is dedicated to faithfully and impartially:

- Providing a safe, healthy, welcoming atmosphere where people can live
- Promoting economic vitality and strategically positioning for the future
- Supporting planned growth and influencing decisions that impact that Nation
- Building an inclusive community with opportunities for all
- Meeting membership necessities through high quality customer service, innovation, a positive work environment, and a commitment to excellence by providing well defined policies and procedures that focus on autonomy and accountability

With the Vision and Mission Statement come goals, strategies and benchmarks but yet we fall short. The Government is getting involved in the businesses of the Nation. This philosophy of the council to act like they can run businesses is and will continue to fail on all endeavors. How? Need I remind you of the last article I wrote for the Chieftain that showed numbers, the amount of money spent on our Section 17 Corporations, over 130 Million dollars in just over ten years! And yet Councils continue to claim they can do better and fix things. All we do is create an exercise in futility and in Four years walk away and say, not my problem until then next election to which now they have a plan. We as voters have to be accountable to our most precious privilege, our right to Vote and lest we forget that Native Americans fought for many civil rights since 1968, that's only forty-nine years. We should all be casting our vote in our local elections and those who do not vote should be held just as accountable for not doing their part. We have had just over thirty percent come out and vote, out of twenty-seven hundred eligible voters, that means less than eight hundred are doing their part. I ask, what part do you need to play in our future? VOTE!

My last big attempt to try and continue serving as a public servant for the Nation was once again unsuccessful. I lost to a guy whom I had called out at a shareholders' meeting. He was a board member, and I actually served with him in my first term, where I had questions I had written about in my op-eds as to the practices of the section 17 accounting practices and lack of ever being audited. As I started asking questions, his comment was, "I don't know why he is asking all these questions. When I was on council, we just listened," a point that was untrue while me and my former colleagues served alongside this particular individual. In fact, many times, he sat silent and rarely provided positive input, well, minus the full-blood comments about people. But I stated, "If the gentleman does not want to participate in debate and help this body, who should be asking questions at this shareholders representative meeting and not just criticize after the fact while they sit in their next office meeting, then they too can join you at lunch since it has been served!" I guess I struck a nerve because the next thing I knew, he had filed against me and was a candidate for the seat I represented. Well, whatever he said in his campaign did the trick. He beat me, and I bowed out gracefully. As I then struggled to finish my term, issues were still red-hot against me, and then the home issue, I was feeling the aftereffects of things and now finally beginning to process these thoughts that I had tried to repress. My last day, I went to my last duly called meeting to then call for adjournment so that the newly elected officials could be installed. I sat at the ceremony trying to look tall and confident, but I was fighting the desire to want to slouch and hang my head. My very last comments were to thank the membership for their confidence in electing me and that sometimes when you treat people with kindness and compassion on a consistent basis, they can depend on you and in turn maybe even create a lifelong friendship. I thanked my two colleagues I had served with for four years and turned to look at each and every one of the newly elected members of the council and wished them congratulations and left, saying to them, "You have a wonderful opportunity in front of you. Do what's right. Use the torch that is being passed to you to light the way and not burn down the house." I recognized some people in attendance and also thanked them for keeping me accountable to all my words and then left the stage to go home.

My time and seventeen years of being associated in the public sector of the Jicarilla Apache Nation and community of Dulce came to a close, and after five losses, I felt I would never be able to serve again. That was a tough thought to process as I still had the stigma I just left, which to me was unfinished because even though I proved in every aspect that I did do my job, I had shared information, and I was not a thief, I knew that my name would continue to be sullied, and my reputation would carry a mark, and then I had to go home and swallow my feelings, put on a happy face, and be the best dad I could be. That part came easy, and I did a pretty damn good job. Ask the kids. Wait, don't ask them!

The last few months of the year were fairly easy to handle because I was still in the loop of the government's dealings, and did

I ever feel like I could still give an opinion as to keep the promotion of holding the government most accountable? I was at the Nation's administration building on business, and I found myself in a conversation as a large group of people congressed outside the meeting chambers, waiting to address their officials about money from the settlement.

Since all funds JANCO had been awarded, the 1.6 million and the 100 million, again only in spirit as it never was deposited in JANCO's account, I was very unhappy that around that time of the JANCO dismantling, the government was supplementing the Nation's operational budget with money from the settlement, and although I voted for the use of funds, it was my duty to make sure the nation had a budget. And since calculations forecasted as shortfall, the only place to get money, quickly, was from the Nation's portfolio, which I personally did not want to ever do, so the only logical and feasible place to get funds for the budget was from the settlement. I was even more upset and then offended because the role of council member for the Nation is to create, promote, and protect the laws and then to create economic development and business opportunities that would create revenue for the many benefits nation members receive, and to kill the one saving grace that could have really helped and then have no contingencies to replace or help avoid the issue that would now be faced annually in trying to establish a operational budget without going to the "piggy bank," what I call the portfolio, was a breach of duty.

I made the comment that if the government was not going to be responsible and not inform the people as to the truth as to what is really going on and then have the audacity to use all the settlement money as a way to pretend everything is fine and dandy is, in my opinion, ludicrous and irresponsible, and then not properly, I was now fuming. If you do not want to be proactive and do your job as a leader and find better ways, like JANCO, to create better-vetted revenue streams, well, I say give the settlement to the people and let them at least do what they want to do with their fair share. There was some grumbling but never when the chambers were never wall-to-wall standing room only. Those big tough comments about tribal members not deserving this money and that all they would do is drink and buy drugs were now null and void as the large group met with their government. It took a couple of hours to listen to the crowd before I asked to be recognized by the chair so that I could read the draft resolution I crafted and prepared in advance of the meeting, to then call for a vote. It was unanimous, and the membership received a very nice holiday bonus from the settlement money, and from my vote all those years ago to hold the federal government responsible for their lack of fiduciary duty that they complete botched, I was happy. Yes, JANCO could have done much more with that investment, but the people were properly compensated in my book and now again in this book.

I was corralled into another meeting about the rumor that there was more settlement money and that the membership was entitled to it. I sat in the back, and I could see two of the sitting officials turn to each other and smile. I kept my composure and just listened. It took strength to just sit there as I heard a few officials try to answer questions. Many of those answers were completely wrong, but I still didn't say a word. I waited for an opportunity to leave the meeting, and when that time came, I quietly slipped out of the meeting. When I got home, I sat on my chair and thought about what I just witnessed. It really bugged me, so I felt, once again, I needed to address my concerns and, in that, also try and share information once again, so I wrote he following op-ed:

> I recently sat in the November 9, 2018 Legislative Council meeting and six Council members, two not in attendance, addressed a petition request to distributing distribute over seven thousand dollars which was also requested to be added to the December 2018 Per Capita distribution. I watched puzzled as Junior and Senior Councilmembers sat motionless and quiet while two freshman members tried to present to the 30 or so members in attendance. When asked about transparency in sharing the Settlement

accounts transactions, it was stated on record that the members are incapable of understanding or receiving information so sit back and ask no questions. I choose to not chime in as I really felt that my comments would not have made any positive impact so my thought was to add some finality, maybe closure to how the settlement came to be, what has happened to the funds as of September and how this settlement could have helped generate millions of dollars for the future financial stability of the Nation. Since early 2000 the Nation officially entered into two breach of trust responsibility lawsuits against the federal government both for the mismanagement and the miscalculation of tribal of funds, oil, gas and timber sales, which were held in trust and were supposed to be able to generate income for the Nation in the from form of sales, interest and other investment strategies to be done by the Department of Interior or Bureau of Indian Affairs to which practices were not handled very responsibly nor was the fiduciary duty of BIA ever practiced, this led to the loss of millions of dollars of potential growth over the time period. The lawsuit addressed the years the accounts were held in trust prior to the Nation taking hold of its own financial future and invested the remaining funds into the Stock market in the 1980s, this is why we have one large nest egg on Wall street. Since then this one nest egg has been the main account that the Nation has depended on to save, fund and preserve for the inevitable future. The lawsuit has gone through a couple of law firms from the time it started with the Nordhaus law firm. Nordhaus began gathering financial records from the Nation and BIA, many of the records were held in storage and took time to request and compile complete records but the tumultuous task was done. When things change, ideology and ignorance ensue, so the 2006 newly elected council unfortunately assumed, speculated and then fired the Nordhaus firm because they heard that the firm was stealing, a false charge that has never been proven but nonetheless, the change was made, then a new law firm was hired, the Holland and Knight law firm. The lawsuit continued and there began an exchange of information and the H&K law firm took the lead including subpoenaing individuals within the Nation, like the Nation President, Controller and our illustrious local BIA Superintendent. The process continued and the Nation was in years of being in litigation to which the Nation lost a Supreme Court decision loss, 7–1 on a claim that the Nation should be allowed to view trust related documents held by the Department of Interior. Regardless, this was a setback on the basis of this lawsuit but the legal bill kept climbing, around the mid twenty-million-dollar mark with no real victory in sight and even if we did win, was the Nation going to see a payment and by when? In 2016, I was told, by some individuals associated with people in high places, that President Obama, before the end of his second and final term was going to fulfill his promise to elevate the status of Indigenous people, by settling as many Tribal breach of trust lawsuits. Once this information was learned, calls were made to verify before reacting and a meeting was set up between former Secretary of the Department of Interior Ken Salazar and myself to discuss, one, that this was true and two, what and how did the Nation

needed to do to benefit from this once in a life-
time opportunity. Although nothing is guaran-
teed, we discussed that this was factual and that
there was a very high chance that we could finally
end this chapter of Nation's lawsuit of the Federal
Government. One big issue I had was that the
Nation had already spent over twenty million
plus on this lawsuit and this could have gone on
at the cost of millions of dollars more but if there
was a way to stop this and gain some restitution
then by all means this needed to be discussed by
all ten members of the government. Philbert Vigil
Sr., Bilford Vicenti Sr., William Muniz, Martin
Perea, Wainwright Velarde, Adrian Notsinneh,
Lillian Veneno and myself met with Ken Salazar,
now a partner of the Wilmerhale Law firm out
of Washington D.C. and Mr. Robert Rosette of
the Rosette law firm, in the chambers to listen,
debate, strategized and agree to go after a settlement. One of the biggest kudos we did, was to
request from our new law team, the need to hire
them but pay all legal fees based on a success rate
rather than by billable hours. A success rate is an
agreement between firm and client on a percentage of what can be charged for legal services, this
ensured that the law firms obtained the highest
payout, in our case of any legal judgment at a
percentage of the award rather than be billed for
every meeting, phone call, email or those high
reimbursable costs, after all, the more money the
Nation received the more the law firm would be
able to receive, so we agreed to a three percent
success rate, negotiated I might add, down from
six percent. All in agreement, we moved forward and just over two months for the Nation
accepted one hundred and twenty-four million

dollars with ONLY three million dollars paid, based on the agreed three percent success rate, paid to the two reputable law firms who were paid one and a half million dollars apiece, a very small drop in the bucket considering the prior legal costs to date. It is important to note that "The Settlement" was not for one hundred and twenty-eight million dollars and we did NOT pay twenty-eight million dollars in legal fees for this settlement!

This Legislative Council, named above, also recognized the need to address and then create new standards in how the Nation and Legislative council deal with our existing and any new tribal businesses. It is not only irresponsible but disheartening to have so many short falls within our enterprises and corporations in which there is NO barriers to stop government encroachment which includes the utilization of the "good ole boy" system which continues to come at the cost of losing millions and millions of dollars. Our discussions allowed us to decide that we needed to sit down and have a retreat in order to properly come up with a growth plan not only to stop the financial bleeding but to generate many more financial nest eggs creating financial stability well into the next twenty years. Whether you know or agree or disagree, the oil and gas industry, which directly affects the Nation, has been and still is in a recession and we have seen and felt significant drops in our assets which is can impact the wealth, making things like our budget uncertain in sustaining the current benefits of the membership.

In order to address the Nation's current and future financial crisis and make sure there was a huge barrier between politics and business, the above Legislative Council, approved Title 26, JANCO (Jicarilla Apache Nation Corporation) to finally have a better plan which also had the highest of standards and accountability also built into this code, so, there was no room for any white-collar crime. This also meant that the Nation would no longer be solely dependent on an ebb and flow industry like oil and gas and now there was a strong plan to increase the amount of money needed for both for the People and the needs of the people, like increased Per capita, more homes with no mortgages, health care, infrastructure and new and improved municipal buildings. Don't get me wrong, the Oil and Gas industry has sustained the Nation for decades but there is so much more opportunity outside the boundaries of the Nation that not only would create stronger revenue streams but could make the Nation a much stronger powerhouse politically in Santa Fe and Washington D.C. Although there is a desperate need to separate business from politics, The Legislative Council still was still involved and to some degree maintained some control over JANCO because they had the power to review, appoint and find vetted individuals who would make up the JANCO Board of Directors and the LC also maintained the power to transfer or allocate any Nation capital or assets to JANCO, so that revenues earned were much more profitable allowing more money to flow back to the Nation for the benefit of the People, including the creation of jobs and better opportunities like providing a funding source for entrepreneurs. The above named Legislative Council then took measures to adopt processes to appoint to the first Board of Directors of JANCO by sending out a country wide request for proposals for proven, background checked professionals which were then selected. Over twenty submissions were received most all applicants had proven records of performance and experience in leading their respective tribes and businesses with financial growth and expansion. Once the Board was officially approved, by LC resolution, the work began and the new board set out to first find a Chief Financial Officer to make sure there was financial and fiduciary accountability demanded by all JANCO members including the Board, next there was a need to find a CEO, Chief Executive Officer, whose responsibility was to lead this new innovative corporation of JANCO to expand and grow, reporting to the Board and more importantly making money securing the Nation's wealth. The Board needed a CEO and hired Allen Bedell who then hired COO, Chief Operating Officer, Shannon Jones and Stephean Becker who was the corporate controller and hit the ground running by immediately looking for new business opportunities and begin the restructuring process of existing companies owned by the Nation. Shannon Jones recall's the many new opportunities and wanted to share just some including the discussion of engaging in one of many investment opportunities in the Oil and Gas industry that initially was being presented to the Nation's government, known as the Branta II deal, and this exploration company proposing doing business with the Nation's government that would have resulted in approximately around the amount of $76,000,000 to 250,000,000 million dollars of net revenue to the Nation. However once the JANCO team evaluated the financials of the deal and reworked the contract including increasing the ownership percentage of the Nations portion, this deal was then forecasted for the Nation, through JANCO, to make approximately $425,000,000 million dollars of net revenue.

Additionally, JANCO looked at all the current Oil and Gas companies doing business on the Nation lands that had fallen in violation of the production agreements they had agreed to which was to drill on the land rather than cap and abandon wells stopping the flow of oil, gas and money. JANCO begun reviewing and discussing the need to recall these contracts, if done, would have increased the number of wells under the control of the Nation. New technologies were also being looked at to purchase that would have then allowed the JANCO to begin producing both diesel and high-octane fuels in large quantities. Initial projections showed approximately 2,500 gallons per wellhead daily. This would have led to the development of many new jobs, which would include a JANCO owned trucking enterprise that would haul the fuels produced. Along with the development of this additional enterprise the corporation had begun looking at plans to development a gas fired, wind and solar plant to produce green energies that would be tied into the national power grids and allowed the Nation to become one of the first tribal nations to produce sustainable green energies. In order to accomplish this monumental endeavor the development of a small city would have been established down near the Tipi's Casino area to support the management and daily working operations of the energy plant. As word began to reach other tribes that JANCO was looking for investment opportunities, vetting processes began as well as the negotiations to fund several tribes as they moved to increase their businesses. The investments were all limited to 24-month contracts that would generate large monthly returns to the Nation. The tribe's prominence was quickly spread among the investment network and we were being selective as to what opportunities that were the best advantage to grow the Nation's wealth safely and with minimal risk. This would place the Jicarilla in the position to become the developers of one of the first nations to create a fully tribally owned investment lenders to other nations. JANCO had also begun the search to purchase our own banking network to further the growth of the Jicarilla Nation. The Executive officers had been approached by private companies to loan monies to expand current profitable companies which would increase the overall wealth of the Nation. This not only included interest on the loans but also royalty monies being paid to the Nation as the companies' products were being sold for a period of time after the maturation of the initial interest loans were paid. JANCO also looked at the development of current holdings that the Nation already owned to maximize earnings on these respective properties. One such property was the Chama Land and Cattle Company located in Chama. This property only showed gross revenues of $4.5 million dollars in the last year that we were in business in 2016. The payment back to the Nation for that year was $250,000 dollars. The expansion of other capabilities on the property could have easily surpassed the previous revenues to bring the Nation millions more in revenues as well increasing many jobs to the members of the Nation. These projections placed revenues well beyond $25 million dollars with the integrity of the property being protected and preserved. There were also opportunities to work with and invest in many potential business opportunities including plans with the neighboring community of Pagosa Springs. The leaders in both the town and the county had extended tracts of lands for the building of a large shopping plaza that the Nation would have owned for generations to come. One project that was discussed was the building of a 28-acre Votech Technical School, which would have provided an opportunity for both learning and skilled trade jobs for both communities. It also would have produced workers to develop affordable housing developments that were being planned on lands that the corporation was being provided by the town and county leadership. These are just a few of the many opportunities that were looked at and evaluated by JANCO. In addition, the many new opportunities that JANCO was evaluating, the team also began the process of restructuring the existing companies owned by the Nation. The team started with JAECO, the Nation's oil and gas company. The team completed a detailed review of JAECO's, revenues, expenses and assets and began developing a plan to restructure the company. The JANCO team was planning on reviewing each of the Nation's existing companies develop a restructuring plan for each company, and then execute those plans. The goal was to first stop the financial bleeding and then turn the companies into profitable entities that would be able to contribute to the Nation's wealth. It was because of the settlement JANCO was proceeding, the initial budget was presented, discussed and approved by the LC at that time and if not rescinded, the settlement money was approved by resolution to been invested into JANCO, the Nation's new holding company and could have been able to leverage another hundred million, now making the coffers of JANCO over two hundred million dollars, to make millions of dollars monthly. Not only would the investment be returned to the Nation but also the opportunity to build wealth would have created these much-needed revenue streams.

Unfortunately, JANCO was shut down with no warning by then President Wainwright Velarde and then concurred by the newly elected Legislative Council members, William Julian, Jr., Shane Valdez, Sherryl Vigil and Incumbent and initial voter William Muniz. The loss of revenues to the Nation cannot be measured in terms of monies but in the loss of jobs to tribal members, free homes and other mutual growth of our community of Dulce, halting the building of any legacy in avoiding more money issues like we are encountering now. There was rumor, speculation and lies told about JANCO, many came from the government but no one made anno attempt to ask questions nor ask for a copy of the newly approved Title 26, so a vote was made to kill the concept and JANCO itself with no replacement plan or strategy! In an attempt to slander my name, the newly elected LC targeted me and made-up stories that I was stealing and squandering money given to JANCO. Well as I said earlier, JANCO's code was created out of all the negative issues our current corporations and enterprises currently encountered, including mismanagement of funds, breaching corporate charters and other questionable practices but rather than call a meeting to ask questions of JANCO's Board, controller and Chief Financial Officer, all who passed a rigorous criminal and corporate background checks, the LC paid thousands of dollars for TWO forensic audits! It is my pleasure to report that there were NO findings and every dollar that was invested by the Nation into JANCO was properly accounted for, in fact both audits proved that any and all allegations of impropriety on me, were found to be false, by the way the remainder of all funds left in JANCO's bank accounts were returned to the Nation, might I add most likely the largest return of money given from a Nation corporation, back to the Nation. At no time were the JANCO officers brought in to give any explanation or update of any business plans that the corporation officers.

One could say that the Nation won the lottery and in doing so did not share accurate information or any strategies but rather acted like there were no issues with our current finances that are only derived from Oil and Gas and the one nest egg in the stock market. The one hundred- and twenty-million-dollar breach of trust settlement instead was used to offset the Nation's budget, around the thirty-six-million-dollar mark for the calendar years of 2017 and 2018 and was being looked at for the 2019 budget shortfall again with no strategy to preserve or growth this new money, especially after dismantling JANCO, as far as I know, there was no regard or respect of current colleagues, predecessors or the people, so it was because of this shady tactic, using all the settlement money to offset the budget, it was time that the membership needed to know the truth, I said "if you are going to act like everything is fine and you are going to use all the settlement money… let's give money out to the people!" Which was done in December of 2017 and two more times this year. You're welcome! This money distribution was not done because of the election, it was not done to retaliate, it was done because it was the right thing to do which is why you need to demand information from your government.

Merriam Webster defines Spite as petty ill will or hatred with the disposition to irritate, annoy, or thwart (to treat maliciously), it also defines rumor as talk or opinion widely disseminated with no discernible source. In 2015 I wrote an article highlighting the need to find better ways to separate how economic development and how all business is conducting by the Legislative Council, to which I also received flack for but it showed that the Nation's government could not, has not and did not have any understanding or concepts of business strategies to warrant any returns on these investments, at that time in 2015, the Nation's LC had given over one hundred and thirty million dollars, within the span of that ten-year period, to our own Corporations and enterprises with less than one percent returned to the Nation's coffers, that means that over that time, the Nation received one million dollars from that one hundred and thirty million, in the real world, those corporate members would be fired or in jail. Strong leaders understand how to balance emotion with reason and then in turn make decisions that positively impact others, all financial resources, respecting our customs and our most important Natural resources, the people they represent. Making good decisions in difficult situations is no small feat, these types of decisions involve change, create a possible perception of uncertainty, anxiety, stress, and most certainly create unfavorable reactions of some. We have adopted a democratic process by electing tribal leaders but we should always keep in mind that politics should never be based on party affiliation, size of families or hearsay and ego but that the role of an elected official is based on the concept and action of a republic, to which the ultimate power lies with you the membership who vote for officers and representatives who are responsible to you!

We have to understand that it is both a privilege and right for all tribal members to request and receive Jicarilla Apache Nation government information deemed public information! For any one Council member or should I say public servant of the Nation, to go on record and state that you as constituents cannot handle receiving information because they fear you will share it, is not only disrespectful but irresponsible! I say this because the oath of office is not just a sound bite, it is a promise, a swear to the highest of powers, God and you, that now appointed, elected officials will hold themselves to the highest standards of the constitution, ordinances and all laws with no bias or ignorance because of family or friends or any discourse because "they heard" or "think" and refuse to ask any questions to not only hear firsthand but assist in any decisions to help make better decisions rather than have spite tell them

243

they are not to stand on their own convictions. We have twenty-six Articles with various subsections within our Constitution and twenty-four Titles, again with various sections, also known as Ordinances that are permanent law and thousands of resolutions that are temporary law and although my opinion are acted like memos rather than the substantive use of the law but I digress but more importantly our current laws were created for the best interest and integrity of the Nation's government and members.

Within the comprehensive laws we have both an article within the Nation's constitution and title, of our permanent law, that specifically addresses the of sharing of information, they Article 10 and Title 19 Section 3. No one is above the law and denying tribal members the opportunity to request information for the purposes of transparency simply to hold the government accountable, is a huge abuse of power! If elected officials are saying you elected us so trust us but we will keep you in the dark, I have to ask if we are becoming lawless, so maybe rather than breech the oath of office and Nation's laws, rescind all laws, at least that way the government will quit consciously breaching the law and blaming you or others in doing so! Now that may not be feasible or responsible, but we should not accept this very bad practice of don't ask don't tell. We know that there are tribal members who have the right intention and skill to honor the oath of office and All ideology and professional background should be welcomed because the beauty of our electoral process is the diversity it's brings but never forget, the only "power" a Council member has is to follow and enact law

and approve a presidential budget and always and
only in a duly called meeting set by the President!

It's time to Request a copy of your constitution and ordinances, there are even copies on
CD-ROM for your computers, the most important thing we can do is educate ourselves about
our laws, sure we voted for a person to represent
us as a government official but the same demands
made of the membership should be more so of
any official, remember, an informed tribal member is powerful tribal member.

I had never before used names in such a personal manner, but I
was angry, and the membership had a right to know at least my side
as a sitting leader. I also thought my swan song should be more in
your face, and then the membership would want to take the imitative
and ask questions of me or the government, but nothing much happened. My article gained no momentum, and I grew more depressed
and beaten. It was a matter of time, but as I predicted, my name
was once again being tossed around and now by the newly elected,
some of whom I had been extremely helpful with as far as including their input in reports and speeches during lobbying efforts or
helping create artwork using Photoshop and many other things that
I had problem helping with, and I never said no, and never did I
not ask for input when needed. But I also knew the mentality was
to criticize without directly asking questions and then relying on a
group that were now the seniors was also not going to be favorable.
I was really letting their comments get to me, and at the same time,
I tried to ignore because I knew what was true and not, and that
could be proven with some research of the meeting records, but it
began to pick at me. I felt I needed to say something because what
I was also hearing was that I was going to be brought up on charges
for JANCO. I thought bullshit, so I wrote this and had a hard copy
delivered to each sitting member of government.

I hope you are well and I hope I have a few seconds to capture your attention. I continue to hear that I have been charged with stealing money and that you all, the LC, were going to press charges on me?! This stated by one of your new sitting colleagues this morning.

Well, I say please pursue because if you had any factual information showing I was a thief, you would have done so already! I also ask that if you do press charges then let's do so in a vetted environment that will give the most credence to fairness and impartiality because your opinions unfortunately have already put you in a category of slander and it's a shame that the draft Ordinance addendum to the Criminal code of Defamation was not passed because we could have tested it out on the already made comments from you leaders, both publicly and stated on the record about me, which is I am told accessible by request of meeting minutes to the Nation's Secretary.

I also ask then if you pursue charges then let's also put on the table the Special Investigator report that was done in August and completed in September of last year on the allegation of Abuse of Power as well as all audits of JAECO (Jicarilla Apache Energy Corp) and ANC (Apache Nugget Casino).

Lest you think I am crying foul because I lost the election, I assure you I am not but maybe I should honored to continue to be in your minds when you have so much work to do. You know I am completely accountable and transparent and if you scoff, that is just a defense mechanism making you feel less guilty of what I am saying in this email.

I have not once defamed you nor spouted any rumor about you, I know what I say and how I say and who I say it to and if you want to have a grown-up professional conversation, then invite me to the table, otherwise try to remember your roles and responsibilities as well as your experience as professionals! Your time as an official is winding down and you still have a wonderful opportunity to build a new not sit idle and point the finger, you have done that far too long and at some point, you might get tired of making me your scapegoat just start now by doing your job.

Have a wonderful weekend, as a professional curtesy of a former colleague, I hope I get a response from you.

All my best!

I had not heard any more about my name and JANCO after the letter, and I would be lying if I said I was still not angry. In fact, now that I had more downtime, I tried to deal with all the emotions that began to reach up out of the layers of dirt I tried to bury them under. I had stayed on the high road while I was still working and even managed to hide from the infidelity and estrangement from the marriage. I had not filed for divorce for over eight months, and it wasn't because I was feeling like I wanted to reconcile, but what I now know was that I was trying to keep some harmony with the person I dedicated my life to, and sure, there were issues, and I was passive aggressive and moody and never received affection, but I still felt that I was committed. And when she moved out at my request because the clandestine behavior was not working for me, I even bought her a Keurig coffee maker as an apartment-warming gift. By the time I actually understood my lack of trying and taking things for granted in the marriage, it was too late. Choices were made, and that time made me face even more reality as a man, dad, husband, and someone who lived in a glass house as a public servant. I remained respectful to the ex-wife and never fought for sole custody. I asked for joint, and even when I became the sole provider for the kids, I didn't even ask for child support. The very short moments of rage were quickly replaced with clarity and avoidance of what I call ripple effects. Any negative behavior could have shown the kids that I not only was being hypercritical but also continue down the path of unhealthy coping, so in my mind, I needed to be the example of what I was trying to teach the kids, even when bad things happen. But facing, communicating, and then doing your best to act in a positive manner or not react in a negative could keep us all grounded, and that way, we could be able to process emotions in a much healthier way even in their adult lives.

I endured and made it through that tough time, even when I thought I was losing the battle. It also made me shed some pounds and begin to be a better man with my words to the constituents I dedicated part of my life to and especially to the kids. It was challenging, and together we grew as I gave my permission to them to also call me out on my bullshit and attitude, and boy did they. So to me, that showed that they were processing and learning, and it is a wonderful feeling to know that even your children can be treated as equals and not just people who, because they are younger, have to abide by all my rules just because I am Dad and, even more so, when I was inconsistently not following these same rules of the home.

I still was in a pretty big depression about the issues from work, I mean my former job. I tried to be fine, but I was still asking questions about hearing my name and that I was stealing and that I was a bully because my only agenda was to get my friends' jobs so that they too could take from the Nation. It was preposterous, and I took it extremely personal, which in retrospect may have been me adding more fuel to an already moot issue. Before we left office, I was feeling spiteful and let my ego get the best of me. When elected leaders leave office, there is a chance they take their work vehicles with them. I guess it's a reward for doing a great job, although extremely questionable as to job performance. I really could see how anger gets the best of a person and then makes one feel like they are owed. I had not taken my work vehicle from my first term, nor did I take my work vehicle from the term I had filled. In fact, the only thing I had requested from my first term was the laptop I was assigned because it was becoming obsolete, and it had all my documents on it. I guess after all the accusations of me being a thief, the home issues and the continued cloudiness of just trying to keep walking straight finally made me crack a bit. I wrote an executive order for the president to sign, awarding the vehicles we were assigned as donations for doing the job. I wrote the executive order to also try one more attempt at showing the allowances that the offices of the president could do to further help the causes of employees and departments, and the other famous Jicarilla term would hopefully gain less and less power, which was "I have to ask the council." I had told my colleagues of my intention and received no qualms. The document was signed, and the registrations were transferred, and for the first time in my political tenure, I had a capital purchase. I wasn't all that proud of my actions and thoughts that led me to thinking of such a thing with the executive order vehicle request, but I told myself, "Fuck it," which was a phrase I rarely used in my business life because it never ever fared well for me and was always bad for business. Case in point, tax season came around, and I was going through the mail so I could gather all my tax info to file. Lo and behold, I received a 1099 showing that I had earned income of over $16,000. I was confused and was good about saving receipts, and I couldn't figure out where this amount came from. I sent my tax information to my tax preparer, and it was then that I found out I now owed taxes on over $15,000. I quickly called my tax preparer and said, "How? Why? What is going on?" Turns out, my former colleagues recanted on the executive order donation and gave me one last "Fuck you." I knew there were no freebies, and although shocked, I paid the amount, and therefore, the right thing was done. If I wanted my vehicle, I had to pay for it, and it was the right thing, and I could then feel better because deep down, I was free from the feeling like I was trying to sneak something by the system that I loved and respected.

I was now Mr. Mom, and I actually loved it. I would clean, cook, and have more open dialogue with the kids. I was learning how to play guitar and even playing drums and signing with a band. Things were getting on track. I even joined a Facebook page that a community member created. That was a private page for the purposes of sharing what was going on in the community, but it would soon become a platform for banter, criticism, and trolling of people and politics. I actually was pretty happy I found a place where could chime in when I read posts that either asked questions or were on the cusp of becoming a rumor. I thought, *What better place to engage in good debate, possibly even educate membership on some of the questions floating around?* I actually felt that I was bringing some good, and I did know that I wasn't just going to be giving my rant or an ignorant opinion. I would quote laws and give background information thinking it was helping people in an attempt to gain some feeling of buy-in so that there was a means to want to help themselves. And this to me was a good avenue to have and to share insight, especially since the government was notorious for not sharing information, and maybe a means to show that I was not who I was being labeled to be. That part is self-serving, but I also really just wanted to have the members know more and in turn educate themselves to form better-informed questions to the government. My joyous feeling of helping didn't last very long. I soon found out that people just wanted to complain, and no matter what I said, shared, or tried to inspire, it gained no momentum. I decided to accept that my mental status was more important, and I needed to rebuild what I let crumble and that this particular Facebook page was not the way to find sanity. So I wrote this message and unfollowed the group.

> Saying something for the sake of creating angst is not only irresponsible but doesn't do a whole lot of good for positive outcomes and it only really speaks to the character of a person and faking it never really works out as an advantage. There have been many comments made about loving the Nation and all people, well, then maybe it's time to prove that, If you really love your Jicarilla people then could serve as an open, positive platform to help share and show others what is going on and how they can be empowered

to also help, anything less than is just an act and a bad one at that. There are many here on this page who want to know, to see, read and understand, simple dialog that either informs or inspires!

I applaud anyone who steps up and does something, not just those who run for office, or have served in office but those who work hard, do what needs to be done and ask for nothing in return! This by the way is not about being a candidate is really about promoting and practicing the GOLDEN RULE for the benefit of our community and not just talk about it! It seems fairly Easy to troll, sitting behind a screen acting like you're doing something but that's just an act, a facade derived from insecurity which speaks to the character of a person and karma will find you, just remember to not play the victim when it does.

If you really care, then take a stand, listen, learn and understand the concept of "it takes a village!" Ask questions as to how the many variables make up the big picture that have provided positive outcomes, then ask how you can help! You will then see for yourself how you are adding value and not just more confusion. perpetuating the same poison you say you are rallying against.

Some critics here, have not once ever personally had a one on one conversation with me but those who did were treated with respect and there were a lot I conversed with who still contact me today and I am most humbled and appreciative for that!

We ALL should be just as accountable as you are demanding of leadership, you too have a responsibility to NOT be mediocre, you to have a responsibility to help your fellow member regardless of your opinion, that means placing others first and providing some good by helping make things better including squashing hearsay and rumor! If you are wanting instant gratification and easy answers, well you might be disappointed, good things take hard work and effort with the dedication deserving of being a leader in your own right. The rules are there, use them to show and teach them so we avoid the same cycle of behaviors.

I show up every election because I know how to help and despite losing, I still show up always willing and ready to help, I challenge you to do the same!

You do not have to like what I say, you do not have to agree with what I say but I do try to bring facts that are based from valid sources either be it from research or our own existing rules/laws and the allowance of exercising the rules/laws with the clear intention of positive outcomes! There are NO instant answers or easy answers for that matter, I can say and answer because I have done the hard work and made your commitment to be able to say my words but it will still need hard work and dedication from ALL of us to make sure what is built is maintained with the understanding of why, that way there are no surprises, only momentum forward!

Lastly, I used to feel that I had to comment on every issue, to help but I can see from prior comments, there not landing and that's ok, I will still do my best to inform with what I know and there's a saying, "the biggest communication problem is some do not listen to understand, they listen to reply" and there are a lot of People

here who are watching and though they may be
silent, they definitely are listening!

During the downtime, I was very surprised to know that my
story had struck some interest in a young director from France.
About four years ago, during a snowstorm, a vehicle carrying a film
crew was passing through Dulce, and because it was dark and snow-
ing, they decided to stay the night and ended up at the only hotel in
Dulce. They went to bar to get something to eat, maybe have a drink
and relax before leaving the next morning. There at the bar, they
met my brother. My brother is such a strong extrovert that he could
initiate into any conversation and then be welcomed to sit and talk
more, and that was what he did. They talked, and he shared some
information about Dulce and, by the end of their conversation, had
went home and delivered some food he had prepared for dinner that
evening. Somewhere along her journey, she felt a connection with
Dulce and wanted to film a project here, and my brother had told me
about his meeting, and I told him to pass my contact info along, and
he did, and she contacted me. I asked about her project. She shared
her vision and her connection she made during her first stop that
night during the snowstorm, and I was more than happy to assist in
any way I could to help with her project.

While serving in public relations, I had written executive orders
for other film crews to film on the reservation, always felt that it was
a positive to share the wonderful history and even maybe inspire students to try their hand in filmmaking and at the very least see how
this craft was done. The only one unsuccessful in procuring permission was for a show that chronicled extraterrestrial events and other
myths and conspiracy theories. The host was none other than former
wrestler, movie star, and governor of Minnesota, Jessie Ventura, a
very cool guy, and we even joked about wrestling. I'm a big guy, and
he was a big guy but really cool to have met him and chat with him
on politics. I wrote an order, again sharing what my intention was to
my colleagues, for this new director, and she had permission to film
throughout the reservation.

During her trip back to Dulce, I had made sure she was both safe and sound by making sure she had chaperones just in case she was confronted about why she was filming. She had brought a camerawoman and sound engineer. I figured she was in great hands as I had told people of her intentions and that she was allowed to film throughout the reservation and made sure she had a copy of the signed executive order. I can't exactly recall when we actually sat down in person and talked, but I shared my background of living on the reservation at young age, then my parents uprooting to attend college. I told her of my elementary days as a bully, and then when we moved and I began middle school, I felt I was being punished and shown that my bully mentality was not good and that I became an introvert day 1 of middle school. I mentioned my high school days and working in a blue-collar job and felt that I was not tough enough to hang, so I went to school in Florida. I talked about moving back to El Paso after graduation and then finding the only job I could, which was working in a gentleman's club as a bouncer and then disk jockey, then into radio and eventually back to Dulce, where I said I would never ever move to. I told her about being an accountant and not loving that but then found the beauty of politics and the ugliness of wearing the label of politician and then having the brand seared into my skin of half-breed. I said, "Haff-breed," using a Native accent. Somehow, she must have been interested or impressed because, all of a sudden, her vision for her film changed because I was going to be the main character of her film, with my life being the storyboard setting. What a trip! They filmed. The kids, my brother, and I followed direction, and she was very impressive to watch. All of the crew were just fantastic, and they filmed a movie, a documentary that would later be shown at the Paris Film Festival. Well, that is until the pandemic shut down the world.

Once again, the Nation would find itself in yet another special election for the office of president. The candidate who beat me in the first special election resigned from office, so there was a vacancy for office of president. I debated running for the chair but felt it important to keep taking a stand, pursuing the passion I found with politics and a desire to push a positive, empowering, accountable agenda. I knew, I felt, that if people saw consistencies in protocols, rules, and the replacing of condensation with kindness and good faith, there could be real buy-in and therefore create strong morale within the workplace, but by this time, I was also becoming more and more cynical. I had run positive empowering campaigns before and still fell short but was also proud as to the same number of voters who saw something in me and stuck by me in all the elections. That number was consistently around three hundred, and that to me was not only a great indicator that people desired, themselves, positive consistencies but saw that I could do my best to promote and help deliver. I decided that even though I was out of office for several months, I felt strong enough to step forward and try once again to win an election, and by this time, I was beaten down more than ever but wanted to keep sharing the same message from prior campaigns because I knew that I couldn't promote consistency if I was not following the same strategy myself, so I wrote this:

Good Citizens Who Don't Vote, Elect Bad Politicians! Here's What's Really Going On And What This Means For You And Me

I wrote the article on integrity not to complain or to climb a top my soapbox but to remind us all that we as a community deserve fairness and the highest of standards. Trust is the most important ingredient in any relationship! Trust is something to be expressed not only from the government but all members and with Trust comes honesty and honesty should never be censored. When we hear trust, the first reaction is to let our ego's lash out trying to make ourselves feel better, when were here honesty we try and argue, complain and blame others again to make ourselves feel better. Honesty must be the highest priority and we should not ignore the power this gives us to never forget our place and our roles and responsibilities to ourselves and people around us. We have been fooling ourselves thinking that we have to ignore conflict by ignoring honesty because we feel that we have to please everyone because we don't want to create conflict because we fear relationships will fall apart, instead we sugar coat, or accept and then are subject rumors. Conflict is rewarding because without conflict there can be no trust. Conflict exists to show those who are truly here for us, unconditionally, and those who are here for their own benefit. There is an old saying…"no one trusts a yes person!" For a relationship to be healthy we all must be willing and able to both say and hear no! Without this agreement and understanding, boundaries break down which then allows those negative values to dominate others!

I Trust You

I am writing to let you know a little about me. I have been proud and privileged to work as a public servant for the Nation and through this experience have learned many things from my colleagues—some what to do, and some what not to do including accepting honesty. I credit my former 2002–2006 colleagues, including and especially my "mentor," Mr. Merlin Tafoya Sr. to whom I extend my most sincere thanks and gratitude, as well as those colleagues I had the privilege to serve with more recently, Mr. Notsinneh and Mrs. Veneno. We took an oath to uphold our Nation's laws and policies and while our positions were not always popular and even condemned, at times, they were appropriate because they followed our Nation's laws. Although some took issue with this mandated practice, most embraced it and were grateful to know that they would be provided with due process and treated with fairness.

Together, We Can Make a Change For the Better and Do So With Integrity

So with that, the Office of the President deserves a leader who can be trusted and to embrace, promote and execute the letter of the Nation's law "to a T," and not circumvent based on emotion or political motives.

Article V, Section 1 of our Constitution provides that **"[t]he powers of the government of the [Nation] are divided into three distinct departments: the legislative, the executive and the judicial; and no person or group of persons charged with the exercise of powers properly belonging to one of these departments shall exercise any of the powers properly belonging to either of the others, except as this constitution or an appropriate Tribal Council enactment, may otherwise expressly direct or permit."**

Despite this clear language, we have allowed the encroachment of these powers by past and present leaders to tarnish and blur the laws and our Nation. We deserve a leader who can un-blur lines but also be the bridge to make sure accountability is of the highest of standard. I have been asked to put my name in for the remainder of this Presidential term and, frankly, I have been on the fence. I personally went through a lot in the last two years of my Legislative Council term, enduring the slander, being "black balled" and the subject of various attacks on my character from the current Council.

I can honestly say that it has been firm commitment and allegiance to perform my professional and personal endeavors with integrity, which allowed me to remain professional and stay on the "high road" without straying off the path of honesty and righteousness. I have come to enjoy my life as a single father, being home to cook, clean and laugh with my children. I have learned to accept challenges and adversities in my life and choose to embrace my shortcomings, stop complaining and take action that has given me a much more empowering and optimistic outlook on life. I have even begun to play drums in a band and have occasionally shared an adult beverage with people at Trophies Lounge. I have no problem living in a glass house. However, I do not want to change who and what I am. I know the importance of commitment and I can serve effectively and competently as President of the Jicarilla Apache Nation, with a level of integrity and dignity the Office deserves.

I'm not quite sure which direction to go. What would you do in my situation?

I have been fully prepared to sit out of the upcoming 2020 elections and possibly the 2024 and I would have never predicted another vacancy of the office of Jicarilla President, but this is a very important election aside from the short time frame to finish this term. So, my final question to you is this, "are you willing to support and elect me to serve as President, if, yes, then I am asking for your vote and as a token of good faith and allegiance of your commitment for effective leadership, good governance, adherence of the Nation's constitutional laws and most importantly to ensure that our government serves with integrity; and to pledge your vote as informed members to become engaged, proactive, empowered, and informed in the matters of governmental affairs, in order to promote goodwill, and understand the importance of the economic wellbeing and security of our Nation and its members.

I have good news and bad news.

I know there will be those critics and naysayers who will condemn my letter and even attack me shamelessly on rumors. However, this is not just about me, your pledge to vote shows that you are ready to deserve a government that is no longer tarnished and deceitful and that we are all finally ready to take a stand with a candidate who is objective, who will urge you to ask questions and seek the truth, who will communicate and share information from convened meetings, speak out against the practice of spreading rumors based on hearsay, discourage retaliation based on emotion and retribution, and most importantly, inspire us all to be proactive citizens of our beautiful community.

Here's what's really going on and what this means for you."

I think we can all agree that the future is our children. As such, why are we waiting to promote—or even demand—accountability? It is important to state that no one person can fix all our problems but having a leader that recognizes the difference between good and bad problems is one way to help ensure fairness for all and to abide and stand for the laws of the Nation. Today is your day to help stand in unity with a strong, open-minded leader who can serve as the vessel needed to remind and be reminded that **PEOPLE UNITED** can create a stronger, healthier and thriving future. If we can get one thousand members or more to stand and vote with us, we can show that the people are the real power and that they have chosen and will stand and support a leader who has proven to be and will continue in the future to be an effective, open minded, honest, empowering and account-able leader.

Unfortunately, only 30 percent of the Nation's eligible voters voted in last year's elec-tion. If you, the great people of our Nation, want better, then you must not be complacent, you must not complain, **you must act**. I ask that you stand with me, realizing a better future for our Nation, our children and community. If you won't make a personal commitment, then sit at the mercy of no progress, negative governance, the lame duck status quo and worse, the promo-tion of a lack of integrity, accountability and sta-tus quo! The destiny of the future of our great Nation is in your vote!

I thank you for your consideration and thank you for your willingness to get involved. God bless the Nation, the membership and ALL of you who live and work in the wonderful com-munity of Dulce.

I had lost another election! I was at a loss emotionally. My mind went into a deeper depression, and I just sat in my chair replay-ing scenarios that I thought I should have done or not done. I was becoming the definition of insanity, but I loved politics so much that I was obsessed. I had no interest in even looking at the Nation's administration building and even for business reasons avoided going. I even separated myself from being in public. It was a rough time and again dealing with almost every emotion at once, now that I had no chance of winning a seat in government and no job, but I still felt it was important to try and share what had be done to date, as both a reminder and a hope that all that had been done in a vetted, proactive manner would continue. I also thought this may be my last opportunity to serve in any capacity just to help, and yeah, still near a profession I adored, I wrote one final letter:

Mr. President Elect,

I know you just got back from your vacation hopefully it was first class all the way!

I send this letter which will not only attempt to highlight some aspects of what has been done to date and at the same time, respectfully this email be my last attempt to showcase the topics and individuals contained in this email including hearing any political agenda you might have. I know you have been dealing with administrative matters and there I am sure are a lot of different pressing matters that need your attention but in being positive, not impossible because you do know the job. Maybe it's my fault for never coming to you in person during the election or after and I apologize but I do give you tons of respect. What we haven't had a chance to talk about is why I even wanted to run for the office of the President but I ran because I know I could handle the job better than any Executives we have had to date, excluding you sir because I know that my agenda would have first and foremost had empowering, accountability and autonomy, by the way, I am not saying this to be disrespectful! I'm just letting you know that we have a lot of similarities and desires and we want to make a positive impact during our tenures. I look back and I am proud to have personally grown so much since we last worked together in 2004 and then again in 2008. I know that I can do my job, so when I send an email like this I am doing so as a proven professional equal! I say this with honesty and sincerity, to date, the Nation has hired some real assets who have truly helped set up, protect, enhance and assist the Nation in what we have done to date, unfortunately these assets, have also been false accused of wrong doings and from that have been falsely labeled as having no ethics or scruples but I can say that all their work can be produced and substantiated.

The biggest challenge to date was to respectfully show how the Nation needs to separate business and politics, this new concept was done so through presentations, discussions and even approvals for what is now the Nation's new Holding Company, the Jicarilla Apache Nation Corporation (JANCO). JANCO has been approved by the LC, with a majority vote I might add and via the Bureau of Indian Affairs (BIA) process so it is a newly approved Ordinance. In trying to update and show why there was even a JANCO, the LC sat with the Rosette Legal team, sat with the JANCO Board and the Corporate Officers before they were let go but really never wanted to hear, in my opinion and were looking at this new model as a very bad thing even though as you heard and saw, the JANCO audit proved otherwise and I will still challenge any one of our enterprises and corporations to try and show the same standards, through their own much needed audits. I can say for a fact they will show shortcomings, why, because JANCO was born out of these failing business practices and JANCO was designed to set real viable polices as well as to never repeat these same failed business practices that our current "for-profit" organizations are doing. The Nation's government subsidizes our for-profit entities and has done so to the tune of 130M in the last ten years, the LC also hires and fires and protects key certain key employees of our Section 17s and Enterprises, there are No boundaries and at this level, there should be. I don't want to sound condescending but just the term "for-profit" means that these businesses should be self-supportive and revenue generators for the Nation and most importantly allow more lucrative Rates of returns for the Nation. Because of these shortcomings and lack of boundaries, the government then feels it needs to assist, so then our businesses become political and no longer independent, leaving room reaction rather than facts like generated revenues. Boards or General Managers, CEO's should be held accountable and the LC as owners, should only be involved by simply developing policies and other written policies, creating consistencies and clear lines rather than the continuation of politics. Many tribes are already implementing this new business philosophy and are being much more successful, Tribes like Ho Chunk, Seminole, more locally, Ohkay Owingea, Southern Ute, Northern Ute and many others. If we allow this commingling, we cut the rate of success from 80 to 90 percent to less than 20 percent. JANCO was created already knowing and learning from these shortcomings but it also sets up better guarantees utilizing much better business standards. JANCO is the new standard and pinnacle of progress for the Nation, yes, it is unorthodox from what the Nation has done and change is scary but from what we already know, our government should once again be the front runners in Indian Country but if we continue to allow the mentality that the government can "fix" everything, we will certainly failure. As we currently financially sit, there is NO way the Nation can absorb anymore liabilities without having to go to the Nation's portfolio to bail us out. In fact, we already have gone to the till and used 34M from the 124M Breach of Trust settlement money we received last September just to subsidize the 2017 budget! In fact let me tell you how we even received this settlement, the Rosette Law firm, who by the way was already working for the Nation and hired through an RFP process, has a ton of contacts and one of those contacts was former Department of Interior Secretary Ken Salazar. Ken told Rosette that President Obama wanted to leave a legacy with the tribes by settling ALL Breach of trust suits. Rosette called me and I told Ty, he balked, so I picked up the ball and told Rosette to go forward, by the way all along the way the LC were kept in the loop and gave consensus to also proceed. In moving forward Rosette arranged a call from Ken, from there we met and we had dinner, he gave me the background on the inside information and it seemed feasible. I told Ken that we had been spending a lot of money in this current law suit but also knowing law suits are expensive but then the topic of hourly billing came up, as I was complaining about the firm working on this case and said Holland and Knight has billed the Nation a total of 25M since taking over this case in 2007. So Ken, Rosette and I talked about a success rate, meaning the more money the Nation received, the more money the law firms got and there was no need to bill hourly, it made sense to me and it also made the firms work twice as hard to get the most successful win for the Nation! As we began to move forth, the discussion of the success rate started at 6% then was agreed by all parties to be at 3%, again, to which the LC approved. So as negotiations proceeded and we went back and forth on settlement offers from the Feds. The settlement offers started coming in at 20M, we said No, then it went to 50M we said No, then it went to 80M and the talk from DOI and The US Treasury dept was that was it, we still said No, all the while being informed every day from Rosette, so then the offer went to 100M, we said more, finally, the offer went to 124M with a solid that's it, as the Feds had no more permission or room to negotiate, so we accepted! From that 124M the 3% successor rate was 3M, a drop in the bucket from what H&K was charging for every call, email and we settled in less than 60 days, which was a far cheaper way to accept this offer, rather than continue to fight for other possible 10 years with H&K and because of Rosette and Salazar, we had a cash settlement that was almost as equal to the entire law suit for total timber breach of trust law suit. If we did not make the move, based on the inside information, we would most likely still be paying H&K, still be in litigation with NO guarantee that we would have even settled much lees received a check in an acceptable timeframe. During the waiting period of the negotiations, the JANCO Board/corporate officers were working on several deals and other than the initial start-up cost of 1.6M, the Board along with the Corporate Officers presented an opportunity to get the best rate of return on what I called a "monetary gift" from the Federal

Government and invest this money into JANCO. The JANCO strategy was detailed but in its simplicity, was to use this settlement money as a capital investment allowing JANCO to then use this fund as collateral, where even just sitting in the bank would have generated 8% interest safely, rather than possible losing millions because of the volatility of the stock market. JANCO could have then leveraged from that money and could have had in excess of 90M to use for all sorts of viable, vetted business ventures JANCO had lined up, some of these ventures generating, 20, 30 and 40 percent rates of return. But now the 120M was just lumped, into the pot of the Nations portfolio and is now subject to the volatility of the Market, not to mention we had to take money out of the settlement to subsidize the 2017 budget and will most likely have to do so again for the 2018 and 2019. I will say for the last time that the Rosette law firm was instrumental in moving the Nation forward, not only in this opportunity with JANCO, department policies, the housing issues and in lobbying efforts in D.C. and I say this with great passion and full respect, Rosette has and will prove their worth, please give them an opportunity to show you personally. As an example of better strategies, one of the reasons the LC wanted to adopt a telecom/IT committee, was to help viably research, vet and find other resources and companies who could fairly assist the Nation either monetarily or structurally in making sure we could either joint venture or recreate our own Telephone/ Broadband company and between the IT/ Broadband committee and the Rosette firm, they did! I ask you to please allow a simple conversation with the IT/Broadband committee and Rosette firm, to hear and see firsthand what they have done, including any billing concerns. Any of the negatives that were stated will reflect that their professionalism and reputation was a strong positive. Through their level of understanding and working in Indian Country and vast network of contacts, the Rosette firm really has assisted in putting the Nation at the front of these line, it is to our disadvantage that we have stalled but I say this respectfully, let's not lose our place or this momentum have a sit down with the firm.

Mr. President, the iceberg is down the horizon but we are moving steadily in the direction of the iceberg, but through a good strong administration, proper planning and understood roles and responsibilities, we have time to start steering this large ship in a different direction but if we do not consider and allow an approved out of the box idea like JANCO work, or for that matter, any other properly structured plan designed to separate business and politics, we will eventually hit the iceberg. This is my opinion but at the same time I have witnessed the LC's involvement and when it works its great but when it's not working, it is very destructive. To date, business development at Jicarilla has primarily consisted of the LC and comments such as "I heard", "I think," "We don't need," "it's only going to cost this much" or "we can fix it after we buy it." Decision making like this is nonexistent in other places and is very irresponsible and should not be an acceptable practice anymore. If we do not find a way to truly separate business and politics, the government will continue to vote on all business opportunities, like the recent proposal of Black

Hills, based on emotion, hearsay, popularity, and ego and that only does one thing, spends and wastes money and creates more liabilities for the Nation. Right now, we have a positive business, that has been approved at all levels of governance, a model that is also being utilized in Indian Country because other tribal governments are also failing at trying manage business and politics and JANCO is ready to do its job and can and will create the much-needed protocols for success and longevity like any Fortune 500 company. JANCO's board stands ready to even handle all board work if things need to start quickly, the JANCO Board is just asking for an opportunity to sit down with you and show you. The LC have to many other issues to deal with, issues that are that are being neglected and left on the table. Yes, our laws have sustained the Nation all these years and yes we are more proactive than other tribes but we also need to amend and address our laws addressing the dire social issues we are now encountering. Social challenges such as substance abuse, suicide, truancy in schools, theft, lack of homes, the lack of Infrastructure and the most important structure that ties all these things together, the budget. Every election we hear the government say that they can "Fix things" and at the same time critique their predecessors by saying everything to date was wrong and that things need to be fixed and know that they are at the table, will make sure they do a much better job but wiping the slate clean and reinventing the wheel every four years, especially with no history as to why and how, not only becomes expensive but creates further social issues and deflates communal moral therefore only further adding to the long list of community shortfalls. The role of the LC is to create and set laws and approve a budget, you as President have the real authority to create a strong agenda, set goals and reinforce these boundaries of when and how the LC should interact or should not with department and or administrative issues. The Nation has shown that it can no longer do things from the inside or at the level of governance, we need new philosophies and more importantly better business practices and standards and this can only be with the separation of Business and Politics.

Lastly, I hope you were able to glance at the folder I gave you, there is a lot of really good info in there and I know you can pull from it. We have paid for work that has been shelved and some of that information I provided can help set the responsibilities of government in motion. The job of President and Council members is complex and most forget that we, as elected officials, have a fiduciary duty to be professional, to create polices, laws, structures that will benefit long term. I am confident to say that, you Mr. President, even though you have inherited a table full of issues, you have also inherited a proven team and we have been diligently with this strong team like Rosette, Jenny Dumas, In house legal and countless others who have been ignored and criticized, these teams bring sound judgments and professionalism and have proved their value, have completed their assigned tasks and have helped the Nation successfully move forward.

Maybe I should quite while I am ahead but this next bit of information is also important to share. The final analysis of the funds of the CDX deal have been reconciled by both internal and external key players. After paying the debt and bank fees, the Nation still made millions and it could have made much more if at the very least these key players would have been allowed to see this deal to completion using the parameters of this deal to even allow a second set-up deal and new agreement with EnerVest, who bought the leases, when CDX went bankrupt, in fact because of opinion's made from Legislative Council members in 2006 and to date, ended up costing the Nation millions because those transitions that were set up to be successful like the hedge, were changed without any consideration or opportunities to extend these terms, because those terms were altered, JAECO was no longer in pole position to become a partner, the Nation lost out on the gas marketing with ABQ Energy because no one was monitoring the work, and the Nation absorbed a ton of costs ranging from legal fees, time and waiting until 2016 to even refinance those existing bonds. The good news is through good governance and a strong team, the Nation still made a profit of $37 million on an investment where the Nation borrowed 100% of the money, that sir is a pretty good return. I will continue to say the CDX deal was a very good deal! I know it's tough sometimes when things are done and we have to play catch up midstream but the LC at that time, those inaugurated in September of 2006, came in stating this deal was bad because we hedged and we locked the Nation into rates that were unacceptable and wrong. Comments like that were made without even asking for background information on the deal or even why there was a team to professionally assist as to make sure ALL decisions were going to be positive and there were based on the money the deal made. The LC at that time (2002–2006) discussed this deal over and over and then determined that we alone could never craft the language needed to make this deal successful. So we compiled a team consisting of local and independent experts. The initial transaction was structured to allow the Nation to lock in a certain level of profits no matter what happened to gas prices over the life of the transaction. Profits would come from the fact that the Nation borrowed money at a 5% interest rate on the bond financing and then essentially got an 11% return on the money when you purchased the gas from CDX for the life of that transaction. Based on expert opinions, we even took the position that it would be allowed to keep certain severance taxes on that gas as the Nation now owned that gas. The combination of these two terms was designed to provide about $45 million in profits to the Nation. Nothing comes easy and if things sound too good to be true, maybe there are but that's why we needed an independent study conducted. There were a number of risk factors in the transaction, the questions that arose were, would there be enough gas produced in the field to get the amount that the Nation had paid for? In order to make sure we had a solid yes, The Nation had a separate and independent analysis of the field done by Cawley Gillespie which showed there was an average of 1.2–1.3 times as much gas available each year and there was about a 35–40% "tail" which was in essence a contingency in case there were earlier shortfalls. Again, wanting to properly vet we decided to receive another independent analysis ensuring that we would have strong coverage and that there was enough gas for the Nation to get what we for paying for. One of the questions we didn't know was, what happens when gas prices go up or down? To make sure we had a consistent number, it was discussed that the Nation would purchase gas over a long-term period at a fixed price of $4.05 per MMBtu. But since we had known that the Nation would not get all the gas at once, it was agreed that we would have to sell the gas at the market price when it was delivered to the Nation or JAECO each month. So how do we make sure we come out ahead against the volatility of the Market, meaning, if prices went up, the Nation would make more money but if prices went down, the Nation would get less money. We then decided with the input and recommendations of the team, that we would RFP and then received proposals from JP Morgan, BP and one other group, that I forget but to help take away the risk of market's gas prices going up or down. The three groups bid on the commodity hedge and BP was selected because they provided the best price and the best terms. In fact, BP was about $2–3 million better than the other bids from the other parties. This is a great example of how the LC worked diligently with its team and this resulted in finding the best hedge partner. So now, with the hedge, the Nation really did not have to worry if gas prices went up or down. If prices went up, you got more when you sold the gas that month, but you paid more or got less from the hedge. The hedge allowed the Nation to lock in its profits. The third question we had was, would the Nation be able to sell the gas each month? The answer was yes and the Nation worked with Mr. Brian McNiell to sell the gas into the market. Mr. McNiell did a very good job but the newly elected LC members began to question motives and also wanted to have someone closer to do the marketing and moved the job to ABQ Marketing. These events led to what I am calling the downward spiral of this deal and loss to the Nation's coffers. In fact, there was even an audit of the entire CDX transaction around 2009. At that time, the transaction was within about $300 of being exactly as forecasted and another fact, because we had made money from this deal, aside from what was left in the bank account, the $37M, the Nation had used certain profits to work on Nation projects. So why revisit the CDX deal, two reason, the first, it keeps being stated that it was a very bad deal but yet no one can say exactly why, second, creating a strong team independent of just the LC increasingly helps make solid business decisions. The Nation at that time, had good partners, including factoring in JAECO, to reap the benefits of selling the gas at market, agreeing to a hedge that would then take away the risk of falling gas prices and most importantly, making sure the Nation had independent engineering reports from the market leaders verifying our resources in the field for longevity. The way the Black Hills deal was presented, I'm sorry to say, factors in nothing like the above, to be fair, it looks like Mr. Davis did have an independent review done but questions still arise to me and others that overlook any possible liabilities to plug any wells in that area, does that affect the values if we did not take this into consideration? Were gas prices used that were factual meaning present numbers for gas, rather than padded numbers, making it look like there was a higher value of return. I can honestly say I do not know but by not making sure we have the right players and strategies to help and we do not change the way the LC get involved and sequester outside business dealings, we will continue to lose millions rather than gain.

I have not been one to be a lame duck and maybe at least in my mind, my professionalism and niceness have been mistaken for weakness. That's the furthest thing from the truth, I am passionate about my role as a LC member and I know my role and I have mastered it. I told you that the new LC members should step up well in my opinion, I have not heard any reports from the tasks assigned and I ask if they have moved anything forward, with all due respect, maybe they have and have reported to you directly but as you know information and communication are vital but at times absent, so I say, if you need to move something, I will volunteer, I can be a part of any team or I can do it solo but I will get things done. I pride myself on knowing my role and job as a LC member and knowing this role and job is a very important part of being a Public servant, we all should be factual and respectfully vocal and I feel strongly that if I have ever say anything out of context or emotionally, You will tell me, that being said, I will make sure they, we, I and you get the job done in a manner that is positive.

I thank you for your time, you told me while we had a brief chat in my office, that you had a new perspective by being away from political office. I completely understand how you feel, as this is why I am so adamant about this separation of LC roles and responsibilities and it took a long time but we now have a law on LC polices and standards, it's in the info I gave you in the folder. I know I said a lot but I hope you use your strong instincts to schedule meetings to sit and hear firsthand, the value Lilian, Adrian, and yours truly have helped create, especially in the absence of the much needed Executive leadership from the past 6 years. There is a trust factor, you have to trust me and vice versa and I hope you know I will never state anything that is negative or unproven, so I reiterate, I am sending this email as a proven equal, not as a family member nor out of any personal obligation or personal relationships, you taught me to be respectfully forward, to be strong and stand by my convictions, even if people do not like hearing the truth. I do that and I do so in a manner that is both factual and historical. I am blessed to have been given the opportunity to learn from good teachers, I will always be the student but I know I am also ready to stand as the teacher.

Thank you again for your time and consideration.

I never received a response or acknowledgment. Maybe I was desperate. Maybe I felt one last Hail Mary would show that my efforts for improving and further securing self-determination would propel the Nation and the members and community of Dulce forward the next one hundred years but felt deflated and then began to dig myself into a hole. No one could talk me out of climbing out despite some accolades of my service.

I look back in this memoir, and terms like *council, self-determination, sovereignty, tribe,* and *Nation* seemed so foreign. I remember knowing the concepts as I sat at the table and began learning, not really chiming in, absorbing and listening to comments, concepts, and opinions, many of which had ranged from specious and emotional, but then there were many comments and strategies that had clarity, logic, and reasoning, and I began to see how that logic was paramount especially in this position of representing as an elected official. I wanted to know more, especially how our tribal constitution was being used and not being used. I began to quote constitutional clauses in my debates and presentations, and that would now become my method of operation. I feel it important to note that, during my first two years as a council member, I did let the title get to me, not necessarily in an entitled way but in a cocky way, especially since I did spout the law. But at the same time, I began to see that it was not that simple. I had to balance emotion, perceived entitlement, and the labeling of being considered an outsider. There were a few times I may have tried to force points, maybe feel like I had to show someone they were incorrect in their translation of protocols and policy, and realized after some sage advice that I had to change tactics and how I perceived protocols and policy. The sage advice I received was from a colleague I truly value to this day. We were in a discussion in the tribal chambers, and no matter what law I was citing, one member was completely resistant. His rebuttal was not of current law but of traditional law and, yes, valid. My thoughts ranged on those now-established laws, which were the Nation's constitution, established in 1934, and the following twenty-six ordinances that followed collectively through the decades. So yes, traditional law had some merit but no precedence as the bands of Jicarilla prior to agreeing to one established document had similar but different cultural traditions, cultures, and subtle language dialects. After all, there was an agreement made in the 1930s that would unite the tribe as one and create one document that would also secure this agreement to govern the governed. It was always off-putting for me to hear, "We never did it that way" or "That's not our way," when in fact the agreement to establish one unified body to serve was indeed established based on a traditional model but with the understanding that no one would be above others, therefore creating equity. But these types of comments usually were always followed with the jab of blood quantum.

Using blood quantum as a be-all end-all comment was in my opinion a cheap shot that bordered on ignorance, but because I was told I was less than, I had to find better ways to present and vouch my comments for progress. In my debates, I would always mention and reference the law and usually was received with blank stares and again the usual rhetoric of "That's not how we do it." It was at that time a dear colleague leaned over to me during a recess and said, "You can hit a donkey in the head with a two-by-four to try and get him to move, and it will not budge, and the only one getting tired and frustrated will be you." That advice still rings true with me today, and when I feel like I need to change my tactic and strategy, I stop forcing and use my comments for the record.

Sovereignty would be my new platform and not just to stand on when boasting or sit on when it didn't suit me. I could see a clear vision of how this given concept could change the way tribes were viewed, treated, and how they could help not only their own but also all those communities around them, including counties and states. In my vision, I saw the political clout this new advantage could bring to the community, again as well as those neighboring. I could see the Nation moving away from the glass box it seemed to encase itself in. I use the analogy of a glass house because the typical description of a glass ceiling prohibits moving up. I felt the Nation added those glass ceilings all around and therefore prohibited any movement in any direction.

That was not a disrespectful critique. I base my opinion on the current laws indoctrinated and sworn to uphold since the 1930s. I applied all my concepts and now law creating on the laws, and if there was an opportunity to amend for the purposes of growth, then that's how I referenced in my draft resolutions or ordinances. There is a code that I based almost all my concepts of economic development on. After all, I was an elected official, and my title came with the responsibility of creating, upholding, enforcing, promoting, and developing law and developing economics both micro and macro, and when I discovered this law that was established in 1993, I thought, yes, I have a foundation to help me do my job. This title, code, ordinance was created for the purposes of

- having a lower dropout rate for high school students;
- encouraging graduates to attend and graduate from trade schools and colleges;

277

- increasing motivation for self-improvement;
- lowering unemployment rate;
- reducing employment burdens on tribal government;
- having better availability of health care, retirement, and insurance;
- increasing self-esteem; and
- producing high tribal morale and pride.

I didn't know it at the time, but this ordinance was my vision, and my goal was to do all I could to make sure I honored this intent. For some reason, there is a disconnect about how the "leadership" interacts with, provides for, and assumes responsibility of the unfortunate; it is backwards. There was a running joke I heard and even took offense of. It went along the lines of, "If you wanted to show how success was measured, do the opposite of what Jicarilla's government does." That comment made me incensed, how we were not, as a group, providing for this powerful allowance and a reminder of what it means to serve. I got close, my vision was coming true, and the tribally owned holding company was the baby. It was going to kick-start and create meaningful employment opportunities for members of the tribe; it was going to bolster the reservation economy and make certain educated members have professional employment both on and off the reservation because the holding company planned on procuring land, businesses, and new development both on and off the reservation. This new out-of-the-box, tribally established, not federally established company was going to be a new force of nature for all Indian country but absolutely Jicarilla! JANCO was the catalyst to 100 percent enhance all economic well-being and provide permanent employment to tribal members and any person who wanted to work, but the vision and mission I so desperately fought for, lived for, and stood for were not meant to be, and I see this beautiful land the community of Dulce resides on, and it seems so barren. Businesses are shut down, there is a huge beautiful new building and the community center, and yet its doors remain closed to the public. Sure, at some point, the doors will open, but there was a plan in place to make certain the building was constructed good. All issues would be professionally resolved, and the deadline would be strived to be achieved. The plan was changed. My assumption was, "That's not how we do it. We can do things ourselves," and yes, we can, but based on no outside input, no questions as to how and why the plan was applied, changes swiftly happened, and there seemed to be a myriad of issues keeping the doors closed. Again, the law states a council member is to create and improve, not disrupt based on speculation, rumor, spite, or other concepts that "white people do," when in reality, we as Natives have mastered, internally, criticizing our own race, family, and lifestyle. When your community maintains an approximate 40 percent unemployment rate and is and has only one source of income, with little to no long-term planning and little to no promotion of entrepreneurialism, well, it can create a slew of issues that will and have incorporated social issues. Yes, that is my opinion, but ask someone from the community, and let's see how many share my opinion about the standards and qualities that should be provided, living within the boundaries of reservation land.

I feel I can finally smile now, but it was like another relationship had ended, and I had little to no opportunity to find a replacement, much less a chance to even court a new prospect to even try and build a new professional relationship. I was now applying for unemployment benefits. As a tribal member, I was receiving a monthly tribal payment. In fact, I would even get more upset as to feeling that my job was to help all members, and I did that by writing the amended per capita schedule. Per capita was a fund set up to provide a fund to all enrolled tribal members as a benefit from the tribe's economic growth, like a dividend paid to shareholders, and this amended version was working and, if nurtured as the law stated, would have created even better returns paid to the members on an annual basis but unfortunately became stagnant, still there but remained capped. My children are not eligible to receive any tribal benefits, but I was so grateful to get a monthly payment, despite my anger and frustration to have the bills get paid monthly even with one check.

The days flew by, and I stayed in my rut or what I know was depression. My desire to find employment was very thin. I created this fantasy that I was going to wait for another election so I could once again run for office, and if I did get a job, I would not be fully committed because I would find myself declaring my candidacy, and I didn't want to be a job jumper. It was actually an emotional battle going on in my head. I couldn't find the closure I so much needed. I kept asking questions of myself, and my mind let me burrow deeper into the void. I wanted to know, and right now, how I could have lost and then how could I not be in a relationship. It was a tough time, and I tried to keep busy, but when I wasn't cooking, cleaning, or running errands, I was slumped in my chair, flipping through channels but staring through the television.

I never knew that I could fall prey to depression. It didn't matter what form or amount. I was having brain fog, and all I could concentrate on was this feeling I had for revenge. Sounds crazy, but I kept playing scenarios in my mind if and when I might have run into any sitting member of the government at that time, what I would do, what I would say, could I cuss them out, and would I get in their face to confront them on the lies they brazenly talked about me. The funny thing about the mind, it definitely created some plots, and in these plots, I was badass. I would be making my point and having these people bow at my feet. The reality, well, common sense brought me back to being grounded. My core, my gut, always had been calibrated correctly, and it was that inner core voice that kept my mind at bay. It allowed my mind to fantasize, but it made sure my heart and body never did anything that would cause me embarrassment or bring harm to anybody. I still thank this gift that has allowed me to live but also let live and knew, I am a firm believer, wholeheartedly, that karma would reward or penalize, and I always did my best to stay in its good graces.

The last year and a half of my 2018 term was also challenging when it came to dealing with family. The kids and I had our back-and-forth times, but by this time, since the estrangement of my wife in the latter part of 2015, we had a lot of time to adapt to our new dynamic, and I was doing much better in my communication and working daily on theirs. It was a much bigger issue dealing with the family outside the house. I had aunts, uncles, and cousins, whom I placed on a pedestal, who were spreading vicious lies about me. To be fair, it was not all my extended family. Most were very kind and supportive, but the handful whom I felt were, as the kids say, ride or die completely disowned me. I can recall the first issue I had, in my first term in 2005, a family member who had been working as an assistant treasurer and kept asking me when the council was going to make changes and who might be considered a viable candidate for this appointed position and why I am not pushing more for my family member. My comments were that I had no confirmation of any change and that I would never overstep my authority to circumvent any process. I further stated that I completely believed in her talent, skill, and expertise, and that should be the basis to obtain any position or advancement, not just having a council member pushing just because there is a misunderstanding of what ability the council can really do and what they can't or even shouldn't. My comments did not land, and the retort was, it was done before, and I did acknowledge knowing of such practice. But I also said that was still wrong. I added in my conclusion comment, "Keep doing the great job you are doing. There will be rewards from the hard work and dedication, and if we all become cynical, we could easily lose sight of what it is we are doing and for whom. Besides if anyone is going to be cynical, it should be. I made that comment confiding in a person whom I had many conversations with and simply making a loose point that as a government official, some comments are forced as to quickly get something done for people despite ignoring the protocols and policies set in place. I later found out that my comment on being cynical turned into I was in charge, and all of a sudden, I was a big shot and that if I choose to get something done, I would, which was the furthest thing from the truth. But it caused a rift in that side of the family and lingered for a while. Well, maybe *festered* is a better word as I would soon find out who also was calling me a thief based on the JANCO concept. I had wondered how a relationship that was very positive had gone sour. I couldn't quite put my finger on things, and that was because I was literally blindsided that a family member, who was in an appointed position as treasurer, was so critical of me and my position and duty of creating opportunity as a council member. All of a sudden, it all became clear as to who was writing letters about me and giving half-truths. I could not understand why this person was so against such a powerful document. I had even asked for input as to how things could be improved from this particular person, and there were some really good insights that was built into the ordinance of JANCO.

It was on the trip to Washington, DC, to meet with the secretary of the Department of Interior to sign the final documents accepting the settlement between the Nation and the federal government, where I finally found out one of the sources of disdain and criticism and how this family member's opinions were being told to not on the newly elected council members but other professionals the government worked with and alongside of. This was the text message that confirmed my suspicions, and I was upset. I still tried hard to stay on the high road. (Note that LR is me and T is the treasurer.)

> LR—I have to ask because I felt I was blindside a bit to which I have nothing to hide but if there is an issue with me, my role, whether it's JANCO or travel or whatever, I hope we can talk like we used to before. I don't mind protocols being put on the record but a call to me would have cleared up many things.
>
> T—Since u reachd out i was doin as president ask me. I dnt like tis whole tng wt JANCO its a sick deal & i cnt support it. Its jus anotr utility authority deal all ovr again. Wat hapnd 2 u leon. I was all 4 u. I lobbied 4 u during election & the more i bcome familiar wt janco now i no why myself r sean was nvr nvited 2 tese mtgs wt janco bcuz the rug was being pulled out frm evy1. Ur a very good speaker yes but i c how its used 2 ur advantage. Im disappointed. <<insert emoji>>
>
> LR—Well I'm sorry you feel that way but JANCO will be the saving grace for the nation. JANCO is supposed to be separate on purpose

because of the limited expertise the nation has. Yes we have smart people working for the nation but unfortunately no one could ever create the much needed income through high leave deals that the nation needs to climb out of this financial crisis. I'm tired of the band aide approach. I will also say as treasurer, the ball was dropped with Wells Fargo. Your job was to monitor all fees and transactions and it took the LC almost selling its assets of the hotels and by the way a very bad non negotiated offer was presented with your endorsement and no due diligence, to really clean the crap of the Windows. Your job as treasurer was to protect the presidents from bad business practices and unfortunately that did not happen because the Wells Fargo agreement was signed in 2008 with very bad non negotiated fees and practices, that are being reflected today by congress. Once it was cleared up, it showed that there was never any oversight or accountability of Wells Fargo, other than a rubber stamp. Whose job is to secure those finances? Not to mention monitor and question the hotels management company! JANCO will work because it eliminates all political BS to which you complained about almost daily from the last administration but it took guts to take a proactive approach and do whatever necessary to save the nation. If you want to learn more about JANCO ask! if you think it's a bad deal that's fine but please do not dispense unfactual information, that not only discredits your reputation but it is very irresponsible as a leader and whether you know it, you're a leader and I have no problem promoting the need to separate business and politics and being on the record every time I speak about it. Being a leader sometimes means taking a stand whether there is support or not and I have no problem standing up for what needs to be done. You can take my response any way you want but know that there is a mutual respect and if you want to take the low road and say Leon is so mean, then by all means that's your choice but one thing, Leon has the balls to push forward and the LC now is just as strong in doing what's right and I am so happy and believe me I welcome the new philosophies of the LC.

T—Wow leon u wl stop at nothing & ny1 tat gets in ur way! How can u tell the people tat janco is good wen ur ceo jus sat n front of the council sayng only him & u hav access 2 the bank acct! I am not goin 2 continue tis conversation wt u! LEAVE ME ALONE!

LR—You need to grow up and open your eyes! And I will not leave you alone as we work together and your job is provide guidance and info to the LC. So if you have issues with me, pull need to put the aside and be a professional.

T—I wl talk 2 my supervisor abt tis. Talk abt professionalism? U should b telling all tis 2 me n front of council like u sid u hav no problem being on record. In my defense i do rport as i did & i do recommend but its only recomends whether presidents or council take it n2 consideration i hav no vote or control. So if the ball dropped its not all my fault! Coming frm a man who jus praised me on the record 4 my work jus contradicts ur stmts as well and shows the kind of person u R!

LR—Talk to the President. In fact if you heard correctly he gave his endorsement. And I stand by my word of who you are. If I ever wanted to say anything negative I would have especially for the record. We all have a job to do we are all part of a team but we also have different roles and responsibilities and trust is crucial. I will let you have your moment towards me because one, my job is to create, not sit back like many other LC before and if I make friends great but all personal relationships have lines and business always prevails. Talk to the president and he will follow up with me.

I grew more and more on the defensive, not because I felt that what I was standing for was wrong or in any way illegal but because I was really sick and tired of this irresponsible practice or slandering one's name simply because of speculation and spite, dare I even add ignorance because no one asked any questions or even wanted to participate in any dialogue when invited. I felt that I needed to share my text exchange between the treasurer and I because if any of the professionals who managed funds and whose fiduciary duty was to help the Nation not only be proactive but protected needed to see any of JANCO's documents firsthand to vouch questions and then come to some conclusion on their own, without heard conjecture and not to agree or disagree, but to see that one new approach could be proven to be more advantageous than the same old status quo that had been inconsistent because the government changed quickly and was subject to allowing opinion to ignore and attack facts. I sent the following email:

First, thank you for your professionalism. As I stated to you many times, I value good people and make it a point to pull good traits and apply those traits to myself, this has made me grow as a father, partner and man.

That being said, a wise man used a perfect analogy in our last meeting in Albuquerque. This wise person said, and I apologize for summarizing, but it went something like this. "you don't go to the butcher and ask how he cuts his meat, we expect a great product because that's the butchers job. We also don't go to the butcher to ask if we should add more fish to our diet." Point being you know what your role is and you have a duty to do that role as not only a fiduciary but reputation.

In continuing with the analogy, JANCO gives you those cows, your role is to butcher and distribute and not try and sell more fish.

Ok, my point, I know you see the value of a better way to generate money, I know JANCO is the vehicle so you did your part. JANCO does have strategies and a very diverse wise Board of Directors. So we appreciate your endorsement and say thank you but getting deeper involved in how JANCO gets you the product, well I will say this, has put many avenues in place as to due diligence questions, there have been companies that the nation currently work with who will not only questioned as to services and fees again because of reacting on how to recycle money but I have received emails not from JANCO but we also have done our own research that also start questioning fees.

This separate but much needed relationship needs to happen. Your endorsement needs to happen and you are my main question is why do you need to know the intimate details of how JANCO will move? JANCO has every avenue covered as much as can be, it has so many safe guards that one could question is this a true independent company. The Board has structure more than ever before of than any Council official, we have Compensation and allocation/distribution committees and we have and can do our homework.

We have nothing to hide, ALL companies who are working for the nation will always be in question especially in crisis and you know as well as I, we are in a crisis. So with the utmost respect, I ask do we want to keep battling every year for questions that are being asked when in reality no one wants to ask questions to listen, they ask questions to react.

I leave you with this. I was getting some very off-putting signals at the last Council meeting last week so I sent a text message to the Nations treasurer and here is how it went, mind you, not one call or one question by the way I purposely sent this as an email to show my transparency at risk or not and state roles and responsibilities…"

I received one comment back that stated, "very interesting exchange there. Thanks for keeping me in the loop. Personally, I think JANCO could be a game changer for the Nation. I really didn't fully understand it until yesterday so I'm glad I was there for the presentations. Between you and me I think that some of the new council members are questioning it and instead of voicing their concerns are having the treasurer do their dirty work. As you know I don't pick sides. I'm a professional and work on whatever the wishes of council or the president are. I will give my opinions if asked but my primary responsibility is to implement what has been approved by council. I will continue to look after the best interests of the nation and hope I can continue this relationship for a long time. I have enjoyed working with you as you get things done. As you know, this is the

best plan of action to save the nation so if you can
help, it will help do good!

For what it was worth, at that time, that one simple statement
made my whole month!

I had somehow found myself in other issues with my younger
brother and mom, and it was weird. I must really be clueless, or
maybe I do block things out, and then when I snap out of it, I'm
sitting there wondering what happened and maybe then playing the
victim. It was on a business trip to Arizona where I had decided to
take the kids with me on my trip so the kids could visit and I could
do what I needed to do, and when all was said and done, they would
have had a mini vacation before heading home.

Every other trip seemed pleasurable, and my brother was very
generous with allowing us to stay with him and his family, but it was
this time that things went south, as they say. It was this particular trip
where the kids and I caught the flu. I was taking one to urgent care
and then the other, back the next day. Needless to say, I then caught
the flu, and there was no way I was able to drive the eight hours
back home. The mini vacation was extended four days, and then
my daughter had lice, and that turned into a huge fiasco, with strip-
ping bedding and towels and pretty much everything in my brother's
house. I was doing my best to take care of the two youngest kids who
were running fevers, and at the same time, I was really trying to hurry
to feel better so we could leave. The flu was bad enough, but the lice
was the straw that broke my brother's back. I can't exactly recall if he
ever said anything directly to me while we were still in his home, but
I could absolutely relate if there were eye rolls and strong attempts
to hold back and not lash out. I look back and realize we could have
checked into a hotel room, but I was very sick.

Three days went by, and I got enough energy to say, "Let's go."
We loaded up the car and gave hugs, and of all times, I had bought
a gallon of Tito's vodka and a large decorative champagne bottle. I
don't recall exactly why vodka and the champagne bottle were for
novelty because it was huge. I began to load the car. All I heard was
crash and pop! I don't know how or who, but the two bottles I had

right next to the car that was parked just slightly inside the garage, literally in arm's reach, got knocked over, and the champagne bottle literally exploded like a bomb and shot glass and bubbles everywhere. The vodka bottle sustained some handle damage but did not succumb to the same fate as its alcohol companion. It was all I could do to not just jump in the car and burn rubber out of the driveway, and out of the corner of my eye, I saw my brother's reaction, and I did not want to make eye contact. I think I even blamed my oldest son, to which I felt really bad. I asked for a broom, coughed, wheezed, and sweated as I swept up chunks and shards of glass that now was ready to be embedded into someone's foot. I seeped and swept, and it felt like I was doing nothing. There was so much dark-green glass all over the garage floor and driveway. I asked for a mop, and it was then that my brother said, "Don't worry about it." I got the kids in the car and hauled it as fast as I could, still coughing and sweating from the flu. I was absolutely apologetic, and if the tables were turned, I would've been just as angry. We got to a town called Payson where we stopped at the local urgent care, and I took my oldest in, and I told the doctor, "It has been a hell of a tough week. Whatever meds my son needs, prescribe them so we could please get home." The doctor prescribed rest, and I laughed and said thank you, and we headed home.

It might have been a week later when I received a call from my brother, and he was candid and told me how angry and frustrated he was and said that it was probably for the best that I and the kids no longer stay with him in their home if and when we ever came to town and that if we did come to town, that maybe we could have dinner and call that a visit. I didn't react, and I kept my composure. After all, I could understand the mood, and I actually invited being yelled at but was not expecting to be read the Riot Act. I calmly said, "I understand," and I was glad he spoke his mind. I told him I was very grateful for his hospitality, and I wished him well. I left him with the comment far be it from me to offer advice, but I had hoped he didn't spread himself so thin with things because his health mattered, and stress can be very disastrous. I said my goodbyes, and that was that. I tried to process what just occurred, and there was a small part of me that thought, *Fuck him*, and then there was the other part, larger in thought, that felt sad and accepting of his feelings.

I hadn't talked to him since that phone conversation, and I had not heard from him either, and I gave a wide berth. I knew I would see him eventually, and when I did, I was hoping to talk and maybe even get some apologies, but like most times growing up, apologies were replaced with, "Get over it," much tougher to say and even try, but I am doing my best to keep traveling on the high road. But high road or not, I feel like I am traveling through dense fog, and why would we not want proper communication and even mea culpas if and when we may be wrong? Another question I have not had answers to, and I am not just smiling and shaking my head as I find my own peace to the answers I provide to my own questions.

During the initial part of my separation, my mother was getting ready to retire, and that brought on a happy moment because with work and traveling out of town quite a bit, I was so nervous the first time I had to leave for an overnight meeting. I had asked my middle brother if he was okay with staying the night with the kids and then just making sure they did what they were supposed to do—get up for school, pick up the house, try not to argue and fight, and have good meals. My brother was so generous with his time, but I felt guilty asking him to stay overnight at my house with kids every time I had to go on a business trip. He actually told me that the kids would be fine and that the oldest should be stepping up and balking at first. I told him I agree, and from that moment on, Nic was the man of the house. I had to go to Washington, DC, and it was all I could do from canceling my trip and then, when I was at the airport, calling every two minutes. What I did do was purchase a security camera, and every once in a while, I would open the camera app and screen-shoot an image of the kids and send it to my son, with the message, "Dad's watching you!" I was really proud of the kids for all pitching in and doing what it took to be responsible, and I also knew my brother was five minutes away, but I would be lying if my mind didn't create worst-case scenarios. Thankfully, nothing ever happened that required an emergency call.

My mother and I had an interesting relationship. She was very caring as I mentioned and very smart and supportive, but as I replay all the events that may have led to issues, those awesome qualities, many of which I have, came with strings, strings I also have. I can't quite explain how we got along, but it was at times like oil and water, but there were also great times that were fantastic when oil and water would mix, but it took some serious shaking to make the two ingredients come together and look like they were mixing well. But when the shaking stopped, the oil and water became separate, but we always seemed to make the best of being around each other. I think early on I used evasion as my way of trying to avoid my anger toward my mother and then would allow dispassion to make me feel like I was making a point and deep down feel like I would be asked if I had a problem and if I would like to talk. I never was asked that question, and I think that further enraged me, but I didn't want to lash out even though I really tried to push the envelope. I never felt like I could also bring up my emotions as I would be met with what I can now call manipulation. If I did bring up an issue that I had a problem with, the first comment would be, "Oh, come on!" "Yeah, right" and "You don't know what I had to do to survive." I had heard things but never deep issues, and that, I think, was her way of feeling like she was in power, and therefore, I learned how to not to have positive conflict resolution. There were and still are no apologies. There are gestures in the form of attempting to want to engage in some dialogue, like poking and the sad eyes, but it's still a "get over it" mentality.

After my mom retired, she came to stay with the kids and I, and I was grateful. I still had a year and a half to serve, and I would no longer be overly worried about my two- and three-day travels. I call the time together our honeymoon stage because it was fairly decent and pleasant to exist under the same roof and under my roof as the power shift had been in my favor because it was my home, but Mom knew how to be a good guest for short-term visits. I can't exactly remember how long we were living under one roof, but the house seemed to be shrinking, and by this point, I was really in a much better mindset with really trying to not react, voice my concerns, and add an opinion with an attached fact as to try and avoid any emotional projection, but I was also going up against the master of the deflect, respectfully saying. She is a classic example of trying to defuse my comments!

There had been a buildup to the eruption, and prior to the crazy night Grandma unleashed her fury, she and I had some very good dialogue. We talked about our feelings, and we, at least I thought so, made some resolutions as to try and continue treating each other like professional equals and not like she was above and I was lower because of age and the hierarchy of her being the mom, and that was that, a reliable term. But using that as a point of validity was in my opinion not understanding what respectful communication was trying to provide. I could sense some tension, and it was reminiscent from the holidays where we had visited my aunt, my mom's sister, for Christmas and New Year's. I felt my agreement to myself to try and just exist as peacefully as I could in the company of my mother, but I don't know if she knows that she can be a lot to be around when she gets moody and feels like she is no longer the center of attention. That's my loose diagnosis, but she can make a sunny sky black as night when she gets into her mood, and I would look at her and think, *Didn't we talk about this, and didn't you give me permission to call you out when you get into this moody mode?* It was very confusing to me because we had, at least I thought so, a mutual understanding and agreement to draw attention when we were both acting wrong, so I did what I do best, and that was go into ignore mode, and that made things worse as it fueled her anger. But all I could think of was that anything I did do would only press more buttons, so I shut down, and that made the holidays pretty tough to get through. I didn't have the kids that year as they were with their mom for the first time since she left, so all I had was my phone and my willingness to not speak. By the time we all got back home from the tense holiday, things were even more tense in the home. It was evening where I heard a yell at one of the kids, and this was not the first time there was an issue between her and my daughter and now my beautiful boy, where I then got up from my chair and went to see what was going on. I asked, "What's going on? Why are you yelling at Dom?"

That was it. I saw her eyes squint, and she walked toward me and said, "What I say to MY GRANDSON is between him and me." I said, "Well, no, when you yell like you did, that will get my attention, and I will make sure that nothing bad will happen next." She scoffed and said, "Please, who do you think you are?" I was starting to chuckle, which I think was out of some weird coping mechanism. What was I going to do, fight my mother? She did get in my face and started calling me a pussy and said, "No wonder you don't have anybody in your life." I said, "If you hit me, all I can do is call the police because I will not do anything else." She laughed and said, "Oh, look at the big councilman calling the cops. Fuck you!" I went back to my chair and heard her ranting by the kitchen sink. By this time, the kids came out of their rooms and were like, "What's going on?" I tried to use my phone to video her yelling at me, but she caught me and said, "Go ahead and tape me, pussy!"

The next day, I got up for a meeting. I had mulled over the nights events and wondered how I would approach both conversation and behavior when I got home later that day. I actually was calm. I made the decision I would not react or revisit some of the hostility, and I actually felt good for my mom. I knew she had huge amounts of personal baggage, and maybe that stemmed from my father, and since she never released those pent-up emotions, I was the next closest person who was the size of my dad, a male, and looked like my dad. I really felt like it was a good thing, and I felt even better that I did not react and create further angst. I parked outside the house and felt ready to see what was happening inside and was ready to talk, but she was gone. My mom had called a friend to pick her up, and she packed all her bags and left.

It would be months before I reached out to her, and we would talk about that night. I didn't offer too much as to what really happened or what was said. I think I did tell her about her calling me a pussy, but I also feel now that may have been a way to punish for my still-hurt feelings. I forgave her, and we had some great dialogue, that is until she came to visit my brother and I. And by the time she came to my house, she was once again moody and pretentious. I felt I couldn't handle another round of Grandma, so after she left back to Arizona, I told myself I needed to cut ties for a while. I called it detoxing, and although I really relied on her to be my go-to for a pick-me-up or to review a document for her very insightful input, I had to relearn how to adjust and rely solely on Leon and no one else. That was a powerful time that made me grow three feet high with my own peace, but more importantly, I had to stand alone for the first time I could think of as I had no crutch, and since that day two years ago, I have not had a conversation with my mom since. I've sent birthday texts and holiday wishes but no dialogue. She tried one time to talk to me during a Thanksgiving visit where she stayed with my brother and his family and he invited us to have dinner with them, and I went, but I had a bout of anxiety and thwarted off her attempt to poke at me and give me the sad eyes in an attempt to garner my attention so that I could be the engager of some dialogue, but I stood tall and shook my head no. I miss the good parts, but I still don't think I am ready to be in the same room with my mom. But she is a strong personality, and I thank her for all the many talents she passed onto me and even those traits that are questionable. Well, they too serve a purpose when I need them, and one day, I will see her and offer a hug and most likely continued forgiveness, and I sent her this message on her birthday, to wish her well but to also share with her my thoughts and not just make her feel like I was purposely ignoring her but really trying to rediscover who and what I am so I could be understanding and forgiving.

Good evening,

This may be a non-personal way to reach out but seems like the most rational way for the moment.

I will try to explain my distance and have a hope that it's is understood but if there are layers of emotion, then, that's both fine and understandable, or as much as I could try to understand as I can't tell you how to feel and Vice versa and that's not starting this email out negativity, it's starting it out with some for lack of a better word, ground rules.

I felt I had to detox from a flood of thought, emotion and feelings, I didn't feel like I was a powder keg but I did feel like a dung that covered a mountain of debris and I kept tripping over it but ignoring because I felt that's the rug I had since birth and how dare I even touch or move it! There's a metaphor there. In that I needed to realign my values and that meant cutting off people, including you. It was almost an intervention and I felt that if I kept agreeing and relapsing, well that enables my behavior and others and it was not quite chocking me but it left me clouded and placating even dissembling because I didn't want to be the one who regressed in understandings, agreements and assumed roles as a dad, son and brother. This distance had allowed me to self-reflect with no deflection or worry or having to abide by rote behaviors and values. Although having great values and judgement, I am grateful I was able to learn from your teachings/guidance but that also made things assumed, in my opinion, as to the hierarchy which I was not jibing with.

The long, short of it is, I also felt dependent on other people's opinions and direction and that also made me addicted to questioning myself in an attempt to please and not create and contention but that also became my crutch! It weighed heavy on me which is why I mentioned enabling and dissembling. I don't know what their message is meant to do but I do hope it received in a fair and open minded manner, as I put myself in the reverse of things to try and be understanding even though we as human nature tend to react based on our egos and that is good at times but also damaging, in my opinion.

Being distance is important for me and although it may seem negative, has been quite positive for emotional growth and new clarity. I wanted to share these thoughts months ago but I wasn't ready and maybe I am not ready now but much better to be able to cope with fall out and disdain, from anyone.

I am at a loss for words as I feel saying more will only be redundant and I do not want my thoughts to be misconstrued as criticism as it is not but if it is, it is constructive as it has helped my mind. I never thought I was weak and having these feelings and being able to explore them has been strong and snapping out of emotions is and was much harder to do as I can see how depression can be a tough joke to climb out of. Mika (My daughter) asked me a question for her schoolwork or during this project may have also been talking with a friend, but she asked what is depression? I asked her what she thought it was and she started saying "I don't know how people get depressed, couldn't they choose not to be?" I started to give her a rote response but caught myself and simply stated, I don't know if it's that's easy, I told her, it is ok to express feelings and emotion because they help us be able to think about things and our thoughts are meant to help us not whether if people agree or disagreed with our emotions, remember, that happiness is an emotion and that life is a balance, so if someone can feel depressed, then chances are they can also feel happy and if we practice that, like all things we practice, we can make a habit and be able to adjust when we have bad days. It made me realize that I don't know shit and that I faked most of my life and tried to conform when I am not a conformist, that's a deeper explanation but I also realized that contradiction and hypocrisy is part of human nature and that we all exude those qualities and chastise ourselves and others which creates more conflict than just agreed acceptance, again deeper conversation for another time.

That's where I am at these days. I send this note with pure intention absent of acrimony, again maybe not good timing but it's like trying to stay sober, again metaphorically speaking.

I wish you a very happy birthday and continue to stay safe and healthy.

This was the first time in a very long time that I have had to stand alone. I have always had some support, from family and being in long-term relationships, but this time, I was to walk alone, reflect much more, and then decide as to how I would keep walking forward. I felt I always had a plan in my life, but after seeing the therapist when I was separated, that somehow made my mind open new doors. Things I had locked up were now being exposed, and one after the other, all my repressed emotions became brighter and brighter, couple that with whatever healing I was trying to do. I used to be a hurry-and-get-over-it guy, but by now, I needed answers and became ravenous with my quest to obtain answers as to try and help me understand and then be able to traverse forward with acceptance. I have always needed to find out the whys and hows and then formulate a strategy to then know how the outcomes could be. It was and is still a very strange demand I made of myself to then keep mulling over and over. I would finally realize or try to accept that no matter what I did, I relied way too much on being rewarded, not monetarily but by acknowledgement, and it became Pavlovian. I craved positive reinforcement and had become a people pleaser even at the risk of allowing disdain. I felt that any reaction would be an opportunity to invite and engage in some dialogue because together there could be a mutual understanding. I would push and press, and maybe that explains the op-eds; maybe that explains my inability to leave things rather than force outcomes I had no control over.

I had decided that if I was going to start something new in my life, I would go out and have a drink at the local bar. The first few times, I was literally sweating. I kept thinking what people will say, how will they react, what if I killed my political career. Sounds pretty crazy, but I was trained and had developed my own internal wall against the same people I was to speak up for. In my quest to untrain what I taught myself, I took those steps, yes, to the bar, past the restaurant where everyone could see who was coming and going, and thought, *Boy, you're going to make this test difficult*. I put on a no-care face and smiled and even engaged in some conversations with people and joked that I really needed a drink after being on council; sounds stupid now because I couldn't be truthful to people if I wasn't even truthful to myself. But I was determined to move past these rooted feelings, and it was weird but nothing bad. In fact, I had very good conversations with everyone I spoke to and created no expectations in those conversations, just talked and listened. It was fun. I forgot what fun was, and it was good to know that I too could even have fun.

One evening, I was talking to a dear friend who was tending bar, and it was a slow night, so he and I were just chatting and laughing, and he told me, "Hey, why don't you run for the school board?" I laughed and said, "Yeah, I had thought of that before," but my comment was more of a blow-off comment than a consideration. I left later that night thinking more about the conversation we had about the upcoming school board election. I thought, *Okay, Leon, if you are on a new path and you have been out of the arena of politics for a year now, that may be an opportunity to help you and the school.* Some time went by, and I had not really made a commitment yet, but what I was now seeing was that there were no candidates filing, and I thought, *Wow, no one wants to run for this opportunity*. And as I look back now, maybe I forced myself and convinced myself that I really should do this. I thought, *What the hell, it was time to file as a candidate for the Dulce Independent School district election*. I showed up to the county clerk's office, and to my amazement, there were sev-

ﾉ

eral other people who told me they were not running, which is why I forced myself to do so. But before I went inside the building, I sat in the parking lot and thought, *Do I really want to do this?* I looked at my daughter, who had accompanied me on the ride over, and asked her, "Do I really want to do this?" She said, "Yes, you should. You will do great and really help." I smiled and thanked her for her kind and generous words, and she smiled, and together we both walked inside to complete my paperwork. I was now an official candidate for the school board election and at the same time coming to terms with emotions I tried to black out from my past job and did okay. After all, I was still relearning how to walk tall again.

Losing elections is tough, and it took me a while to realize the cliché that losing is winning. I called bullshit on that phrase, but upon further self-reflection, that statement somewhat rings true. I actually had to try and rediscover my internal strength. I had the ability to adapt, and I knew how to be a good politician, diplomat, and be of service. There were issues, moments, and times I felt I was not, yet I still stepped up to try, and despite the comments from some, there were many others who saw what I didn't see in me, and they believed in me, and I was not only grateful but also more determined to stand alone, if need be, and keep bringing the best I could. I had proposed many different, even unorthodox approaches to trying to inspire the voters to feel like they could know their worth and value of being more involved in what their government was doing or not doing. The last special election for the presidency, I wrote a letter to my opponent, inviting him to a debate, and he never answered me. There were no responses. The member Facebook page I talked about earlier was abuzz with comments that made me out to be a bully because I wanted to hold a debate. I was really just trying to get people to be able to feel involved, and I may or may not have lost because of that invitation, but I was still preoccupied with my angered emotions that I forgot to maintain my inner balance, and that was what I think made me feel inept and in turn defensive and self-loathing.

During the school board primary, there was an invite to hold a debate of the candidates, and five of the candidates showed up, and there were a couple of dozen voters in the audience. I was elated and maybe even a little perturbed in thinking, *Oh, now you want to hold a debate.* But that feeling was soon replaced with joy at what could be in the future of all elections. I even made that comment to the teacher and those high school seniors for creating such a positive precedent.

The night of the school board election, I had discovered I won and by a good number. I was ready to learn and do what I could to help just by simply endorsing the policies and protocols. I was invited as a school board member elect as I had not been officially installed yet, but I attended my first work session with my new colleagues and the interim superintendent. We sat at a large table, and I bore witness to the same one-sided, egotistical, spiteful, finger-pointing I just left a year and a half earlier. I sat there thinking, *What the hell did I get myself back into?* I even got called out as someone who was not a team player because while I was serving as a council member. I had been very vocal about the encroachment the Nation's government was doing to a separate governmental agency that had its own separate rules and laws, and rather than have a well-built bridge to help the school district in a respectful and consistent manner, the Nation's government would just criticize and put their two cents into how staff operated and how staff were hired and fired. There was really no understanding of roles and responsibilities, just chaos and destruction derived from emotion and opinion. I tried not to chuckle, and I didn't even object. I tried but soon caught myself and tried to redirect back to what the school board was currently charged to do and tried to create a dialogue as to what the board could do. I don't know if my comments landed, but I said them anyway.

I was installed as an official school board member in December of 2019 and began my first meeting in January of 2020. I sat through my first official meeting as a school district representative and just observed. It was fascinating to me. I had some minor insight as to the inner workings as I had scheduled a meeting with the interim superintendent just to meet him and listen to what was going on to date, and there was also the constant turnaround of school superintendents, and I knew that once again there were continued practices that were proving to be detrimental to progress, so I just wanted to try and promote accountability, and I wrote this statement to help inform and remind all that we are a team and we all need to understand that the rules, whether we agree or disagree, are still rules that need to be obeyed.

I had the privilege of being sworn in on the hallowed grounds of Dulce, last night at the rescheduled DISD School Board meeting. I am also the new school board President and sit eagerly to help bridge the much important relationships needed for student success. I will use positive dialog for viable positive outcomes and ask that we all understand that concerns, comments, and emotion can be inputs that some might feel deserve instant demand. Although important, it is again a reminder that we concentrate on positive outcomes.

I personally like the all the high standards, rules and accountability the school and school board members have to abide by, in my opinion if this high mandated standard was adopted at the tribal government level, it would be a game changer as to what and how your Public servants lead especially with having to be transparent.

That being said, I hope you understand that if and when you share your comments and or concerns with any school board member, it then begins a series of motions, governed by the New Mexico Statutes Chapter 22, the New Mexico School Boards Administration and The Family **Educational** Rights and Privacy Act (**FERPA**) which is a federal law that affords parents the **right to** have access to their children's **education** but only their children not anyone else's. Which means if you comment on an issue and another parent or person overhears your conversation could be breaking the law of FERPA. Now I want to assure you that the safety of our students is paramount but please let us not forgot there is a proper and safe way to log any and all comments or complaints and they have to start with the Superintendent who is also bound by law to help in a proficient, ethical and timely manner for any and all follow up as to provide an adequate response and fair solutions.

I encourage you to attend School board meeting and at the very least review the meeting minutes by asking directly or checking the schools website and continuing to stay positive and optimistic.

Great things are on the horizon and they begin with adults who are able to help guide our students to also do the right things by the rules.

I'm not sure how my comments were received. After all, I was hearing comments that I was the new guy and that I had no experience when it came to matters of the school. I smiled and thought, *Well, that could be true, but I also took an oath of office to the laws that were approved by the state government, and despite my opinions as to these laws or behaviors, I had a responsibility to endorse, enforce, and promote these policies.*

It was after the school board work session and my first official meeting that I felt it important to present comments on goals, objectives, and expectations of both the superintendent and the board. My first draft was garbage because I rushed to make this first meeting, but I refocused and took my time and compiled remarks and quoted statutes that the district had to follow and handed out my thoughts along with what I proposed as goals and objectives that could be discussed on the record and even have a possible vote to approve better recommendations rather than goals that were minuscule, like no more assistants to the assistants and other internal personnel issues. That was the job of the superintendent who was hired by the board to do the job, not be micromanaged and paid to follow orders of the board. Plus having goals that were also in line with the New Mexico Public Education Department, the state agency that has direct oversight of all school districts in New Mexico, and to help try and give, the then superintendent, an opportunity to have some insight that could be used to help provide more tangible results based on approved objectives and, in this approach, created ways to provide measurable results rather than forced or coerced results, which really only produce more inconsistencies, in my humble opinion. But that was also the consensus of the very first training I attended by the New Mexico School Board's Association, which in its own right is a sanctioned organization designed to help after you pay dues as a member but offers no real accountability as to ensure the highest standards for districts and their stakeholders, but I digress. This was the letter I submitted for record:

My synopsis as a Dulce Independent School District (DISD) School Board (SB) and proposed Goals and Objectives.

Please understand that any opinion's and or comments will always be directed at the whole, hopefully never preachy and if anyone feels that my comments are directed at them personally, well then maybe subconsciously your actions have contributed and exacerbated to the long-term issues we are facing. I support and welcome any dialog, I also understand the most conversations might come from frustration and emotion, especially if you as a person, have felt that you were not heard or felt that the system that was supposed to help, let you down. We can no longer blame but if we do, we should all share the blame. As representatives, public servants of this fraternal order of elected SB members of the board of education, we have to understand the

VITAL, CRUCIAL and IMPERATIVE role, that we undertook. We sit as one voice for the benefit of those we represent, of our stakeholders, our students, staff, teachers and parents/guardians and students, of the Dulce Independent School District. As SB members, we swore to abide by the Oath of Office to the Ethics and Governmental conduct. We then have to provide a respect and service to the rules with the intention that we ALL create a positive showing of efforts being made as to become a beacon of light of our elected roles and responsibilities and even limitations and do so to ensure the utmost professionalism and fairness in fulfilling any goals and needs of our stakeholders because "Every student has a right to learn in a safe, caring and supportive environment."

Understanding the importance of upholding the oath of office allows all parties to understand and also honor the letter and spirit of the law. We know as individual SB members that we have no AUTHORITY to act alone, demand, coerce or offer preferential treatment of any of our stakeholders. Any breech of the oath is not only illegal but destructive and disruptive. If our actions are not pure and lack standards, our actions then give perceived permission for others to mimic our behavior. If we want our stakeholders to trust us just as we would like to trust them, we have to follow written protocol, follow the proper chain of command and command the highest of standards for all intended rules. Singular interests should not be a variable derived from the basis for personal divisions, personal interests or retaliation, from one person, special interest groups, political expediency, bias or prejudice. If at any time a SB member, staff member, teacher, parent or administrator has breached any rule like following a proper chain of command, your actions have set into motion a cheating of the system which was designed to hold standards and accountability, and too have become guilty of violating the law.

Since we, as DISD School Board members have no local internal guidelines to help govern, we rely on the New Mexico School Boards Association handbook that has adopted the state Public School Code, of Chapter 22 Article 5 of the New Mexico Statutes Annotated, 1978 Compilation. If there is a misunderstood practice or ignoring of these rules, we are at greater risk of being charged as non-compliant as SB members and stakeholders. I ask the question, aren't we all responsible for examining and scrutinizing our own work, especially since we are entrusted to govern and hopefully do so with clarity, free of speculation and hearsay. The argument could then be, that If the rules and laws are respected and understood, then, today, the slate should be wiped clean. Again, I ask, have the letter and spirit of the laws been fostered in an honest, fair and impartial way so that the DISD vision and mission are being practiced reliably? Has the "WHY' and "HOW" been explained to the stakeholders? Communication is a word that gets tossed around and usually ends up becoming used a negative strategy of "passing the buck' for blame because we fail to look at ourselves and often feel that by finger pointing, we are letting ourselves off the hook, especially if one of the major roles is to ensure communication for student success in a safe, caring and supportive environment. If there is no accountability for leadership coupled with no desire to welcome constructive criticism, I ask, then how can we preach achievement, progress and success? Our combined actions, SB members and stakeholders, have to be done wholeheartedly by knowing the value and importance of the system. If WE are not doing our very best to learn ourselves by following protocols, then we ALL are part of the problem. Which then brings us to following current DISD Mission and Vision statements on the website. Are these statements able to be proven and if they have, what is the standard we need to do to continue, if we forget what's at stake then these and other statements we make become meaningless soundbites:

District Mission: Our district will educate, nurture and strengthen all our children to be productive, contributing members of society.

District Vision: Dulce Graduates will be self-directed, capable, responsible, life-long learners, who maintain their cultural identities and creative individualism.

As adults, we have inherited the privilege, dare I say the challenge, to protect, mold, teach and inspire our children! It should go without saying that **"A child's outcome does not change, until adult behaviors change"** and based on that powerful statement, the old adage sits true, **"It takes a whole village to raise our children to which we all must share in the burden"** however **"It also takes a village to tear down and neglect our children, to this we also share this burden."**

I know as one of two new SB members we have inherited a robust and busy schedule but my hope and I'm sure the hope of our stakeholders is that we ALL become part of the solution!

If we as SB members are to make a difference in the lives of our children, we have to stay focused, follow the process and reflect on a dignity that highlights our given authority. We, as adults, have to create an environment that increases teacher appreciation, student engagement and academic achievement so that our children begin to understand the need to be challenged, stay focused and work on becoming emotionally secure. After all, the ability to adopt an infinite mindset is a prerequisite for any current or future leader who aspires to leave any associated organization in better shape than it was found by being a more effective Board. The job of being a more effective board member can be very complex but let us understand that we can do so by promoting, sharing and following the rules so that we have created a warmer environment, become better role and begin rebuilding trust.

We have deep issues that are plaguing us so the time for blame has long past, we all now sit as the catalyst to ignite the spark that allows us to clean up and further build upon the strong foundation we already have, so let's do so with the mentality that long term strategies will always outperform short term "band-aiding" ones with the allowance that everyone know their roles and responsibilities for true measurable outcomes.

If for any reason a SB member or for that matter stakeholder, is unable to practice with a reasonable responsibility, have a total regard for what is in the best interest of the children of our district by allowing those necessary to run the school, have become disinterested in the facts of administrator responsibility, are unable to sift fact from fiction, unable to sort out rumors from realism, and understand the difference, encroached on the proper chain of command in any way, is unable to use good ethical and moral judgment in decision making, incorporate stronger, clearer, measurable outcomes, then we STOP now and NOT rush, by realigning priorities by developing proper structure and allow those to feel empowered, every person will know the importance of their role and responsibility, anything less will do nothing more than kick the metaphorical can down the road for others to deal with. There is some truth in not being able to can't go back and change things from the beginning but today, we can start right now, right where we are and begin to change the ending. We have to ability to inspire, achieve dreams, empower our students to learn more, do more and become more because we ourselves want to do more!

I humbly offer the following suggestions to the agenda items of 5,6,7 of the January 23rd meeting under new business and I hope we can have honest discussion in reaching an agreement to adopt viable, reliable outcomes based on comparable issues that other districts are addressing for their student success.

Item 10 (New Business) #5 Consider Interim-Super Goals and Objectives

As a reminder, Section F (Policy Making) of the New Mexico School Boards Association handbook describes that the board makes policy and the superintendent administers it. This is not the way in which effective boards operate.

In actual practice, the superintendent generally initiates policy formulation and provides the evidence on which the board makes the decisions. The board considers the statement and the evidence and accepts, rejects, or revises the statement. Once a policy is adopted, the superintendent does administer it. The board, however, must continue to receive reports, to evaluate the results of the policy, and when indicated, to revise the policy in light of experience again understood deliverables.

The Standards further require that staff and others be involved in the policy-making, so it should go without saying that part of a board member's responsibility is to see that all policy is established, followed and revised when revision is needed.

Since the purpose of policy is to inspire or help determine the course of action that an organization takes in certain situations, we should then also promote equitable treatment of students, employees, and members of the public, knowing that any deviation from established current SB policy should be infrequent. Otherwise, the policy will be undermined which has been experienced both internally (DISD) and externally (Dulce).

The role and responsibility of the SB is to adopt, implement and share relevant/meaningful Goals & Objectives for DISD, which also falls in line with the Superintendent's answerability and shared responsibility (Sec F In actual practice, the superintendent generally initiates policy formulation and provides the evidence on which the board makes the decisions). In preparing for the first SB meeting and discussions from the

December/January NMSBA conference, I offer the points to be incorporated as DISD's 2020 goals and objectives. It is important to add that the following points appear to be impending at the State level and certainly local level and would then already be easy to command action since we all are speaking the same language in proving accountability of our local district, the State of New Mexico Public Education Department:

- **Yazzie/Martinez**—Identify deficiencies as to create more consistent educational outcomes for students, teachers and community. This in concert with district commitment, preparation and willingness to effectively meet increased funding, resources, flexibility and the accountability necessary to comply with this case. Does or has this SB adopted NMPED directive/timelines to recognize state funding, if yes what has worked, if no then what has not worked, goes to a long-term solution.

- **Early Childhood/Pre-K/Head start**—We need to address and fully understand the need for and support of a comprehensive, well-aligned educational system that begins as early as Head start. Early Childhood education has shown to prepare students for not only inclusion but preparation for success as they grow throw the district. Early preparation for higher education and career pathways will start the need to allow students to begin feeling like they too are allowed to think for themselves and also experience what it is like to be rewarded for hard work and in turn will positively affect their class-mates and then community.

- **SPED**—Since the Special Education Department (SPED) is specialized, decisions flow from the top down, meaning SPED decisions must be made and adhered to in concurrence with all legal requirements primarily spelled out in both State and Federal law and done so with an Individualized Educational Plan (IEP) discussed, agreed to and created by a DISD IEP team with the inclusion of meaningful parental participation and understanding. The goal and objective should be to remedy any financial deficiencies, to apply for and help ensure that SPED students are not just used as a number for the district's budget but are also recognized as student peers, increasing both classroom productivity and graduation rates, better screening devices and standards for identifying both needs of our students who are special needs including giftedness. A recognition of increased salaries for SPED staff/teachers and Care Givers as well as to find ways to train and retain and recruit SPED staff, teachers/caregivers. If SPED students are to benefit from public education then there needs to be a goal and objective to proactively plan for the current student body and any influx of future IEP students, ages 3–21, so that SPED remain proactive and in compliance for both student retention, assimilation and safety recognizing the Individuals with Disabilities Education Act (IDEA) act and Free Appropriate Public Education (FAPE).

- **Community Partnership**—District/ School Board/Jicarilla Apache Nation (JAN) willingness to engage with, understand again and respond with open minded efforts to create ready resources for our students to either properly be prepared to attend higher educational facilities or assimilate successfully into the Nation's workforce. This effort has to be positive and not based on again ego or band-aide input/ responses based on the good old days. If we as adults are not planning for tomorrow or the next 5–10–15 years and as a community proper planning for the growth of employment, families and future students, then we are part of the problem. It is a fact that the future workplace could have as many as 40 jobs in 10 different careers, to which each will then require a retooling of skills. By the way, over 80% of these jobs have not even been created yet! In the next 4 years, jobs could be displaced by technology with over 100 million jobs likely emerging during this same timeline. Whether you like or agree with, the younger generation is here and your positive guidance in homes and at the dinner table are also preparing your children to stand strong and pay it forward.
- **Career Cluster/Pathway Education**— (See attachment A) If this goal and objective is understood especially in utilization of the communal partnership is, the District / SB and JAN commitment in moving forward can help create the important framework for critical Applied Academics, which is as you know is an approach to learning

and teaching that focuses on how academic subjects (communications, mathematics, science, and basic literacy) can apply to the real world will only create a further burden on finances, increased social vices and a growth of the community to which it will not be prepared for. This goal and objective also creates the understanding to help create sustainable, empowered, accountable future Directors, Managers, Parents and Community Leaders.

- **School Safety/ Security/Cyber-Security**—Remedy and identify funding issues and or other funding to improve school safety and security personnel including any and all Capital improvements and equipment, updated and consistent staff training, creating plans to better serve and treat behavioral, emotional and mental services, with measured and continued counseling for student and staff, improved cybersecurity for both protection and technological learning and restorative justice programs which are programs used by tribes, ethnic groups and other communities using an often non-Western process that enables members of the group collectively to respond to and to repair the harm caused by a crime by talking about what happened, the crime's aftermath, and its implications for the future and then arriving at a consensus as to the appropriate consequences for the offender. Restorative Justice Programs include, but are not limited to, circle sentencing, family group conferencing, reparative boards, and victim/offender mediation. If adopted the one issue we as a whole, DISD/Community may want to be cognizant of is if not trusted and have total buy in as this program could also be a disadvantage including short term failing to stop future crimes and the compliant to any powers that be as to avoid imposing harsh penalties.

- **Effective Recruitment of/Growing Our Own Teachers**—First of all, thank you to all Teachers, Care Givers and staff and administrators who have decided to work in our beautiful community and at the same time trust DISD to guide and teach your children, you may not hear it enough but you are valued and welcomed to Dulce. For this goal, we need to support any and all Legislation and our own DISD budget to increase teacher/Care giver salaries and push for better ways to allow current/retired DISD employees to be allowed the opportunity to return to work without penalties as to help with the current crisis teacher shortage issues and also reward and create sustainability for substitute teachers who are currently helping. By also supporting and planning for the expansion and improvement of teacher preparation programs, including planning for future teacher/staff housing, we can maximize, reward, retain and recruit our most precious resources, our teachers/care givers, so that together we have created a stronger feeling of moral and belonging as to help grow future positive DISD initiatives.

As the District/SB and Community our understanding is paramount. It's a fearful realization that we live in a different age. Things of yesterday are completely different than they were in your time and yet in today's world we cannot ignore the other fact, that there is still beauty and love that gives us bountiful blessings, so long as we are all willing to help and offer kindness. By understanding and then wholeheartedly agreeing to these goals and objectives, we are committing to inspiring our children by listening and understanding that they too are just as equal as human beings and they too can become inspired to also help their community by nurturing Realities, Perspectives, Process and Procedure.

Item 10 (New Business) #6,#7 Consider Interim-Superintendent Evaluation/Search

If we are to expecting others to follow the guidelines/rules, stated above, then it behooves us to practice the same and in a much better way. I truly feel that before this evolution begins, the question be asked of our current SB members, have you provided defined measurable's, clearly communicated time lines and encouraged all to follow the proper chain of command, and have you in your role as SB member inadvertently over-steeped your role or responsibility, encroaching on the duties of the Chief Executive Officer, administer and supervisor, deemed that the Superintendent of DISD, after all the SB ONLY oversees one employee, and that is the superintendent and ONLY the superintendent! We have to make sure, we ourselves, not only follow every process of the law but understanding that as Public servants, we cannot taint the system by further created chaos. There are ways of bringing about positive change but doing so based on over steeping only brings spite, ego or title that will then continue to keep us ALL behind, especially if we have adopted presented goals and objectives.

With that, I'd like to add a few questions as to the Superintendent's evaluation:

1. Are we going to conduct these evaluation's with an open mind and positive climate?
2. Are we truly understanding of the Superintendent's job and if yes, have any SB members attempted to interfere with any duties/responsibilities?
3. Has there been fair, impartial, frequent and timely feedback to the Superintendent again things that can be measured and done so by agreed directive in a duly called meeting?
4. If there are viable concerning issues during this evaluation, can your concerns be factually supported with specifics?
5. Is this evaluation being used as a template from a reputable consistence source like the NMSBA handbook and if not, from where was this evaluation designed?
6. Will this evaluation focus on proven performance results/deliverables and not from any bias or hearsay?
7. Will the Superintendent be able to respond to this evaluation in a positive climate?
8. Will this evaluation be limited to the matters to which the Superintendent has authority?
9. Will this evaluation factor in any Board participation, support or lack of support with

the Superintendent in his achievements of
any current SB adopted goals and objectives
done so in a duly called meeting?

10. If for any reason the Superintendent has not
executed his authority, given proper communication and or in a systematic way, have
the factors of what this may do to time,
resources, energy and possible repeated
issues, might cause since, after all evalua-
tions can be described as a way to create a
good, understood working relationship? as

11. Finally, who and at what time would the SB
welcome its own evaluation as to our leadership and achievements with the adopted
goals and objectives?

The proposed goals and objectives never went anywhere and
didn't even make it to the agenda for discussion, much less a vote. In
fact, I would find myself in yet another attempt to terminate a person
charged to serve in the capacity of an executive. The majority of my
new board colleagues were adamant that they were going to get rid
of the interim superintendent because they felt he was not following
the plan of the board. I use that term because most of the accusations
ranged from personnel issues, which is a board no-no, to being ridiculed and yelled at for providing answers some did not agree with.
There is always room for growth especially when it comes to ensuring the highest quality of education for children, but as I alluded to
earlier, school districts answer to NMPED and the governor of the
state, and the two were responsible for inconsistencies in providing
the state's agenda for education, but that is a point that also causes
people, especially board members, to forget or ignore, and it causes
major issues.

It was at one meeting where the board would restructure the
officers, and I had thought, *I cannot sit by and just do nothing, I won't
make my full term, and I didn't want to quit as I made a commitment.*
And the number of voters who trusted me to serve was always on

my mind to make sure they felt they made the right choice, and I would do whatever I could, by statute and moral fiber, to help at the very least and highlight roles and responsibilities and, in that, limitations of all. I decided to nominate myself as school board president. I checked the rules to make sure I was able to give my own nomination, and there was nothing that prohibited such action. The meeting was called to start, and we stood to recite the Pledge of Allegiance and then salute to the NM flag and sat to be called for roll call. The agenda had for-action nominations for new board officers, and I asked the former board president to be recognized, and I said, "I'd like to nominate myself for board president." It got quiet, and I was even thinking, *Oh, shit, what did I do?* But my nomination was recognized, and there was a second and a vote that produced, from what I heard, two votes of yes a murmur and silence. The vote was in, and I got up from my chair and moved to the chair that had a small plaque that said Board President. I was now sitting facing the small crowd, waiting to present to the board, and I thought, *Wow, okay, Leon, you asked for this. Get it done*, and away we went.

This new title has many wonderful opportunities but very little authority to act autonomously, which was great, but the title had brought along some pretty heavy baggage that tried to circumvent process and protocol, and that was not how I saw things, much less ever tried. I kept the interim superintendent in the loop in everything I said or wrote, and I would even have him review my emails before I sent them out so that he knew of my subject matter. And most importantly, I was not out of line. This worked out great, and I felt the interim superintendent welcomed my practice. There was still the taste of blood in the water, and no matter what I said or tried to highlight, the board was ready to get rid of the interim super. I once again came face-to-face with prior emotions I had in the last two years of my council term, tried to rise above, and was beginning to feel like I was once again banging my head on the wall. But this time, I felt the strength I needed was not fully charged, and I was worried I would regress in my mental health. I was met with comments that the super and I were buddies and that I was protecting him and that, because I was new, I didn't know what I was doing or what the rules were. It was crazy, and I was just sitting back listening but contemplating how I would keep pushing forward. I knew I was in line with the rules, and no matter who felt different, all I had to do was show the law, so that was a positive, but being testing was tough. I thought I would at least make sure I was correct in my knowledge, and so I wrote an email to the New Mexico School Board Association's president with a hope that NMSBA could offer ways to help a school district that had a very checkered past. The email read,

Good evening sir,

My name is Leon Reval and I am a school board (SB) member for the district in Dulce.

I have not had the pleasure to meet you official but I have seen you at the last two NMSBA conferences.

I now sit as the DISD SB President, well maybe as I also found out one of my colleagues was questioning the approved agenda item of reorganization but it was both compliant and legal. I was hoping to get some direction to some questions I have, I would be remised if I said I do have my opinions as to proper protocol including transparency, but would feel better if I did have direction about the interim Superintendent (Super) specifically the evaluation. One, does the interim still get evaluated? Two, if there have been no agreed goals and objectives derived jointly with the SB and Super, then I would think the evaluation would be done by the midyear report? Third, NMSBA has a template to help a SB evaluate but does there need to be a certain number of questions that an evaluation should have and is it best to ignore any relevant suggested templates like NMSBA's in lieu of SB members creating their own? Fourth, when would the evaluation have to take place, a duly called SB mtg, work session and if either would that be done in an Executive session?

Lastly can you share any info on a possible Ethics Committee that was proposed last year by the State to create over-site of School Boards and when and how that will be both implemented and enforced?

I thank you for your time and direction and also understand that you may not be able to comment on any of my questions but I'm hoping for some nudging as to try and promote and hold accountability of our Board, District employees and Parents.

All my best.

Response from NMSBA; "Hi Mr. Reval,

I am in receipt of your message and questions. Because we are extremely busy at the legislature and in order to provide a more prompt reply I would prefer to discuss your questions over the phone. Generally speaking, the superintendent evaluation process is spelled out in local board policy. So you may to refer to your local policy for guidance prior to your call.

I will be in the office tomorrow morning and would welcome your call. Please use my cell phone number provided below.

Thank you!

Follow up email: "Thank you for your response Mr. Guillen,

I have reviewed the policy and although not a legal expert am well versed in policy and protocol.

Full disclosure, I have Board colleagues who have a differing opinion and practice of what I am trying to practice and it is in my opinion causing more issues than solutions. My intention to write and have my questions answered, was my attempt to have verbatim responses from someone, like yourself, who has the magnitude and understood need for proper protocol and policy understanding, implementation and understood limitations.

I also know that with SB 668, there is going to be some stronger oversight as to the actions of public officials and this may include board behaviors, who may not abide by the oath of office and oath of ethics.

I appreciate your time and understand the long hours during the legislative session. I will call tomorrow morning and I do look forward to further dialog for the benefit of our student success remaining the priority in our respective districts.

Have a great evening.

I never heard back from NMSBA again. I started feeling like this was bullshit, and that was when I realized this organization was merely ad hoc and had zero authority to do anything for the benefit of stronger oversight for accountability. Even if my email was completely frivolous, in my opinion, a sanctioned organization who takes dues from districts should be able to investigate to make sure the law is followed and that, if my email was indeed frivolous, it could have held me responsible. But if there were issues that reflected breaches in policy, then they could have held better responsibility of those who were committing such atrocities. This wasn't for Leon. This was for students and those who had a duty to provide successes of all students and employees of the district. I was upset and still give no validation to this organization.

The district now has a contracted superintendent, and it was a hard sell, but the board finally went back to an old approach that allowed the cream, as they say, to rise to the top. A large net was cast, and there were about ten very strong candidates for the superintendent job who wanted to work in Dulce. One candidate was chosen, and it was up to the newly placed interim super, yes, the other interim was placed on administrative leave, which, yes, put him out of a job but also paid him the rest of his contract. And now the board would pay for services of the new interion when the contract could have been utilized to finish and complete the job search rather than pay redundant costs, but to make the long short of this hiring process, a selection was made, and it turned out that the person selected spoke to others about his new position in Dulce and heard so many negatives that he recanted and said no to the position. The district's reputation preceded itself, but there was another selection made, and sometimes, things work out in good ways. The district has a very strong super, and for the next two years, yes, there was a discussion to have a two-year contract rather than one so that there could be some consistency for the greater good. I keep my fingers crossed every day and sadly also remain on standby for that dreadful day someone's opinion worms its way into the structure and weakens the foundation yet again.

Since I had been on a pretty good path of shedding the cloak of anger, frustration, and hurt I was dealing with and things were going well, despite the dynamics of the board, but in my new capacity as board member present of the school district, I was proud to be able to promote and endorse empowerment, accountability, and teamwork. I thought, *Okay, Leon, if you feel good, then prove it. Now start working on getting some closure, and that way, you can finally start putting emotions past you.* It was an election year, and the deadline to file was close, and for the time prior, I was determined to not run. But that was what my ego was saying because in my mental battle, I also felt that I had so much to give, and what I learned and applied was vital to at least be a voice to hold accountability. I knew that if I did not become a candidate that I would always have this fantasy that I would have won and, in that, not had the clarity needed to do the duties as a school board member properly and responsibly. I decided to enter into the race, and on the last day of the deadline to file, I went to the bank, withdrew $500, and went to pay my filing fee at the Nation's administration building, the place that I was still trying to find strength to enter. I was sweating. I had some anxiety going to a place that I had loved being in and in my first term helped procure financing for and the much-needed empowerment of the construction manager, a great friend whom I would also serve alongside of in my short term as a council member but now wanted to never step foot in. That day I filed was a test of endurance, and although I tried to force myself to forget my own inner strengths and abilities, a higher power made certain I was able to walk tall. I was shaking and trying to clear my throat so that I wasn't mumbling. I paid, got the receipt, and went to the Election Board office and picked the chair I would run for. The list of candidates was long in all four council positions, and I just pointed and said, "That one." I cannot even recall right now what seat that was, but I did notice later that a good friend had entered the race, and I felt bad because I was so nervous and preoccupied with my worries of who I might run into or what people would think that, in my self-reflection, I posed the thought that I was purposely running against him. I felt embarrassed about my fear but knew I would get closure one way or the other.

There was no lengthy op-ed, no campaigning, just the candidate statement that allowed 250 words to make a statement. Every time I received from the candidate application packet, I would always smile to see the ordinance I wrote that still was being used, and that always made me feel like I accomplished things as a council member. This election was about me and finding a way to move forward if elected or have closure and now face the uncertainty of doing something else with my experience.

I tried to take a different approach with making a statement. I could not, in good faith of both the sanctity of the government and even my continued dedication, just be silent, so I was invited to be interviewed via Zoom, and I accepted. My approach to the questions I was asked was to hit transparency and accountability and hope that these two words would resonate with those who were tuning in to the interview. I really felt I left everything on the table. Not once did I name-drop for either good or bad comments. This was about trying to get the membership to finally get involved and help themselves be the authority in holding their representatives to the highest standards. I had offered to anyone who wanted one a digital copy of the Nation's constitution and laws and had some takers, but I have never heard of any sitting leader, even former, of ever doing that. I was not trying to be martyr or even plot some revenge. This was all about trying to share valuable information ten people swore and promised to a higher power to uphold, and if these ten people did not, then the true power of the people could build stronger cases using statues to make certain the government could show what it does to earn a paycheck.

I lost the election. I didn't even make the top 2 for the general election runoff. That had never happened in all my attempts. I had lost the general but always made the primaries. The reality of "careful what you ask for you just might get it" stared me straight in the eyes, but I had the closure I needed to no longer fantasize about winning and now the challenge of facing a different reality. I look back on a very illustrious career, and even with the clouded emotions, I am most proud of all that was done, and the major or minor part I played in honored the code of what it meant to serve as a councilman.

I smile as I reminisce. I have met so many wonderful, great people whom I value and had the honor of borrowing their great qualities to help me become even more aware of my duties and responsibilities. I really cannot be upset. Politics is a fickle mistress, and she can be inviting and make you feel like a king, but she can also rip the carpet from under you and make you feel lower than low. But I accepted all and everything she gave me as I was deeply smitten, but I chose her. She did not choose me, so I also left on my own terms; that's a powerful realization. I could easily still be holding a grudge, but why? I was welcomed, and I really felt I did what I could. While hindsight can be a monster on the mind, there were some things I personally wanted to make sure were done to help the membership long term. There are definitely highlights that I am most proud of, and no matter how many new buildings my name may or may not be on, I really had a great opportunity to stay in the realm of the political world, and the funny thing is, I always joked that if I did have a superpower, it was ignorance because I had to ask questions and then ask for proof of response and action.

There is not a lot of logic when it comes to serving in office. I am not being critical. When you have a good group who actually has a positive mindset to keep the rules in the forefront, then there is a silent agreement and understanding of always doing right by the rules. But when there is a complete disregard of the rules, then you have chaos. I could never understand how the term *sovereignty* was used with so much prominence but rarely used as a springboard to propel a tribe into the atmosphere for the benefit of the membership. I was asked one time in a meeting what sovereignty was. Now by this time I was at the end of my term, tired and myopic in keeping an open mind, but I answered, "It's a practice that unfortunately has not been used to really help our community." That was an ignorant, pessimistic answer, and I was embarrassed after I went home and recapped the day's events and my behavior played throughout the day. What I should have said, moody or not, was sovereignty was a European concept derived from monarchies that the government used as a term to define how tribes existed within their own societies. In some way, the chief of the tribe was the king and therefore had the authority to make decisions for the betterment and survival of his people. He may have even asked a group of other prominent members of the tribe, like a shaman or a brave, but that was a form of self-governance. Decisions were made for the benefit of all the people, even those that a tribe may have come across who may not have even been Native. If there was good in their heart, then they were assimilated into the tribe. Current tribal government, especially Jicarilla, mirrors the federal structure, so that means people have the power to elect, question, and make certain those elected toe the line. I wrote this short statement so that I could use it in one of my speeches to try and inspire. It was about how rumors were so dangerous that they often became truths because no one asked questions. I tried to make it simple. Follow these three rules to seeing the truth.

Rule 1. Don't believe me. You don't have to believe but think and make choices! I am responsible for what I say, but I am not responsible for what you understand!

Rule 2. Don't believe yourself. Don't believe all the lies you tell yourself, like limitations you put on yourself. Open your ears and open your heart and listen. Let your heart guide you to your happiness, make a choice, and stick with it, but don't just say things. Remember, 80 percent of what you believe isn't true.

Rule 3. Don't believe anyone else. People lie all the time. When you don't have the need to believe other people just to be accepted, you see everything more clearly. People will manipulate your mind. Nothing but common sense will guide you to a clear understanding.

What is true does not need support. Lies need support; lies become exponential, creating a huge structure of lies. And when the truth comes out, most of the lies will dissipate if you don't believe them. The truth will always survive skepticism because what is true is true.

You have the power to make your own choices, so be honest with yourself. You will know that you are always free to make your choices.

I was laughed at and even scoffed at. I went on to say it's easy to make demands of leaders. Maybe you all really want to help change systems and practices that are outdated, but there is also an unwritten rule: we are only responsible for ourselves and our own actions. If you are demanding change, then what change? How will change bring good or bring something worse? If you want change, it has to start within each of us especially those who wanted to stand and be a voice and vision of the people. I was already spent in my emotions, and the last two comments I made to my colleagues was, "We are charged to make sure there is proper economic development for the Nation, not only for employment but financial security." I looked at my naysayers and said, "I'll tell you what, why don't you give me your debit and credit cards, and then I will say, 'Trust me' as I end up spending all your money in your personal accounts with no backup as to how and why." I was met with silence, so I said, "Why don't we put mirrors in every corner of this room?" referring to the council chambers. "That way, when you stand up, the first thing you see is you in the mirror, and then you can ask yourself if you did the very best you could based on the laws that we all swore to uphold." I finished with, "Have a good meeting. I'm going to my office."

That was one of the last work session we had or that I was invited to, but my point was to be forward and with a tone. The job of a representative is to do by the laws in place. Yes, bring your opinion, and if it fits into the grand plan, then great. It will certainly enhance, but when there is a blatant disregard of the protocols and rules for whatever the reason, then nothing good will ever happen, and the glass box, as I call it because it's just not a ceiling, closes tighter and tighter, and there is never going to be a real understanding of how important economics are to any community.

I wrote a resolution, and it was passed by a majority vote. That gave permission for the local newspaper to print the police blotter and court schedule. There was a lot of grumblings in the council chambers about how bad the police were not doing their job and that the social service program was bad and not doing their job. There was never a follow-up of facts when you heard the term, "They are bad," so I thought, *Okay, let me show that part of the responsibility of a legislature is to create laws to help protect and preserve a good, safe quality of life for the constituents and general public.* When the "new bunch" came into office in 2016, the resolution was mentioned, followed by the comment that they didn't know why this resolution passed because all it did was show how bad Dulce is and only tell others our business. I raised my hand and said, "I can explain. I wrote that resolution," and heads once again hung low. I said, "I wrote this resolution to try and show that this body"—I pointed to all my colleagues—"are responsible for helping, ensure departments are properly staffed, funded, and allowed to internally govern themselves along with approval of the executive office, but all this body does is complain, threaten employees, and overrule actions of these departments because of personal reasons. This body does not go out at midnight and patrol the streets. This body does not go into a home where a child or wife/girlfriend or even husband/boyfriend had been hurt and then try to find the best solution for safety, and this body does not ever need to act like we are judge and jury. This resolution was written to show that we are all one community and that if there are way too many issues occurring, then we all have to help one another as family and friends and especially as lawmakers who also approve operational budgets." I heard no rebuttals, and I don't know if that resolution was ever rescinded, but that was just one part of how important the job is, and for individuals who want the job to make sure they know what the job entails and what it does not, if there are many issues that the police department deal with and that the court has to try. I finished with the comment, "Laws matter and should be created to help as a means of serving and then helping the court make sure they have laws to then be able to properly hand down sanctions of those who break the rules. Laws help keep our community safe. I agree that needlessly creating laws is not a solution, which is why I frown on resolutions or, as what they really are, temporary laws, acting like hardened memos." There was and is a very bad practice in my opinion that creates an allowance to pass a resolution to stop or allow something based on emotion and opinion, and in turn, those temporary laws never have a sunset clause or end date, so there could be a resolution that completely contradicts a law that was passed prior or even contradicts a law that currently exists and therefore confuses those who are supposed to abide by these actions.

I feel strongly that having up-to-date, nonambiguous ordinances or permanent laws is the best way to make certain that these things that are needed have the proper teeth to be consistently reinforced and also organic to also be able to grow and evolve as times change.

I had not ever said this out loud, but as I reflect back especially in these writings, I had always felt every election I was a candidate for, win or lose, was always about economics and providing ways both micro- and macroeconomics could help a community thrive and grow. If the government was the only entity allowed to address the needs of the people, well, all I ever asked was, Where are the jobs? Where are the new homes? Where are the programs that can offer hand-ups rather than handouts, and if we have four section 17 for-profit corporations, then how are they doing, and where are the provided opportunities for someone to go into business for themselves? I asked myself over and over if I was the crazy one, the odd ball for even thinking these thoughts. I had been constantly told that I was doing it wrong, and I didn't know how Jicarilla people really are. I could never figure those comments out. I was a public servant. Maybe I was the only person who ever used that description. But since the Nation had its own constitution made up of its own laws and rules—and I even swore an oath of office to promote, uphold and, if need be, build upon for the continued benefit of all members—and if all I did was ask for the correct roles and responsibilities and, in that, write laws, question why there was no consistent accountability, and then write about these issues in an attempt to inform the voters and membership at home and abroad, then why was I here? Why were we all here? I really wanted an answer as to how we as "leaders" were going to provide help with the schools so that our students could buy into why it was vital to get some skill and then have a job ready so that they could then provide the necessary means to help them be adults. They would be able to buy a home and then provide for a family, but things are so hit-and-miss because with each new elected government, the wheel stops and goes backward because now that they are in office, they are going to fix everything but end up doing nothing that address these huge shortcomings for the membership.

I was asked what I had learned in my time as an elected official of the Nation. That's a loaded question, I always felt, since I talked about the roles and responsibilities that are indoctrinated well before a person sits as a representative and, well, after they leave. The tribal council has two major responsibilities while serving in office. One is to legislate laws. The name changed from tribal council to legislative council in the late 1990s to try and make sure that the eight council members know that they are solely responsible to create laws, endorse policy and laws, and have a complete understanding and concept of lawmaking so that there is an open-minded methodology in helping the greater good for safety and well-being of the constituents and community at large.

The other mandated role and responsibility is the creation, endorsement, and protection of economic development. This very important obligation is unfortunately not a major concern and then becomes an attempt to change things over and over with the feeling that there will be better results. I hate to say this, but I believe this is also the definition of insanity. The belief of economics within the reservation is based on a welfare economic model that an elected government is solely responsible for what is considered efficient and how income is distributed. Three or two concepts are grossly misinterpreted and could be why funds are misused, not in the sense of fraud but in the sense of limited growth from other resources or goods. I don't want to turn my comments into an Econ 101 class, but if economic concepts are ignored by those chosen to preserve and promote some type of economic development but may not understand that economies are based from land, labor, capital, and entrepreneurship, and if three of these economic principles are never considered plausible, then how can economic growth and stability become reliable for the purposes of then becoming valid? If sound bites and campaign speeches are trite and boast the importance of the future, which is the youth, and then create the only consistency of redundancy from doing bare minimum, then the future has been set, which will then have very little opportunities to provide jobs, create an enjoyable working environment, and provide any means to strive for the benefit of allowing themselves to improve their own lives. Case in point, let me just quickly talk about one of many problems that welfare economics promotes on the reservation. Homeownership and lack of real ability to become a homeowner are very big issues because when you take away the buzzwords that only create the facade to act like there is no issue, the reality is, there is no ability to own a home! Okay, to be fair, there have been home developments on the reservation, and they stemmed from the federal government housing and urban development program, and yes, people were able to move into homes, and the great thing about this opportunity is that people also do not move. They live in their home forever, and that is a great thing, but when you flip the coin over to see the other side, there is zero value to establish home equity, and therefore, no one can sell or get more value even if they could sell when they add to their home, which in the real world allows for updating more home equity if someone did sell their home. There have been attempts to create homeownership programs, and some homes have even fell into the traditional mortgage model, but the cold hard reality of homeownership on the reservation is null and void. Members are told to pay for what they have, and these comments range from those sitting at the table, and then opinions change as with the electoral cycles over and over. Members are preached to by their leadership, who tell the people there are too many freebies and that they need to pay and be grateful for what the Nation provides, and if at any time the leadership thinks that it will punish the members for something like being in arrears of rent or mortgage payments and the use words like *eviction*, well, that too only adds to further hardship and superfluous problems that will, in turn, fall back on to the decision-makers to readdress and possibly reward those select few who are willing to debate and fight for their home.

If the leadership has no idea of simple economic concepts and why they are important to apply, even within the boundaries of the reservation, there will never be any ability to create more proactive measures to provide consistency and responsibility to provide for today, tomorrow, and well into the future. If the government thinks the only solution is to take membership money and then use these very small funds, like rent and mortgage, to then put it into the large pot called the general fund because they are making people be responsible, and then use the general fund to fund the Nation's operational budget, then the only practice allowed is a continued behavior to not want to do better and therefore allow the practice of taking money from Peter to pay Paul.

Because there is no concept of scarcity, a fundamental issue in economics, council members continue to think there will be infinite amount of money they can rely on like fossil fuels. Oil and gas lie within the ground of the reservation, but the reality is, this one resource is finite and becoming more limited in markets. If the understanding of scarcity is ignored, then how can proper decisions be made to create proper strategies as a means to produce consistent revenue streams from limited resources?

The only thing I could surmise as I thought about those words of me "doing it wrong" was that I was a haff-breed and that I didn't know the culture and that I would never ever be a good leader. I never wanted to be a leader; all I ever wanted to do was to be of service and help shine the light on the foundation that was already built in the 1930s. The first council that established democracy for Jicarilla did so by creating and adopting a very beautiful document, a corpus that was designed to make sure the people had a strong footing to stand on and build upon for some greater good of preparing for an uncertain future. The constitution had clauses that invited and helped all Indian people and, yes, in turn help preserve culture, language, and a way of life that was much better than poverty, disease, and death.

I kept asking how and when those values changed. I had many conversations with elders, and there are two specific conversations that stand out. One I had with a grandma, as I refer to her because of not only her age but also her profound wisdom, about the language dying out, as it was in this current day being referred to, and she got upset and looked me right in the eyes told me, "Jicarilla is connected to the universe. no matter how much time goes by and things change, Jicarilla will still be tied to the universe, and our language and culture will never go away or die out." I developed a lump in my throat, and I said, "Thank you. I may not know a lot, but what I do feel so strongly is exactly what you just said." It was a powerful moment between a full-blooded elder and me, the haff-breed. I never forgot that day. The other conversation I had about being Jicarilla was with a medicine man who is very well revered in the community. He told me a wonderful story that way back then, when the Jicarillas were living on a mesa, they heard a noise. It was a conquistador riding through the valley, and he was hooting as a sign that he was trying to be nonthreatening. The chief told his braves to ride down and not hurt the rider but to see what this was about. There was some dialect exchanged, and the braves escorted the conquistador to the camp, and they communicated. The rider had chickens with him, and to show his gratitude of not being attacked and invited to the camp, he cooked those chickens for dinner. The tribal braves, women, and children sat around the fire and laughed and giggled as the conquistador handed a piece of the chicken to the chief. As he took a bite, the giggling got louder as the group was wondering who was next to eat white buzzards! I laughed and could feel the beauty of his story, but it was his next comment that made me proud. He said, "We as Jicarillas will always be ready to help one another. We will laugh, and we will invite more laughter so that we keep our spirits open to life, the life we thank so much for what it gives us to survive, and even though some people are not Jicarilla, they too will sit with us, and together we will continue to laugh." I was at a loss of words. That's exactly how I felt and, in my confused journey, tried to be something I wasn't, and because I was not poised to know that I was purposeful, that made me react in a negative way that led to my internal self-criticism. I tried to walk, talk, and be a duck, when the reality of what I conclude is that maybe I am a white buzzard, providing substance, sustenance, laughter, and the desire to continue providing some beauty even at my own expense.

The days of using language and culture as a means to hurt one another and then even try and use as a scapegoat to blame for perceived shortcomings only feed the beast of forced segregation, and with the continued spread of internal racism, if this mentality is allowed to turn into a philosophy, we will ourselves have created our own termination! The Jicarilla language and culture are so powerful that it will always be here, yes, like life as things evolve, to some or lesser degree, but maybe even stronger because of such values and traditions. How is it allowable that people who want to run for political office, which is the highest form of serving, use this wonderful platform treat their own people less than?

Every time I heard someone comment about me and my being a haff-breed or chanting that we will lose who we are if we don't speak Jicarilla, I have come to the conclusion that this fear tactic will not be the demise of the Nation. If the Nation falters from where h?
from, it will be because those who wanted to serve their p
perpetuated the allowance of continued corruption a·
am defining corruption as the level of dishonesty and

yes, but in the case of politics and leadership, it is the action of making someone or something feel morally depraved and then felt to be placed in the state of being so! Poverty will also be the next plague, yes, as the state of being financially limited, but more so at the level of being a leader, the state of making people feel inferior in quality or insufficient in amount. We have replaced the beauty of survival as a bad thing when, in reality, it brings us all closer, and in turn, we teach ourselves and our family how to adapt and find compassion. Kindness is natural; hate is taught.

I had many questions about what it means to be a good Jicarilla. Does being a good Jicarilla mean that you feel like you can never succeed? I have seen people criticize a person for being educated, I have seen a person be chastised for having a clean yard, and I have seen people be criticized for wanting to simply help at traditional functions and gatherings. If Jicarilla is truly tied to the universe, then we all owe a great debt to make sure this connection never frays and that to keep this tether strong, we feed it love, understanding, and accountability of ourselves to do whatever is necessary to be inviting and create better outcomes for our children's successes, and that may mean making decisions that allow us to create stronger roots that need to be planted so that we grow and then be able to continue to provide in the most positive ways for a much brighter future because we also know how to nurture our organic way of life.

In my attempt to try and look into the doors that had been closed and reopened in my mind, I still find it interesting how habits can be tough to accept and change. Am I the definition of insanity? Why do I feel I need answers to things I bear witness to and then allow my mind to deject when I don't get any response? I ask myself, Am I upset because I am myself? Am I a narcissist who needs both attention and then feels I have to be right all the time?

I have been blessed with natural talent and the ability to adapt and do good. I excelled at sports in my youth but then never went the extra mile, put in work, but nothing that was making me determined to be the best. I still ask questions of myself and wonder why I ebb and flow with my own commitments of myself, and I had joked that because I am Spanish and Native, that there is always a battle, so

I will be forever ingrained with trying to not only feel I have to pick a side but also feel bad for having to do so. I don't know if I know how to cope with life, but I do know that I tried so hard to change who I am in that I let others change who I am. That is probably the toughest pill to swallow and why I descended into depression. I love being snarky. It was not being critical. It was being witty, and there is a difference. I may have overthought that behavior, but I also had the ability to laugh at myself and therefore should have had the ability to thwart off opinion. So yeah, I guess I can cope, and no matter what I encounter, I also know that I have the compassion, kindness, and professionalism to do whatever it is I need to do.

I was lucky to be the guy people turned to for my two cents, to emcee an event, to want to hang out with, to feel like I was good enough to elect, to even now ask for reference letters. I had never said no when someone asked for help, and as I sat and went through my documents, to have been able to have laws approved and in the books and that have stood the test of time and challenges is really unbelievable. I have been out of work for almost three years now, and I have managed to make ends meet, and yes, there is worry and frustration and unfortunately still very little opportunity to find work. Yes, I can push a broom, but I was made to be of some service, to help and be able to provide an open-minded debate that made sure there was no impasse but as many variables that were positive enough to help be the glue needed to keep things together. I am concerned that I am no longer needed, in the community or in my family, and I know that part of this concern stems from my ego. But there is a hint of truth that allows and comes from the logical, realistic part of my mind that is too concerned with these new uncertainties, and no matter how bad I want answers to questions, I just need to come to terms with who I am, where I came from, how I endured, and now how I need to just stay Leon.

If being a real Jicarilla is based on a process that the federal government used to list and number Native Americans in the 1900s when they put tribes on reservations and then tribal members use this document as some reality to wave in people's faces to gloat, then we forgot that being Jicarilla was not about just being a full blood.

On paper, it was about having a heart and never forgetting the need to always help others, even when things are difficult from disdain and chaos. The stories I heard from all different age groups about what it means to be Jicarilla included the ability to endure and also to continue to be of service. What I forgot or purposely ignored was this feeling of heart and service was inside me all along. I don't want to be a savior. I just want to feed the universe good things like love so that our mutual bond remains ever giving, and now it's been a long time since I felt this, but I feel I finally need to say that this haff-breed is a very proud Jicarilla, Spanish, and everything else in between human being.

As it seems to reoccur during election years, I find myself in yet another conversation about Jicarilla's blood quantum rule, and one viewpoint during my conversation was, in twenty years, all full-blooded Jicarilla members would all be gone and, in turn, the language and culture along with this demographic shift; so why then continue to have a rule like blood quantum, which would feel like the need will feel like it no longer would be based on language and culture preservation but may be based more on what financial benefits tribal members receive? It was a valid point and one I had always keep at the surface of my thoughts when it comes to planning and the longevity of cultivating economics, yes, for the preservation of language and culture; but culture also being defined as the state of continued social traits and activities (i.e., traditions and so) by creating strong revenue streams, we could also create new outlooks for both stability of traditions along with respect of money to be a tool and not a crutch. I still feel strongly that building a consistent and strong local economy would and could do a lot for the moral and personal sustainability of community members and their families, therefore, creating a new tradition of work and effort for the greater good simply by establishing jobs and careers. By the government adding to the coffers of accessible funds, it is helping sustain and create positive ways to further promote the language and culture of the Jicarilla Apache—which, I would safely and proudly express, is a key principle for sovereignty and self-determination.

My thought to the question though was this: I don't think it would take another twenty years. Yes, things inevitably change with time; but it has seemed that money has blurred what it means to be a tribal member, and in turn, a tribe and that concept might have a greater impact on our evolution because we would not grow for the purposes of continued existence. After all, planning and growing will ensure prosperity and will show that we, as a tribe, are able to exist with harmony, provide safety and well-being, and promote the culture and language of Jicarilla for perpetuity.

So if twenty years was the number of the extinction of a full-blooded Jicarilla member, then in my opinion, the clock may have already stuck twelve twenty years ago. The reality of blood quantum and enrollment has really only been criticized by a handful of people. Unfortunately, that handful has been successful in championing this internal segregation, and it has created a negative stereotype of what Jicarilla members are defined as. The current reality seemingly feels that money can be blamed for blinding those who may have forgotten that they themselves may have been registered as *full*-blooded Jicarilla on paper but, in reality, might be questionable if their blood was actually DNA tested. One factor that had made me couch such a thought was most full-bloods I know and knew have always kept open arms about accepting all even those who were not listed as tribal enrollees. They would tell me that they were taught to help, accept, and love regardless, which I interpreted as when growing up in some of the most harshest conditions either by the elements and surviving to the worry of the federal government doing its best to eradicate and neglect, it still never gave any credence to percentages of registered Jicarilla blood. If you were Jicarilla, then you were Jicarilla. End of story! I cherish those conversations and make those who are of lineage and blood feel like they are being taxed for the privilege of being associated is not only wrong but goes against all the stories I heard all my life about being Jicarilla—working together and proving for all only fuels my statement that segregation is not preservation!

In fact, when I think back of my encounters of trying to promote assimilation and being told I was wrong or bad, I still see past the finger0pointing, the labeling of being an outsider and comments like "haff"-breed. In fact as I weed through those comments, I now see that many of those comments came from those who may be questionable as to their own blood quantity, and if they took a DNA test, they too might be surprised of those results of whom they thought they were and are, but I digress.

As significant yet destructive tribal enrollment is, it may be some time before we begin to grow the tribe and find better ways to plan and accommodate such growth but more so for the purposes of stopping the destruction of internal segregation and prejudice, and I remain hopeful that our new generation can see the value of growth; and then we as a tribe will live in perpetuity and still be proud.

I actually was so jaded that I forgot that I had "grandmas" and "grandpas"—nicknames I lovingly gave to those matriarchal and patriarchal members in their seventies and eighties who are of full-blood Apache decent who came to my office. They actually purposely stopped by to talk and actually listen to my comments and, of course, were sponges—absorbing story after story and, although their stories were subjective but we're also relative, addressing the continued need for togetherness, compassion, and growth.

Those are the memorable and powerful moments that I unfortunately shelved when, in actuality, I should have let reinvigorate me to remind myself that I was actually doing a good job as a public servant of the nation's constitution, laws, and culture of the people.

I am a great guy, and as I write this and get ready to add the last period of the last sentence, I picture a slow fade up of a song that I just discovered from the seventies. It is by Stealers Wheel, and the song is called "Star." It hit so close to home for me that I had cried when I read the lyrics. I was in the spotlight, and what do you do when it's gone? What do you do when things change? Am I ready for a new life? Am I ready to start over in a new career? Am I ready to leave the place I vowed to forever hate but feel so in love with? These are questions everyone asks every day, and I guess all I have to do is breath, smile, and unlock that snarky Leon who got stuffed into a chest. Sure, my mind wants to know why, but what I found out in these shared writings is that my mind is good, and I am rediscovering that my being snarky is a good thing, and that's what kept me balanced in my life, and when I tried to change my gift, the balanced side became snide and cynical, and that was never how I have been even when I was tested.

I have not yet come to terms that many other people have issues, that I am special or singled out. I continuously tell myself not to overthink, but that then makes me talk a lot and express those thoughts. The bad thing is that the combination of these behaviors tend to get me into trouble, and yes, hindsight is twenty-twenty, but that can also be a good thing as a means to be able to evaluate and then, if allowed, a do-over, try and do better as one outcome had been gone through and as balance can show us that the other side surely has to be not only different but produce a better outcome. I know I need to continue to practice what I preach, as the saying goes, and I really do try. I don't think I have an agenda. I give compliments when I feel they need to be made. I joke as to provide comedic relief and laughter to help alter moods. I would love to be able to also receive compliments without feeling embarrassed, but I just want to show regard and do so legitimately but without blurred lines.

Yes, I am redundant, and yes, I am verbose because I have always felt that if I am not clear and communication is lost, well, it was not because I laid everything out on the table, and that's all I can really do. I can't force. I can't think for others. All I can do is keep bringing some good. The fact that I shared with you these thoughts was to try and inspire, to remember that commitments are valuable and, when you personally make one, even to yourself, do the very best to honor your commitments. And when you stumble, don't blame. Learn and then get back up and take one step forward and repeat. I have a saying, the words I use and the words I purposely share are not just for you, whomever I am talking to, but my words are stated out loud, to also help me remain mindful of these assertions. I have never ever wanted to blindside anyone, and my angst is to be blindsided, so asking questions and then demanding answers may be my attempt to avoid being blindsided. And yes, I know I need to properly work on better preparing myself on how to be able to handle confrontation better and also accept compliments. All I want is to be able to trust myself and then others without feeling there has to be reciprocation. Maybe I don't not know how to completely say, "Fuck it," or maybe I do but have varying degrees of using "Fuck it" to then ask, well, how do we have better understandings especially if we know of our agreements? I found out that I regress when I am confronted or have to be confronting. My voice cracks, I have shallow breathing, and I may even tear up. I grew up thinking I was weak and that, as a man, I needed to talk with my fists. Well, I also grew up wearing thick glasses, and when my parents agreed to trust me with the expensive purchase of contact lenses, the last thing I ever wanted to do was fight and then run the risk of having to go back to Coke bottle-thick glasses. I figure looking weak and feeling weak is a better outcome than turning green and destroying everything and everyone around me, so I know that my kindness is not a form of weakness, and maybe there will be a day when I have to use my hands to protect. Good thing I have also been blessed with a Mike Tyson jab and harsh knock-power right hand, but I hope I never have to prove that point. I once again begin to find my place, the place I can recall all those decades ago as a child who was born with natural talent and may not have learned how to cope but was taught to always let my strong core values lead me. And if I did ignore my gut feelings trying to fit in, then I can't dwell. I must have had a reason, and it may or may not have worked out at that time, so "fuck it." I am still going to be the person I was then and now, and this person Leon is needs a hug, needs a smile, and despite emotions, will do his best to provide help and be of service.

While I reflect back in this book on many things including the last five years of my personal and professional change, I realized that I was trying to fill a need to be acknowledged and recognized. What does that mean? Well, it doesn't mean what I was supposed to do as far as my job as a representative. After all, I brought new laws such as zero copay healthcare, almost half-a-billion dollars of new funding, towed the line of the laws and those allowances elected officials can and cannot do, and so many other things that really did add value for the community and members. Maybe in my haste to help, I made a mistake in thinking I would be recognized in my merits and outcomes. I may have subconsciously given permission to those naysayers, my colleagues, and their supporters the opportunity to criticize me in the hopes of possibly winning them over. Unfortunately, I left myself wide open and repressed my feelings and emotions and forgot what and who I was as a dad, a husband, and a man. I joke—I tell people that if I was a super hero, my superpowers would be ignorance; so yes, I'd be Captain Ignorant because I have to ask questions, even if emotional. I tend to look past the surface of people, trying to see into their core; and in that, maybe I confuse my kindness with expectation and, in my mind, developed a long-term relationship. I do cherish relationships both personal and professional, and what I am doing now is realizing that these expectations I created in my mind hurt my feelings if and when things change. I then tend to feel that I was used, and there may have been false pretenses in asking for my assistance or friendship. So that has been something I am working on—reestablishing my worth and value and continued dedication to whatever I am asked to do or help with because, after all, I really do want to help, and I don't mind being Captain Ignorant because my superpower will be the ability to listen before I speak and learn as much as I can before I add a comment. After all, I can't preach what I don't practice, and that is a pretty good superpower to have.

I now sit in my cubical, punching a time clock, ahh…the infamous time clock. Okay, I won't soapbox but is the time clock the best use of measuring productivity, or is it a means to remind tribal employees we are pawns and should be grateful we have a job, which really boils down to a useless tool of micromanaging employees… okay…okay. Although very thankful and grateful that someone—the director of the program—sees my value and actually welcomed me to their department, I am happy to be a part of such a progressive and positive program absolutely helping and changing lives and how education is powerful for the community.

Although the job is temporary, it is and has been a huge test of rediscovering courage, fortitude. and respect of a place that I absolutely do love. I now come to a building that I realized I had always admired and respected and, yes, at the same time hid from and despised because of individuals that, in retrospect, seems ludicrous to allow such thoughts to cloud my judgement of what is always supposed to be forthrightly. I remember when we first discussed finding funding to have a new administration building built that would make a statement and serve as a mecca for truth, justice, and community involvement. Unfortunately now, it seems to feel more like an institution; there is security everywhere, the area is quiet, and people are told to hush. No one sitting and visiting with one another, memos are passed around, reinforcing who is the boss and who are to listen. I have always been of the opinion that such memos destroy, only making employees' morale dissipate, treating the workforce like children—only to be seen and never heard. This huge new government facility is a mere façade and shell for distancing from the same people officials swore to be served and be transparent, too, yet, I will always feel like I want to help, use my experience and voice to inspire, and let the membership fight for what's just. After all it is for the greater good. Maybe my ego is still bruised as I slowly accept that my political journey has concluded; and some days, it feels acceptable, and others it feels unfair.

However, there is a plus-side being the low man on the totem pole. I don't mind having to not make decisions or plan or anything else associated with responsibilities. The best thing for me is I also get to bring my son with me to work, and he sits right next to me, watching his iPad and fully content. We do some reading and assignments. I print from some websites, and together, we spend the day at the office, which brings me to a new series of thoughts and concerns—what do I do for Dom's future? his needs and his growth? That is something I need to work on, and I might be being selfish, but isn't he supposed to be with me forever or as long as I can continue to care for him? Being sarcastic, of course, but in all honesty, I know I may have to make a difficult decision for me but may end up being the best decision for him.

I said earlier that I use air quotes when I use the term *leader* because I firmly believe that it is a privilege and not just a title. It is earned, and in many cases, a good leader will never know they had earned that title, but to me, there should be more understanding and respect in any position of authority. Even for a day as an interim or in a term of over a year, bring your best and be able to prove your worth even when you stand alone. I never considered myself a leader but did feel I was always a cog in the machine that helped drive the engine forward. I guess I am a leader, and even at that, I will continue to use air quotes for the *leader* word. Running for public office is a choice—a choice that each candidate has made and fundamentally promised to uphold from the day 1 they paid their filing fee, which inherently means this choice is a promise to the voters that there will be a standard and commitment to the spirit and letter of the laws, rules, and polices when representing, therefore making elected offi- cial's servants of the people. I feel in love with politics, and maybe I did things wrong not by infringing on my oath but maybe creating an expectation that members knew my actions and intentions, and maybe that's where I feel short. I remain proud. Our Jicarilla gov- ernment works, and our system is strong. It's just a shame that a new culture has been cultivated and that—in turn, in my ignorant and humble opinion—has lessened the dignity some elected "lead- ers" have failed to uphold. I need to have music playing lightly in the background while I work, and this song came on, and it seemed so appropriate, so I close with a Stealers Wheel song called "Star." And in my mind, this song has encompassed a life of being in the spotlight and being a positive force that really did do. In my mind, I now imagine a camera slowly zooming out from behind me as I type, like in a movie, and a voice comes on, narrating these last few sen- tences. Song intro begins to play… "I now say to myself the phrase, 'It is what it is'" in an attempt to try and forgive and forget but also to justify my thoughts and my story in this book and that I should also be proud of what I have contributed to, accomplished, and still practice today, including serving with all those I worked with, and also was able to learn from and the ability to also continually learn and apply today. So as I smile, I also feel I have to say, "But what the hell do I really know!"

"Star" plays out as the screen fades to black.

(Record scratch sound) *Wait!* I almost forgot to mention that I resigned for the school board! I know I mentioned my issues but didn't react and, at that time, decided to push through because of commitment; but boy did that change. Maybe therapy is working;

maybe I finally am realizing that I can't solve all the issues or try be the only voice pushing the rules. I mean, I really tired, yet all it did was put me back to a place where I left after leaving my council position in 2018. I knew policy stated that I had to submit a resignation letter in advance of any upcoming meeting and, in true Leon fashion, strongly felt that I could not just submit one paragraph of my intention to leave, so I submitted four pages. Lol! I only laugh because I needed to share my thoughts. I actually was hoping my letter would inspire others to step up and toe the line of the law and hold their District School Board accountable. My letter as submitted is as follows.

Dear DISD Board Members,

I asked myself 4 questions before I considered writing and submitting a letter to the Board, Stakeholders and New Mexico Public Education Secretary.

I pride myself in being able to understand and promote both the letter and spirit of laws and I have made many comments on the record trying to tow that line especially when it came to questionable unprofessional behaviors. I serve with integrity as an Elected official of the Dulce Independent School District (DISD) and community of Dulce, promoting the rules and standards DISD, the New Mexico State Statues and the New Mexico School Boards Association's (NMSBA) rules. I practicing upholding B-0750 BCA—Board Member Ethics, which states:

"As a member of the Board of Education and recognizing that my actions will directly influence the children in this school district, I will:

1) Recognize that there is no authority of an individual Board member either expressed or implied other than during legally constituted sessions of the Board or when representing the Board officially.

2) *Delegate administrative and supervisory functions to the Superintendent of Schools.*

3) *Work through the Superintendent. Make criticisms of school administration and/or personnel only to him.*

(B-0750 BCA) also clearly states that Board Member's will:

- *Recognize that their responsibility is not to run the schools, but to see that they are well run.*
- *Function as a part of a policy-forming and policy-control Board, rather than as part of an administrative Board.*
- *Refer, as far as possible, all complaints and requests to the Superintendent of Schools.*
- *Recognize fully that the appropriate administrative officer is entirely responsible for carrying out a particular policy in accordance with state law and local regulations.*
- *Give all school officials authority in keeping with their responsibilities.*
- *Present personal criticisms of school employees only to the Superintendent of Schools.*
- *Support and protect school officials in the performance of their duties.*
- *Give friendly counsel and advice to the Superintendent of Schools."*

Based on these important policies and at the same time witnessing a selection of the rules, rather than a total commitment of, my answer to my first question, "Is serving as an individual School Board member really mattering?" Based on sitting in the parking lot before meetings, praying for strength, I lean towards an answer of maybe but that is not enough to continue exerting my energy.

The next question was, "Is serving as a representative of my community creating equality and equity for the benefit of ALL stakeholders (Parents, Guardians, Staff/Faculty, Students) really helping?"

NO, I have not felt for a long time like I have been able to positively get my points of accountability across nor have I felt there will be accountability or recourse from actions unbecoming because there is no real way to hold individual board members accountable and I have tried to ask for direction and assistance from NMPED, NMSBA and other State entities that have a hand in State educational matters.

Rather than digress or come off as finger pointing, just watch all the past meeting videos, they are recorded and accessible for the general public on the DISD website.

It is true the best solutions require compromise but when rules, standards and morals are not properly executed or even understood by elected officials, the whole, in this case our district becomes compromised, deprived.

Which brought to me to the answer of my next question, "have my motives and actions been ethical and moral based on the New Mexico State standards I promised to uphold?"

YES, I take my responsibilities extremely seriously and despite the extremely high turnover rate of administrators here, as well continued to comply with district and State policy, my emails and comments are my record and are considered public information for anyone to see.

B-0200 BBA—Board Powers and Responsibilities (22-5-4. Local school boards; powers; duties.) has fourteen specific bullet points that in essence and for the purposes of this letter and violation reflected by you, states two specific main points, The Board shall, in accord with the Administrative Code of the Secretary of Education will delegate administrative and supervisory functions to the Local Superintendent; and refrain from involvement in delegated administrative functions.

I may be wrong but I strongly feel that when a practice circumvents standards, then there is an allowance of blurring the lines set forth in the rules, the foundation then becomes unstable, so when Board members feel like they can micromanage blurring the lines, interrogate and disrespect staff based on speculation, then the line of B-0200 BBA is encroached upon. Crisis management is not only bad leadership but totally erases the fundamentals of what it means to serve and I am choosing to no longer participate in something that is so important that inconsistent, reactive decisions are only making me guilty by association.

Finally, the question that I soul searched long and hard about, "Is there anything I could do to continue to be an instrumental part of the group?"

I have concluded based on my convictions and vast experience as a decision maker, that my efforts are in vain and I have become quite exhausted in only making comments that are ignored, yes, my comments are on the record but not part of the needed strategies the Board are charged to do. I pushed through and continued to serve but these last 2 years and these past few months, have seemingly extinguished my passion of serving in a fiduciary capacity. I take the oath of office extremely serious as well and the code of ethics but my answer is a resounding NO, I do not feel like I can be instrumental!

To the voters, thank you so much for using your voice and power to elect me to this prestigious position, I sincerely apologize that I have even had to consider such an extreme action like resigning but there were way too many answers of No to the questions I continually asked myself. I am grateful for your trust and I hope I earned your respect and there is some hope that you understand that my resignation is not an emotional moment of weakness but a stand I need to take to no longer abstain or vote against poor priorities.

Our district is wonderful and has produced many fantastic students and graduates, some of whom dedicated themselves to give back as staff or faculty but there is a palpable feeling that they too are struggling to understand the actions or their leaders but I am certainly not speaking for anyone. I am absolutely proud to have witnessed their hard work and dedication. I can understand the need to make sure our schools are run properly and I can even accept the passion to do so but in my strong beliefs, there should never be a confusion of what the school board can or cannot do.

I firmly believe that resigning from the DISD school board will allow me greater access to push for the highest of standards as a parent and community member rather than serving as a board member.

I do have one request for consideration, since my school email is public record, I would appreciate a copy, on a Zip drive that I will produce if need be, with all my DISD school emails, both received and sent before my school email account is canceled.

Lastly, per DISD policy B-0450, BOARD MEMBER RESIGNATION, I respectfully submit this letter to the office of the DISD Superintendent, to then submit to the Board, serving as my Official Letter of Resignation from the Dulce Independent School District School Board effective June 13, 2022, citing irreconcilable differences.

Best,
Leon K. Reval
Proud former DISD School Board Member

Not one response, and maybe that surprised me; maybe I had hoped that there would be opportunity to acknowledge the issues, but again, I cannot act like I am the savior. I shared my personal and professional concerns and stated points that were relative to the position of being a decision maker I served and swore to uphold via the oath of office, and that's all I could do. Funny thing though, as I look back, I noticed more gray hair has appeared and ironically not from the daily activities of being a dad and raising kids or worrying about income from but sitting across the table arguing about consistency and standards.

Looking on the bright side, I have finally embraced my "haff"-breed moniker, and I have nothing more to prove to anyone other than myself; and so yes, I walk tall to my Monday through Friday in the building I do see as a place of justice to my cubicle to begin my work day, and I do keep a chip on my shoulder. However, it is invisible and only now serves as a personal reminder that, if confronted for any reason, I don't have to provide a retort or prove myself to anyone; all I have to do is remain humble, grateful, and simply continue to get older, grayer, and wiser and just love the community this "haff"-breed and his quarter-blood children call home.

About the Author

Leon K. Reval is a Native American tribal rights advocate, a member of the Jicarilla Apache Nation, and a former elected leader of the Nation's Council. He has led many initiatives for the Nation—from asserting its sovereignty, protecting tribal assets, to bettering the general welfare of his people. He spearheaded litigation against the United States for its breach of trust responsibilities and mismanagement of tribal resources, which resulted in the United States' payment of over $120 million to the Nation. In addition to being a dedicated father of three children, he is an accomplished public speaker and works tirelessly advancing Native American rights throughout the country.

Printed in the USA
CPSIA information can be obtained
at www.ICGtesting.com
LVHW050704100823
754633LV00001B/43

9 798885 058339